INTERMEDIATE KOF
A GRAMMAR AND WORKBOOK

Intermediate Korean: A Grammar and Workbook comprises an accessible reference grammar and related exercises in a single volume.

This workbook presents twenty-four individual grammar points, covering the core material which students would expect to encounter in their second year of learning Korean. Grammar points are followed by examples and exercises which allow students to reinforce and consolidate their learning.

Intermediate Korean is suitable for both class use as well as independent study.

Key features include:

- clear, accessible format
- many useful language examples
- all Korean entries presented in Hangul with English translations
- jargon-free explanations of grammar
- abundant exercises with full answer key
- subject index.

Clearly presented and user-friendly, *Intermediate Korean* provides readers with the essential tools to express themselves in a wide variety of situations, making it an ideal grammar reference and practice resource for students with some knowledge of the language.

Andrew Sangpil Byon is Associate Professor at the State University of New York at Albany, where he teaches courses in Korean language and civilization.

Other titles available in the Grammar Workbooks series are:

Basic Cantonese
Intermediate Cantonese

Basic Chinese
Intermediate Chinese

Basic Dutch
Intermediate Dutch

Basic German
Intermediate German

Basic Irish
Intermediate Irish

Basic Italian

Basic Korean
Intermediate Korean

Basic Polish
Intermediate Polish

Basic Russian
Intermediate Russian

Basic Spanish
Intermediate Spanish

Basic Welsh
Intermediate Welsh

INTERMEDIATE KOREAN: A GRAMMAR AND WORKBOOK

Andrew Sangpil Byon

Routledge
Taylor & Francis Group

LONDON AND NEW YORK

For my parents, James Ki Yong and Gloria Hye Ja Pyon

First published 2010
by Routledge
2 Park Square, Milton Park, Abingdon, Oxon OX14 4RN

Simultaneously published in the USA and Canada
by Routledge
270 Madison Ave, New York, NY10016

Routledge is an imprint of the Taylor & Francis Group, an informa business

Typeset in Times Ten by Graphicraft Limited, Hong Kong
Printed and bound in Great Britain by CIP Antony Rowe, Chippenham, Wiltshire

British Library Cataloguing in Publication Data
A catalogue record for this book is available from the British Library

Library of Congress Cataloguing-in-Publication Data
Byon, Andrew Sangpil.
Intermediate Korean : a grammar & workbook / Andrew Sangpil Byon.
    p. cm.
  Simultaneously published in the USA and Canada.
1. Korean language—Grammar—Problems, exercises, etc. 2. Korean language—
Textbooks for foreign speakers—English. I. Title.
PL913.B965 2009
495.7'82421—dc22
2008053381

ISBN10: 0-415-54714-8 (hbk)
ISBN10: 0-415-77488-8 (pbk)
ISBN10: 0-208-87590-7 (ebk)

ISBN13: 978-0-415-54714-7 (hbk)
ISBN13: 978-0-415-77488-8 (pbk)
ISBN13: 978-0-203-87590-2 (ebk)

CONTENTS

PREFACE

Intermediate Korean: A Grammar and Workbook is a sequel to its sister volume *Basic Korean: A Grammar and Workbook*, and it likewise focuses on providing an accessible reference grammar explanation and related exercises in a single volume. It is designed for independent English-speaking adult Korean-as-a-foreign-language (KFL) learners who intend to maintain and strengthen their knowledge of essential Korean grammar and for classroom-based learners who are looking for supplemental grammar explanations and practices. Consequently, this book differs from existing KFL materials whose primary purpose is to help KFL learners acquire four language skills, such as listening, speaking, reading, and writing as well as cultural knowledge.

The layout of this book also differs from those of existing KFL materials. For instance, a typical KFL textbook chapter may include model dialogues, followed by vocabulary lists, grammar explanations, cultural notes, and exercises. In contrast, following the pattern of *Basic Korean* and other Grammar Workbooks of the Routledge series, every unit of *Intermediate Korean* focuses on presenting jargon-free and concise grammar explanations, followed by relevant grammar exercises.

This book has 24 units, and it does not take a functional-situational approach in grouping and/or sequencing target grammatical points. Rather it sequences and covers grammatical points according to their grammatical categories (e.g., sentence endings, conjunctives, particles, and so on), so that learners can use the book as a reference material as well as a practice material. The exercises at the end of each unit are designed primarily to reinforce the target grammatical points.

All Korean entries are presented in Hangul (the Korean alphabet) with English translations to facilitate understanding. Accordingly, it requires that learners familiarize themselves with Hangul, before going on to the book. In addition, when translating Korean entries into English, efforts were made to reflect the Korean meaning as closely as possible. Consequently, some learners may feel certain English translations do not reflect typical English usages. However, the direct translation approach was employed for pedagogical purposes.

Preface

In writing this book, I have been fortunate to have the assistance and support of many people. I would like to thank my colleagues in the Department of East Asian Studies at the University at Albany, State University of New York, who were supportive of this project. I am grateful to anonymous reviewers for their constructive and valuable comments. I would like to express sincere gratitude to Sophie Oliver for initially encouraging this project and to the editorial and production teams of Routledge—Andrea Hartill, and Samantha Vale Noya—for their advice and support throughout the process. My thanks also go to Neil Dowden for his careful and thoughtful copy-editing service and to Kathy Auger at Graphicraft for her kind assistance during the final stage of production. Finally, as always, my special thanks go to my wife, Isabel, who, with her optimism and encouragement, makes it possible for me to do what I really love to do. Of course, I bear all responsibility for any shortcomings and errors in the text.

UNIT 1
The intimate speech level and the plain speech level

The intimate speech level

The intimate speech level is in general used in the following situations: by adults when addressing children, by parents when addressing their kids, by children when addressing their peers, and by adult friends when addressing their childhood friends (or friends whose relationships are close enough to switch to the intimate level from the polite level).

The intimate speech level ending is ~어/아. The choice of ~어 or ~아 is the same with that of the polite speech level ending ~어요/아요. ~아 is used after a stem that ends in a bright vowel, 오 or 아 (e.g., 찾다 "find" => 찾아), while ~어 is used with the stem that ends in any other vowels (e.g., 배우다 "learn" => 배워). Consider the following examples:

	Polite speech level	Intimate speecsh level
가다 "go"	가요	가
배우다 "learn"	배워요	배워
가르치다 "teach"	가르쳐요	가르쳐
먹다 "eat"	먹어요	먹어
하다 "do"	해요	해
있다 "have/exist"	있어요	있어
이다 "be"	이에요	이야
아니다 "not be"	아니에요	아니야

As seen above, one can generate the intimate speech level from the polite speech level, simply by removing 요. One exception is that the copula 이다/아니다 takes slightly different forms: 이야 instead of 이에, and 아니야 instead of 아니에.

Just like the polite speech level ending ~어요/아요, the intimate speech level ending ~어/아 is used for all sentence types: declarative, interrogative, imperative, and propositive. For instance, consider the following:

매일 뛰어 "(I) run everyday."
매일 뛰어? "(Do you) run everyday?"
매일 뛰어! "Run everyday!"
매일 뛰어 "(Let us) run everyday."

Koreans use contextual elements as well as intonation (e.g., rising intonation for a question) to figure out what intimate speech level ending
~어/아 is used for a specific sentence type.

The plain speech level

The plain speech level ending sounds more blunt and direct than other
speech levels: deferential, polite, and intimate. The plain speech level is
primarily used in the following three contexts: When one addresses a child,
his/her childhood friends, or younger siblings; when the speaker talks to
himself/herself or wants to draw the listener's attention to information
that is noteworthy or provoking; when one writes (e.g., personal essay,
prose, newspaper articles, academic papers, diary, and so forth).

Unlike the intimate and the polite speech levels that use the same
endings for different sentence types, the plain speech level has different
endings for different sentence types, as shown below.

Declarative

~는/ㄴ다 (for verb stems)

가다 "go"	간다
먹다 "eat"	먹는다
공부하다 "study"	공부한다

~다 (for adjective and copula stems)

춥다 "cold"	춥다
깨끗하다 "clean"	깨끗하다
이다 "be"	이다

~었/았다 (for all predicate stems in the past tense)

앤드류가 학교에 <u>갔다</u> "Andrew went to school."
날씨가 <u>추웠다</u> "The weather was cold."
방이 <u>깨끗했다</u> "The room was clean."
그 남자가 한국 사람<u>이었다</u> "That man was a Korean."

Interrogative

~니/(으)냐? (for all predicate stems)

가다 "go"	가니? (or 가냐?)
먹다 "eat"	먹니? (or 먹냐?)
공부하다 "study"	공부하니? (or 공부하냐?)
좋다 "good"	좋니? (or 좋냐?) / 좋으냐? (for writing)
춥다 "cold"	춥니? (or 춥냐?) / 추우냐? (for writing)
깨끗하다 "clean"	깨끗하니? (or 깨끗하냐?)
이다 "be"	이니? (or 이냐?)

~었/았니/(으)냐? (for all predicate stems in the past tense)

앤드류가 학교에 <u>갔니</u>? "Did Andrew go to school?"
날씨가 <u>추웠니</u>? "Was the weather cold?"
방이 <u>깨끗했니</u>? "Was the room clean?"
그 남자가 한국 <u>사람이었니</u>? "Was that man a Korean?"

Imperative (only for verb stems)

~아라 (after a stem that ends in 오 or 아)
~어라 (after a stem that ends in any other vowels)

가다 "go"	가라
먹다 "eat"	먹어라
공부하다 "study"	공부해라

Propositive (only for verb stems)

~자

가다 "go"	가자
먹다 "eat"	먹자
공부하다 "study"	공부하자

Note that the plain speech level imperative ending ~어라/아라 and propositive ending ~자 are used only for verb stems, and they are not conjugated for the tense.

Exercises

Key vocabulary for Unit 1 exercises

가게 store
가방 bag
가르치다 to teach
강의 lecture
건너다 to cross over
경찰관 police officer
과일 fruits
공부하다 to study
공연 public performance/play
그리다 to draw
그림 painting/picture
기다리다 to wait
기분 feeling/mood
깨끗하다 to be clean

나쁘다 to be bad
날씨 weather
내려가다 to go down
누나 older sister
느낌 feeling/mood
느리다 to be slow/to be sluggish
다리 bridge/legs
닫다 to close/to shut
달다 to be sweet
담배 cigarette
던지다 to throw
따뜻하다 to be warm
따르다 to follow
떠나다 to depart/to take leave of/to leave
뜨겁다 to be hot (water)/to be heated
로맨스 romance

마시다 to drink
마치다 to finish
만나다 to meet
머리 head/hair (of one's head)
먹다 to eat
멀다 to be far
문 door
믿다 to trust/to believe
바쁘다 to be busy

받다 to receive
발 foot
배우다 to learn
버리다 to throw away
버스 bus
범인 criminal
보내다 to send
보다 to see/to watch/to read
빌리다 to borrow

사과 apple
사람 person
사무실 office
사진 picture
소포 package
손 hand
시험 test/examination
신다 to wear (shoes/socks)
신문 newspapers
싱싱하다 to be fresh
쓰레기 trash/garbage
씻다 to wash

아니다 not be
아래 the base/the lower part
아버지 father
아침 morning
아프다 to be sore/to be painful
양말 socks
어렵다 to be difficult
언제 when
열다 to open
열쇠 keys
영화 movie
외치다 to shout
이번 this time
일 work/matter/errand
일본어 the Japanese language
일찍 early
읽다 to read
입다 to wear (clothes)

자다 to sleep
자전거 bicycle
잡다 to catch/to hold
재미있다 to be interesting

접시 dishes/plates
조용하다 to be quiet
좋다 to be good/to be right/to be beneficial
주다 to give
주말 weekend
중국어 the Chinese language
집 house

차 car
찾다 to look for/to seek for
창문 window
책 book
친구 friend
커피 coffee
크게 aloud
타다 to ride
팔다 to sell
프랑스 France
피우다 to smoke
하늘 sky
하다 to do
헤어지다 to get scattered/to be separated/to break up
흐리다 to be cloudy

Exercise 1.1

Conjugate each verb or adjective in parentheses with the intimate speech
level ending. Then translate the sentence, as shown in the example.

> Example: 학교에 (가다) / imperative
> = 학교에 가. "Go to school."

1 다리를 (건너다) / imperative
2 문을 (열다) / imperative
3 차를 (팔다) / propositive
4 쓰레기를 (버리다) / declarative
5 창문을 (닫다) / imperative
6 공연을 일찍 (마치다) / imperative
7 접시를 (빌리다) / propositive
8 발을 (씻다) / declarative
9 일찍 (자다) / propositve
10 자전거를 (타다) / interrogative
11 느낌이 (좋다) / declarative
12 강의가 (재미있다) declarative

13 프랑스 사람 (이다) /interrogative
14 일을 (하다) / imperative
15 경찰관이 (아니다) /interrogative
16 집이 (멀다) / declarative
17 사과가 (달다) / declarative
18 머리가 (아프다) / interrogative
19 하늘이 (흐리다) / declarative
20 과일이 (싱싱하다) / interrogative

Exercise 1.2

Conjugate each verb or adjective in parentheses with the declarative plain speech level ending. Then translate each sentence.

 Example: 서울에 (가다)
 = 서울에 간다. "(I) go to Seoul."

1 아침을 (먹다)
2 중국어를 (가르치다)
3 누나를 (기다리다)
4 물을 (마시다)
5 소포를 (받다)
6 일본어를 (배우다)
7 사무실이 (깨끗하다)
8 버스가 (느리다)
9 커피가 (뜨겁다)
10 이번 주말에 (바쁘다)

Exercise 1.3

Conjugate each verb or adjective in parethensis with the interrogative plain speech level ending. Then translate each sentence.

 Example: 슈퍼마켓에 (가다)
 = 슈퍼마켓에 가니? "Do (you) go to the supermarket?"

1 언제 가게 문을 (닫다)
2 어디서 친구를 (만나다)
3 언제 (떠나다)
4 어디서 (공부하다)
5 담배를 (피우다)
6 열쇠를 (찾다)

7 날씨가 (따뜻하다)
8 시험이 (어렵다)
9 기분이 (나쁘다)
10 집이 (조용하다)

Exercise 1.4

Conjugate each verb or adjective in parethensis with the imperative plain
speech level ending. Then translate each sentence.

> Example: 우체국에 (가다)
> = 우체국에 가라. "Go to the post office."

1 다리를 (건너다)
2 아래로 (내려가다)
3 가방을 (던지다)
4 창문을 (열다)
5 아버지를 (따르다)
6 앤드류를 (밀다)
7 양말을 (신다)
8 셔츠를 (입다)
9 손을 (잡다)
10 크게 (외치다)

Exercise 1.5

Conjugate each verb or adjective in parenthesis with the propositive plain
speech level ending. Then translate each sentence.

> Example: 도서관에 (가다)
> = 도서관에 가자. "(Let us) go to the library."

1 사진을 (보내다)
2 그림을 (그리다)
3 범인을 (잡다)
4 신문을 (읽다)
5 일을 (마치다)
6 택시를 (타다)
7 커피숍에서 (헤어지다)
8 로맨스 영화를 (보다)
9 책을 (주다)
10 쓰레기를 (버리다)

Exercise 1.6

Underline the correct English translation of the Korean phrase below.

> Example: 자전거를 타자.
> (Let us) ride a bike / Ride a bike.

1 Page 19 를 읽어라.
 (Let us) read page 19 / Read page 19.

2 손을 씻자.
 Wash (your) hands / (Let us) wash (our) hands.

3 문을 닫아라.
 (Let us) close the door / Close the door.

4 돈을 빌리자.
 (Let us) borrow (his) money / Borrow (his) money.

5 방에서 나가라.
 Go out from the room / (Let us) go out from the room.

6 녹차를 마셔라.
 Drink green tea / (Let us) drink green tea.

7 숙제를 주자.
 (Let us) give (them) homework / Give (them) homework.

8 청바지를 입자.
 Wear jeans / (Let us) wear jeans.

9 영어를 배워라.
 Learn English / (Let us) learn English.

10 런던으로 떠나자.
 (Let us) leave for London / Leave for London.

Exercise 1.7

Finish the following translation using the intimate speech level and the sentence cue provided in parenthesis, as shown in the example.

> Example: "What kind of movie do (you) want to see?" (무슨 영화를 보고 싶다)
> = 무슨 영화를 보고 싶어?

1 The movie begins at 2 p.m. (오후 2 시에 영화가 시작하다)
2 Be quiet. (조용히 하다)

3 (Let us) clean the house. (집을 청소하다)
4 Where do (you) meet Tom? (톰을 어디서 만나다)
5 Where did (you) go? (어디에 가다)
6 (He) quitted smoking. (담배를 끊다)
7 The weather was clear. (날씨가 맑다)
8 Buy some wines. (와인을 사다)
9 How long did (you) wait? (얼마나 기다리다)
10 (They) taught English in Korea. (한국에서 영어를 가르치다)

Exercise 1.8

Finish the following translation using the plain speech level and the sentence cue provided in parenthesis, as shown in the example.

Example: "(He) attends the University of Hawaii." (하와이 대학교에 다니다)
= 하와이 대학교에 다닌다.

1 (I) major in economics. (경제학을 전공하다)
2 (He) traveled in Seoul last year. (작년에 서울을 여행하다)
3 The coffee is hot. (커피가 뜨겁다)
4 Is (he) a Canadian? (캐나다 사람이다)
5 Was the subway convenient? (지하철이 편하다)
6 Are (you) happy? (행복하다)
7 Open the window. (창문을 열다)
8 Throw the garbage. (쓰레기를 버리다)
9 (Let us) have the confidence. (자신감을 가지다)
10 (Let us) sing a song. (노래를 부르다)

UNIT 2
Sentence-final endings
~지요, ~군요, ~네요

Typical sentence-final endings are speech level endings, such as the deferential, polite, intimate, and plain endings. However, sentence-final endings also include various sentence-final suffixes, such as 지, 군, and 네. These suffixes, combined with 요 "the politeness marker" can serve as sentence-final endings that convey the speaker's various psychological states or attitudes. This unit introduces three sentence-final endings, ~지요, ~군요, and ~네요.

The sentence-final ending ~지요

The sentence-final ending ~지요 is a one-form ending that indicates one of the following four mental states or attitudes of the speaker: (i) seeking agreement, (ii) asking a question with a belief that the hearer has the answer, (iii) assuring information, and (iv) suggesting. The speaker's intonation (e.g., falling or rising) as well as contextual factors involved (e.g., referential and situational contexts) determine which among the four moods or attitudes the ending indicates.

(1) Seeking agreement (with a rising intonation)

Consider the following two examples:

폴이 매일 조깅을 해요? "Does Paul jog everyday?"
폴이 매일 조깅을 하지요? "Paul jogs everyday, right?"

Notice that the ending ~어/아요 in the first sentence simply asks the message in a straightforward manner. On the other hand, the ending ~지요 in the second sentence indicates that the speaker seeks agreement while asking the same question. Here are more examples:

오늘 저녁 6시에 만나지요? "(They) meet at 6 o'clock this evening, right?"
어제 학교에 왔지요? "(You) came to school yesterday, right?"

(2) Asking a question, believing that the hearer has the answer (with a rising intonation)

피터가 몇 시에 <u>돌아와요</u>? "What time does Peter return?"
피터가 몇 시에 <u>돌아오지요</u>? "What time does Peter return?"

Again, the ending ~어/아요 in the first sentence simply asks the message in a direct manner. However, the second sentence with the ending ~지요 implies that the speaker believes that the hearer has the answer. Here are more examples:

저 사람이 <u>누구지요</u>? "Who is that person (over there)?"
열쇠가 어디에 <u>있었지요</u>? "Where was the key?"

(3) Assuring information (with a falling intonation)

네, 내일 <u>떠나요</u>. "Yes, (they) leave tomorrow."
네, 내일 <u>떠나지요</u>. "Yes, (I assure you that they) leave tomorrow."

The first sentence with the ending ~어/아요 simply states the message. On the other hand, the ending ~지요 in the second sentence indicates that the speaker assures of the referential message. Here are more examples:

영국의 수도가 <u>런던이지요</u>. "(I assure you) that the capital of England is London."
네, 어제 약속이 <u>있었지요</u>. "Yes, (I assure you) that (we) had an appointment yesterday."

(4) Suggesting (with a falling intonation)

추운데 창문 <u>닫아요</u>. "(It) is cold, so close the window."
추운데 창문 <u>닫지요</u>. "(It) is cold, so how about closing the window?"

The first sentence with the ending ~어/아요 is a direct request. However, the second sentence is a suggestion because of the ending ~지요. Here are more examples:

테니스나 <u>치지요</u>. "(How about we) play tennis (or something)?"
점심이나 먹고 <u>연습하지요</u>. "(How about we) practice after eating lunch (or something)?"

The honorific suffix ~(으)시 can be optionally used along with ~지요 to make the suggestion sound more polite, as shown in the following examples:

선생님, <u>가시지요</u>. "Professor, (how about we) go?"
책 좀 빌려 <u>주시지요</u>. "(How about you) please lend (me) the book?"

The sentence-final ending ~네요

The one-form sentence-final ending ~네요 is used to indicate the speaker's spontaneous and immediate reaction, such as unexpected surprise and/or realization. The ending ~네요 is used only for the declarative statement sentence type, and it may be translated as "Oh, I see/realize that..." Consider the following two examples:

존이 한국말을 잘 <u>해요</u>. "John speaks Korean well."
존이 한국말을 잘 <u>하네요</u>. "(Oh, I see that) John speaks Korean well."

Notice that the first sentence simply conveys the message in a straightforward manner. On the other hand, the second sentence with the ending ~네요 indicates the speaker's spontaneous emotive reaction. It denotes that the information which the speaker hears or observes (e.g., John speaking Korean well) is unanticipated and/or contrary to what was expected. Here are more examples:

아침을 많이 <u>준비했네요</u>. "(I realize that you) prepared huge breakfast."
토마스가 영어 선생님<u>이었네요</u>. "(I am surprised that) Thomas was an English teacher."
비가 많이 <u>오네요</u>. "(Oh, I see that) it rains a lot."
이 커피가 <u>진하네요</u>. "(Oh, I see that) this coffee is strong."

~겠네요

The suffix 겠 is a pre-final ending that comes between the stem of the predicate and the final-ending. The suffix 겠 denotes the speaker's conjecture or inference about what did occur, what is occurring, and what will occur, based on circumstantial evidences.

~겠네요, the combination of the suffix 겠 and the ending ~네요, is used to indicate the speaker's realization of what will happen in reaction to the surprised or unanticipated information the speaker just encountered. It is best translated in English as "(I guess...something) may/will..." Consider the following examples:

음식이 많이 <u>맵겠네요</u>. "(Oh, I see that) the food may be very spicy."
내일 날씨가 <u>춥겠네요</u>. "(Oh, I realize that) tomorrow's weather may be cold."
그럼, 우리 내일 공항에서 <u>만나겠네요</u>. "(Oh, I see that) then, we may run into each other tomorrow at the airport."

~었/았겠네요

~었/았겠네요, the combination of the past tense marker 었/았 and ~겠네요, is used to express the speaker's surprise or realization about what must have occurred. It can be translated as "I guess that something must have…," as shown in the examples below:

많이 아팠겠네요. "(I guess that it) must have been painful."
영화가 재미있었겠네요. "(I guess that) the movie must have been interesting."
누나 생일이었으니까 집에 갔었겠네요. "Since (it) was (his) older sister's birthday, (I guess that he) must have gone home."

The sentence-final ending ~군요

The one-form sentence-final ending ~군요 is used as an exclamatory ending. It is used to express the speaker's immediate realization to what he/she just perceived. The meaning and usage of ~군요 is similar to those of ~네요 in that both indicate what the speaker just realized. However, there is one subtle difference. While ~네요 indicates that what's been realized or perceived is contrary to the expectation, ~군요 simply expresses the immediate realization in a straightforward manner.

~군요 is used after adjective and copula stems. However, for verb stems, ~는 "the noun-modifying ending for verbs" is used along with ~군요 (e.g., ~는군요). Consider the following examples:

After adjective stems

날씨가 덥군요. "(Oh, I see that) the weather is hot."
한국 음식이 맛있군요. "(Oh, I see that) the Korean food is delicious."

After copula stems

제시카가 일본 사람이군요. "(Oh, I see that) Jessica is a Japanese person."
여기가 존의 집이군요. "(Oh, I see that) here is John's house."

After verb stems

일본어를 가르치는군요. "(Oh, I see that they) teach the Japanese language."
매일 골프를 배우는군요. "(Oh, I see that he) learns golf everyday.

For immediate realization about a past event, ~었/았군요 is used for all predicates.

영화가 재미있었군요. "(Oh, I see that) the movie was interesting."
한국의 수도가 서울이었군요. "(Oh, I see that) the capital of Korea was Seoul."
한국 노래를 좋아했군요. "(Oh, I see that you) liked Korean songs."

For immediate realization about a possible or guessed future event, ~겠군요 is used.

서울에서 어머니를 만나겠군요. "(Oh, I see that he) may meet (his) mother in Seoul."
내일 가게를 열겠군요. "(Oh, I see that they) may open the store tomorrow."
한국 문학을 전공하겠군요. "(Oh, I see that she) may major in Korean literature."

Exercises

Key vocabulary for Unit 2 exercises

가게 store
경치 scenery
김치 kimchi
깨끗하다 to be clean
날씨 weather
닫다 to close
덥다 to be hot (the weather)
맛있다 to be delicious
먹다 to eat
물가 prices

방 room
변호사 lawyer
비싸다 to be expensive
시끄럽다 to be noisy
신혼 a new marriage
아름답다 to be beautiful
어제 yesterday
없다 not have/not exist
여행 trip/travel
오늘 today

15

오후 afternoon
이야기하다 to talk
일하다 to work
자다 to sleep
조용하다 to be quiet
집 house
형 older brother

Exercise 2.1

Finish the following translation using ~지요 (seeking confirmation) and
the sentence cue provided in parenthesis, as shown in the example.

> Example: "Nick is also coming, right?" (닉도 오고 있다)
> = 닉도 오고 있지요?

1 Wendy is a Chinese, right? (웬디가 중국 사람이다)
2 (They) meet Edward, right? (에드워드를 만나다)
3 (You) believe me, right? (나를 믿다)
4 The price is expensive, right? (가격이 비싸다)
5 (You) take the bus over there, right? (저기서 버스를 타다)

Exercise 2.2

Conjugate the predicate using ~지요? (seeking confirmation). Then translate the sentence, as shown in the example.

> Example: 토마스가 사과를 먹고 싶어하다
> = 토마스가 사과를 먹고 싶어하지요?
> "Thomas wants to eat an apple, right?"

1 오늘 날씨가 덥다
2 경치가 아름답다
3 방이 조용하다
4 집이 시끄럽다
5 커피가 맛있다

Exercise 2.3

Finish the following translation using ~지요 (suggestion) and the sentence
cue provided in parenthesis, as shown in the example.

Example: "(How about we) see an action movie together?"
(같이 액션 영화를 보다)
= 같이 액션 영화를 보지요.

1 (How about we) go back home? (집으로 돌아가다)
2 (How about we) order coffee? (커피를 시키다)
3 (How about we) turn on the air conditioner? (에어컨을 켜다)
4 (How about we) make a phone call to Linda? (린다한테 전화를 걸다)
5 (How about we) pay (them) by cash? (현금으로 지불하다)
6 (How about we) buy a birthday card? (생일 카드를 사다)
7 (How about we) borrow a Korean movie? (한국 영화를 빌리다)
8 (How about we) use the subway? (지하철을 이용하다)
9 (How about we) invite Jodie's friends as well? (조디의 친구들도 초대하다)
10 (How about we) quit smoking? (담배를 끊다)

Exercise 2.4

Finish the following translation using ~네요 and the sentence cue provided in parenthesis, as shown in the example.

Example: "(Oh, I see that) it rains outside." (밖에 비가 오다)
= 밖에 비가 오네요.

1 (Oh, I see that) Chris snores. (크리스가 코골다)
2 (Oh, I see that) Abigail sings well. (아비게일이 노래를 잘 하다)
3 (Oh, I see that) Ronald is diligent. (로날드가 부지런하다)
4 (Oh, I see that) Diana went home from work. (다이에나가 퇴근했다)
5 (Oh, I see that) Lidia earned money. (리디아가 돈을 벌었다)
6 (Oh, I see that) the ring was expensive. (반지가 비쌌다)

Exercise 2.5

Conjugate the predicate using ~네요. Then translate the sentence, as shown in the example.

Example: 토마스가 제인하고 커피를 마시다
= 토마스가 제인하고 커피를 마시네요.
"(Oh, I see that) Thomas drinks coffee with Jane."

1 조셉이 집에 없다
2 레이첼이 김치를 먹다
3 니콜라스가 나탈리하고 이야기하다
4 데이빗이 알렉스의 형이다
5 씬디가 아직 안 자다
6 방이 깨끗하다

Exercise 2.6

Finish the following translation using ~군요 and the sentence cue provided in parenthesis, as shown in the example.

> Example: "(Oh, I see that they) arrived (here) already."
> (벌써 도착했다)
> = 벌써 도착했군요.

1 (Oh, I see that) the weather is chilly. (날씨가 싸늘하다)
2 (Oh, I see that it) was very windy yesterday. (어제 바람이 많이 불었다)
3 (Oh, I see that) Boston is famous for lobster. (보스톤이 바닷가재로 유명하다)
4 (Oh, I see that) Julia is a nurse. (줄리아가 간호사이다)
5 (Oh, I see that it) is summer from now on. (이제부터 여름이다)
6 (Oh, I see that) Jim received the bonus. (짐이 보너스를 받았다)

Exercise 2.7

Conjugate the predicate using ~군요. Then translate the sentence, as shown in the example.

> Example: 폴이 도서관에 갔다
> = 폴이 도서관에 갔군요. "(Oh, I see that) Paul went to the library."

1 나오미가 패션 모델이다
2 유럽으로 신혼 여행을 가다
3 오후 9시에 가게를 닫았다
4 해리가 변호사로 일했다
5 물가가 비싸다
6 어제 방이 더웠다

UNIT 3

Particles
보다, 처럼, 같이, 만큼, 마다, 마저,
조차, 밖에

보다

The particle 보다 is used to make a comparative sentence. This particle is attached to a noun that is being compared, and it is translated as "more than" or "rather than." Consider the following example:

제인의 방이 톰의 방보다 커요. "Jane's room is bigger than Tom's room."

Notice that Tom's room is the noun that is being compared to Jane's room.

Adverbs such as 더 "more," 덜 "less," and 훨씬 "by far," can be used along with the particle 보다 to put more emphasis on the comparison, as shown below:

이 옷이 그 옷보다 더 비싸요. "This dress is more expensive than that dress."
오늘이 어제보다 덜 추워요. "Today is less cold than yesterday."
제가 형보다 훨씬 더 많이 먹어요. "I eat much more than (my) older brother."

Here are more examples:

저는 봄보다 가을을 더 좋아해요. "As for me, (I) like autumn more than spring."
앤드류가 누구보다 더 멋있어요. "Andrew is handsomer than anybody."
로날드가 저보다 두 살이 더 많아요. "Ronald is two years older than I."
조지가 프랭크보다 더 벌었어요. "George earned more than Frank."
커피보다 주스를 더 마시고 싶었어요. "(I) wanted to drink juice more than coffee."
이 영화가 그 영화보다 덜 재미있었어요. "This movie was less interesting than that movie."

톰보다 돈을 덜 썼어요. "(I) spent less money than Tom."

브래드가 존보다 훨씬 더 유명해요. "Brad is much more popular than John."

피터가 저보다 키가 더 컸었어요. "Peter used to be taller than I."

처럼 and 같이

The particle 처럼 is used to compare one noun with another. It is translated as "as if" and "like." Consider the following examples:

앨리스가 한국 사람처럼 한국말을 잘 해요. "Alice speaks Korean well like a Korean."

다이애나가 어른처럼 행동해요. "Diana behaves like an adult."

티나처럼 열심히 일하세요. "Work hard like Tina."

The meaning of the particle 같이 is similar to that of 처럼, as shown below:

제인은 목소리가 남자 목소리같이 허스키해요. "As for Jane, (her) voice is husky like a man's voice."

어제는 여름같이 더웠어요. "As for yesterday, (it) was hot like summer."

오늘 밤은 낮같이 밝아요. "As for tonight, (it) is bright like the daytime."

만큼

The particle 만큼 is used to express "as much as" or "to the extent to that." Consider the following examples:

우리 형만큼 똑똑했어요. "(I) was as smart as my older brother."

오늘은 어제만큼 덥지 않아요. "As for today, (it) is not as hot as yesterday."

조지가 윌리엄만큼 골프를 잘 쳐요. "George plays golf as good as William."

이 차가 저 차만큼 비싸요. "This car is as expensive as that car (over there)."

힐러리는 메리만큼 예뻐요. "As for Hilary, (she) is as pretty as Mary."

기대만큼 점수가 나왔어요. "The score came out to the extent of (my) expectation."

마다

The particle 마다 means "every" or "each," as shown in the examples below:

형이 <u>달마다</u> 돈을 부쳐 줘요. "(My) older brother sends (me) money every month."
4<u>시간마다</u> 약을 먹으세요. "Take the medicine every 4 hours."
<u>방마다</u> 텔레비전이 있어요? "Does each room have a TV?"
<u>교수님마다</u> 연구실이 있어요. "Each professor has an office."

마저 and 조차

The particles 마저 or 조차 are used to express "even." Consider the following examples:

<u>토마스마저</u> 파티에 안 왔어요. "**Even** Thomas did not come to the party."
그 학생은 자기 <u>이름조차</u> 못 써요. "As for that student, (he) can not write **even** his name."

The meanings of 마저 and 조차 are similar to that of 까지 "even." However, differing from 까지, the particles 마저 and 조차 are in general associated with unfavorable or unsought contents. Compare the following two sentences:

존의 여자친구<u>까지</u> 만났어요. "(I) even met John's girlfriend."
존의 여자친구<u>마저</u> 만났어요. "(I) even met John's girlfriend."

Although the translation of both examples are the same, the second example with 마저 implies that meeting Thomas' girlfriend was not a favorable event, whereas the first example with 까지 simply indicates "including (even)." Here are more examples:

차 사고로 부인하고 <u>아들마저</u> 잃었어요. "Due to the car accident, (he) lost (his) wife and even (his) son."
<u>당신마저</u> 나를 떠나면 어떻게 살아가요? "If you also leave me, how should (I) go on living?"
빚때문에 집을 팔고 <u>차마저</u> 팔았어요. "Because of the debt, (we) sold the house and even the car."
아침도 굶고 <u>점심조차</u> 못 먹었어요. "(I) skipped breakfast and could not eat even lunch."
그의 <u>여자친구조차</u> 그의 이야기를 안 믿었어요. "Even his girlfriend did not believe his story."

밖에

The particle 밖에 is used to indicate "only" or "nothing but" in English. The meaning of 밖에 is similar to that of 만 "only." However, differing from 만, the particle 밖에 always co-occurs with the negative predicate. For instance, compare the following sentences:

15 달라만 있어요. "(I) have only 15 dollars."
15 달라밖에 없어요. "(I) have only 15 dollars (lit. I have nothing but 15 dollars)."

Notice that although the meanings of both sentences are similar, the second sentence ends in a negative 없어요 "do not have." Here are more examples:

5 분밖에 안 기다렸어요. "(I) waited only 5 minutes."
교실이 반밖에 안 찼어요. "The classroom is only half full."
커피를 두 잔밖에 안 마셨어요. "(I) drank only two cups of coffee."
다음 학기는 세 과목밖에 안 들을 거예요. "As for next semester, (I) will take only three courses."
유니스는 일본어를 조금밖에 못 해요. "As for Eunice, (she) can speak only a little Japanese."

Exercises

Key vocabulary for Unit 3 exercises

기다리다 to wait
낮잠 nap
마시다 to drink
만나다 to meet
먹다 to eat
분 minute
사과 apple
샐러드 salad
생각하다 to think
손님 customer/guest
시간 hour
아빠 dad
어머니 mother
어제 yesterday
언니 older sister
엄마 mom

자다 to sleep
재즈 jazz
좋아하다 to like
주스 juice

Exercise 3.1

Complete the following translation using the particle 보다 and the cues
provided in parenthesis, as shown in the example.

Example: "(I) wanted to drink juice more than coffee."
(커피 / 주스를 더 마시고 싶었어요)
= 커피보다 주스를 더 마시고 싶었어요.

1 Charles is more popular than Lisa (리사 / 찰스가 인기가 더 많아
   요)
2 Philippine is hotter than Korea (한국 / 필리핀이 더 더워요)
3 (I) liked autumn better than spring (봄 / 가을을 더 좋아했어요)
4 (He) wanted to major in literature more than science (과학 / 문학을
   더 전공하고 싶어했어요)
5 Did (you) want to buy a notebook more than a digital camera? (디지
   탈 카메라 / 노트북을 더 사고 싶었어요?)
6 An airplane is faster than a car (차 / 비행기가 더 빠릅니다)
7 New York City is bigger than Honolulu (호놀룰루 / 뉴욕시가 더 큽
   니다)
8 Today is less cold than yesterday (어제 / 오늘이 덜 춥습니다)
9 Does Sam play tennis better than Harry? (해리 / 샘이 테니스를 더
   잘 칩니까?)
10 Does Jane like meat more than Dave? (데이브 / 제인이 고기를 더
   좋아합니까?)

Exercise 3.2

Finish the following translation using the particle 처럼 and the cues provided in parenthesis, as shown in the example.

Example: "That child drinks water much like a hippo."
(그 아이 / 하마 / 물을 많이 마셔요)
= 그 아이가 하마처럼 물을 많이 마셔요.

1 Juice is chilly like ice (주스 / 얼음 / 차가워요)
2 Lidia acts like a detective (리디아 / 형사 / 행동해요)

3 Does Chris swim well like a seal? (크리스 / 물개 / 수영을 잘 해요?)
4 Jerry was docile like a sheep (제리 / 양 / 순했어요)
5 Vegetables will be expensive like gold (야채 / 금 / 비쌀 거예요)
6 John is tall like a basketball player (존 / 농구 선수 / 키가 커요)
7 Sandy is slim like a model (샌디 / 모델 / 날씬해요)
8 Anthony is smart like Einstein (앤서니 / 아인슈타인 / 똑똑해요)
9 Sarah sang the song well like an opera singer (사라 / 오페라 가수 / 노래를 잘 했어요)
10 Thomas will run well like a marathoner (토마스 / 마라톤 선수 / 잘 뛸 거예요)

Exercise 3.3

Complete the following translation using the particle 만큼 and the cues provided in parenthesis, as shown in the example.

Example: "Bill is as rich as Tom." (빌 / 톰 / 부자입니다)
= 빌이 톰만큼 부자입니다.

1 Catherine speaks Korean as fluently as Neal (캐서린 / 닐 / 한국어를 잘 합니다)
2 The kitchen is as big as the living room (부엌 / 거실 / 큽니다)
3 Daniel is as diligent as Philip (데니엘 / 필립 / 부지런합니다)
4 Did Patrick like wine as much as Erica? (패트릭 / 에리카 / 와인을 좋아했습니까?)
5 Rebecca was as graceful as Jennifer (레베카 / 제니퍼 / 얌전했습니다)
6 Seoul is as expensive as New York (서울 / 뉴욕 / 비싸요)
7 This car is as good as that car (over there) (이 차 / 저 차 / 좋아요)
8 Does Philip earns money as much as Adam? (필립 / 아담 / 돈을 벌어요?)
9 The subway was as convenient as taxi (지하철 / 택시 / 편했어요)
10 Edward drank (it) as much as Thomas (에드워드 / 토마스 / 마셨어요)

Exercise 3.4

Complete the following translation using the particle 마다 and the cues provided in parenthesis, as shown in the example.

Example: "Does Hugh jog every morning?" (휴 / 아침 / 조깅을 합니까?)
"휴가 아침마다 조깅을 합니까?"

1 (I) take a walk every evening (저녁 / 산책합니다)
2 Do (you) ski every winter? (겨울 / 스키를 탑니까?)
3 (We) went to the beach every summer (여름 / 바닷가에 갔습니다)
4 Every store will be busy (가게 / 바쁠 거예요)
5 (Let us) meet every night (밤 / 만납시다)
6 Every supermarket sells juice (슈퍼마켓 / 주스 / 팔아요)
7 Each school has alma mater (학교 / 교가가 있어요)
8 Each room had a window (방 / 창문이 있었어요)
9 Every student is studying for the test (학생 / 시험 공부를 하고 있어요)
10 Did (your) friends play golf every Saturday? (친구들 / 토요일 / 골프를 쳤어요?)

Exercise 3.5

Complete the following translation using the particle 마저 and the cues provided in parenthesis, as shown in the example.

Example: "Even Jane was sick." (제인 / 아팠어요)
= 제인마저 아팠어요.

1 Even Sabrina lied (사브리나 / 거짓말을 했어요)
2 Even (my) older sister hid the fact (누나 / 사실을 감췄어요)
3 Even the weather was cold (날씨 / 추웠어요)
4 Even my room was dark (제 방 / 어두웠어요)
5 Even the air conditioner was broken (에어컨 / 고장났어요)
6 Even Matthew did not go to school (매튜 / 학교에 안 갔어요)
7 Even (his) wife will go back to the States (부인 / 미국으로 돌아갈 거예요)
8 Even Monica failed the test (모니카 / 시험에 떨어졌어요)
9 Did even the convenient store close? (편의점 / 닫았어요?)
10 Even Paul will sell (his) car (폴 / 차를 팔 거예요)

Exercise 3.6

Rewrite the following sentence using the [밖에 + negative] pattern, as
shown in the example. Then translate the sentence.

Example: 사과만 있어요.
= 사과밖에 없어요. "(I) have only apples."

1 사과 주스만 마셔요.
2 샐러드만 먹어요.
3 엄마는 아빠만 좋아해요.
4 손님이 7 명만 있어요.
5 낮잠을 1 시간만 잘 거예요.
6 어머니만 생각했어요.
7 재즈만 좋아했어요.
8 어제 5 시간만 잤어요.
9 10 분만 기다릴 거예요.
10 언니만 만날 거예요.

UNIT 4
Auxiliary verbs I

An auxiliary verb combines with a main verb to express tense, aspect, mood and/or voice. For instance, English auxiliary verbs include "can," "have," "may," "shall," and "will," since they combine with a main verb, as in "I can speak Korean." This unit first discusses some general structural characteristics of Korean auxiliary verbs. Then, it introduces how the following three verbs, 보다 "see," 오다 "come," and 가다 "go," can serve as auxiliary verbs.

Korean auxiliary verbs

Korean auxiliary verbs are in fact all regular verbs. However, when these verbs are used as auxiliary verbs, they express different meanings, as shown below:

Regular verbs	Auxiliary verbs
보다 "see"	~어/아 보다 "try (doing something)"
오다 "come"	~어/아 오다 "continue to"
가다 "go"	~어/아 가다 "continue to"
주다 "give"	~어/아 주다 "do for (someone)"
내다 "produce"	~어/아 내다 "do all the way completely"
나다 "occur"	~어/아 나다 "have finished"
버리다 "throw away"	~어/아 버리다 "finish up/end up with"
놓다 "put down"	~어/아 놓다 "do for later"
하다 "do"	~어/아하다 "be in the state of"
지다 "become"	~어/아지다 "become"
말다 "stop"	~고 말다 "end up doing"

Korean auxiliary verbs always appear after the main verb (or adjectives for limited auxiliary verbs). In addition, the main verb is always conjugated with ~어/아 (or ~고 for limited auxiliary verbs). The compounding process takes the following pattern: [stem of the main verb ~어/아 plus an auxiliary verb]. ~아 is used after the stem that ends in 아 or 오 (e.g., 찾다 "find"

=> 찾아 보다 "try looking for something"), while ~어 is used after the stem that ends in all other vowels (e.g., 만들다 "make" => 만들어 보다 "try making something").

~어/아 보다

When the verb 보다 "see" is used as an auxiliary verb, it is used to express "try (doing something)/experience." It is used when a speaker tries doing some action just once so that he/she can explore the consequences. For instance, consider how the auxiliary verb ~어/아 보다 is used with the main verb 배우다 "learn."

> 한국어를 배워 봅니다. "(I) try learning Korean."
> 한국어를 배워 봅시다. "(Let us) try learning Korean."
> 한국어를 배워 보시지요. "(Why don't you try) learning Korean?"
> 한국어를 배워 보십시오. "Try learning Korean."
> 한국어를 배워 봤습니다. "(I) tried learning Korean."
> 한국어를 배워 볼 거예요. "(I) will try learning Korean."

Notice in the examples above that ~어/아 보다 completes each expression and carries all grammatical information, such as tense, sentence types, and honorifics. Here are more examples:

> 김치를 먹어 봤어요. "(I) tried eating kimchi" (lit. "I ate kimchi and saw what it was like").
> 프랑스에 가 봤습니다. "(I) have been to France."
> 오토바이를 타 봤습니까? "Have (you) tried riding a motorcycle?"
> 김치를 먹어 보세요. "Please try (eating) kimchi."
> 존을 만나 보십시오. "Try to meet John."
> 제리한테 일을 맡겨 봅시다. "(Let us) try entrusting the task to Jerry."
> 한국 음식을 먹어 볼 거예요. "(I) will try eating Korean food."
> 한국 맥주를 마셔 볼 거예요. "(I) will try drinking Korean beer."

~어/아 오다/가다

Korean has two motion verbs 오다 "come" and 가다 "go." When these motion verbs are used as auxiliary verbs, both indicate that an action of the main verb is carried out continually. Since 오다 "come" signifies the motion toward the speaker, ~어/아 오다 is used to express an continuous action that comes toward the present, as shown below:

지금까지 혼자 잘 <u>살아 왔어요</u>. "Until now, (I) have lived alone well."

김사장님이 회사를 잘 <u>이끌어 왔어요</u>. "President Kim has led the company well."

저희는 선생님 말씀을 <u>믿어 왔어요</u>. "As for us, (we) have believed the teacher's word."

On the other hand, 가다 "go" indicates the motion away from the speaker. Consequently, ~어/아 가다 is used to express a continuous action that goes into the future.

드라마가 <u>끝나 가요</u>. "The drama is going to end."

가을이 <u>깊어 가요</u>. "Autumn is ripening."

사업이 잘 <u>되어 가요</u>? "Does (your) business continue to do well?"

아이가 엄마를 <u>닮아 가요</u>. "The child continues to take after (her) mother."

Exercises

Key vocabulary for Unit 4 exercises

가다 to go
가르치다 to teach
가정 family
감기 a cold/flu
고치다 to fix
끝나다 to end/to finish
낫다 to get well/to recover from (illness)
논문 thesis
늙다 to grow older
다 all
도자기 ceramics
만들다 to make
먹다 to eat
물 water

바꾸다 to change
병원 hospital
산 mountain
살다 to live
쓰다 to use/to write
여자 woman
영어 English
올라가다 to climb/to go up

음식 food
이제 now
인도 India
입다 to wear

전화하다 to make a phone call
절약하다 to economize on/to save/to be thrifty
조금씩 little by little
친구 friends
한복 traditional Korean clothes
해 a year/the sun
행복하다 to be happy
헤어지다 to break up
혼자 alone

Exercise 4.1

Conjugate the predicate using ~어/아 봤습니다 as shown in the example.
Then translate the sentence.

> Example: 집에 가다
> = 집에 가 봤습니다. "(I) have been to the house."

1 인도 음식을 먹다
2 도자기를 만들다
3 한복을 입다
4 베이징에 가다
5 병원에 전화하다

Exercise 4.2

Conjugate the predicate using ~어/아 봤습니까? as shown in the example.
Then translate the sentence.

> Example: 엘비스의 노래를 듣다
> = 엘비스의 노래를 들어 봤습니까?
> "Have (you) tried listening to Elvis' song?"

1 무역 회사에서 일하다
2 낚시를 하다
3 타이 음식을 먹다
4 한국어를 배우다
5 교회에 가다

Exercise 4.3

Conjugate the predicate using ~어/아 보십시오, as shown in the example.
Then translate the sentence.

> Example: 요가를 하다
> = 요가를 해 보십시오. "Try doing yoga."

1 영어를 가르치다
2 산을 올라가다
3 아파트에서 살다
4 여자친구랑 헤어지다
5 컴퓨터를 고치다

Exercise 4.4

Conjugate the predicate using ~어/아 봅시다, as shown in the example.
Then translate the sentence.

> Example: 도서관에 가다
> = 도서관에 가 봅시다. "(Let us) try going to the library."

1 기도하다
2 선생님한테 부탁하다
3 차를 고치다
4 구멍을 막다
5 에어컨을 켜다

Exercise 4.5

Finish the following translation using ~어/아 보다 and the sentence cue
provided in parenthesis, as shown in the example.

> Example: "(I) tried (doing) bungee jumping" (번지점프를 하다)
> = 번지점프를 해 봤습니다.

1 (I) have been to Africa (아프리카에 가다)
2 (I) will try to study the Korean language (한국어를 공부하다)
3 (I) tried drinking Korean beer (한국 맥주를 마시다)
4 Have (you) been to Sweden? (스웨덴에 가다)
5 Have (you) tried playing a guitar? (기타를 치다)
6 Try to memorize (her) home phone number (집 전화 번호를 외우
다)

31

7 Try (using) the massage machine (마사지 기계를 사용하다)
8 Try making Korean friends (한국 사람하고 사귀다)
9 (Let us) try to learn cooking (요리를 배우다)
10 (Let us) try to repair the computer (컴퓨터를 고치다)

Exercise 4.6

Finish the following translation using ~어/아 가다 (or ~어/아 오다) and
the sentence cue provided in parenthesis, as shown in the example.

Example: "Ice is melting" (얼음이 녹다)
= 얼음이 녹아 가요.

1 (My) older brother brought good news (형이 좋은 소식을 전하다)
2 The dog has run toward this way (개가 이쪽으로 달리다)
3 William has suffered from a cold (윌리엄이 감기로 고생하다)
4 (They) have been receiving help from Robert (로버트로부터 도움을
받다)
5 Water is getting frozen (물이 얼다)

Exercise 4.7

Conjugate the predicate using ~어/아 가다, as shown in the example. Then
translate the sentence.

Example: 영화가 끝나다 (declarative)
= 영화가 끝나 갑니다. "The movie is going to end."

1 우리 할머니는 해마다 늙다 (declarative)
2 이제부터 혼자 살다 (interrogative)
3 행복한 가정을 만들다 (imperative)
4 물을 절약하다 (propositive)
5 조금씩 스케줄을 바꾸다 (propositive)

UNIT 5
Auxiliary verbs II

~어/아 내다

The verb 내다 means "produce/put forth" as in 용기를 내세요 "Put forth courage" or 속력을 내세요 "Speed up" (lit. "Produce speed"). However, as an auxiliary verb, ~어/아 내다 means "do all the way (to the very end)." It is used to express that although a certain task/action is troublesome or difficult, he/she completes the action to the very end (or does all the way). Compare the following two examples:

하루만에 책을 읽었어요. "(I) read the book within a day."
하루만에 책을 읽어 냈어요. "(I) read the book (to the very end) within a day."

Notice that the first sentence simply indicates that the speaker finished reading the book in one day. On the other hand, the second sentence with ~어/아 내다 implies that although reading the book within a day was a difficult task, the speaker did it anyway. Here are more examples:

혼자 고생을 견뎌 냈습니다. "(He) endured hardship alone (all the way)."
결국 지갑을 찾아 냈어요. "Finally, (I) found the wallet."
3 년안에 학위를 따 냈어요. "(He) got the degree within three years."
결국 전구를 만들어 냈습니다. "Eventually, (he) made an electric bulb."

~어/아 버리다

The verb 버리다 means "throw (it) away/dismiss/abandon," as shown in the following examples:

어제 옛 사진들을 버렸어요. "Yesterday, (I) discarded old pictures."
그녀가 남편을 버렸어요. "She abandoned (her) husband."

내일까지 쓰레기를 <u>버리세요</u>. "Throw the garbage away by tomorrow."
친구를 위해서 목숨을 <u>버릴 거예요</u>. "(I) will lay down (my) life for (my) friend."

However, as an auxiliary verb ~어/아 버리다 means "do completely/ end up doing/get (it) done." Compare the following sentences:

내일 편지를 부치세요. "Send the letter tomorrow."
내일 편지를 <u>부쳐 버리세요</u>. "Send the letter tomorrow."

The basic meanings of both sentences are the same. However, the message of the second sentence is stronger than the first sentence, since ~어/아 버리다 adds the meaning of "completeness of the action."
~어/아 버리다 is similar to ~어/아 내다 in a sense that both are used to indicate the completeness of an action. However, unlike ~어/아 내다, ~어/아 버리다 does not imply that the completed action was a difficult task. Instead, depending on the context, ~어/아 버리다 is used to express a sense of regret or relief. Consider the following examples:

지갑을 잃었어요. "(I) lost (my) wallet."
지갑을 <u>잃어 버렸어요</u>. "(I) lost (my) wallet."

Losing a wallet is undesirable. Consequently, ~어/아 버리다 in the second sentence adds the sense of regret, while the first sentence simply states the past action. It indicates that losing a wallet is not what the speaker had expected or wished for. Here are more examples that may denote a sense of regret:

결국 <u>울어 버렸어요</u>. "(She) finally cried."
돈을 다 <u>써 버렸어요</u>. "(I) used up all of (my) money."
나오미가 결국 미국에 <u>가 버렸어요</u>. "Naomi finally went to America."
제 남동생이 벌써 다 <u>먹어 버렸어요</u>. "My younger brother already ate (them) all."
금붕어가 <u>죽어 버렸어요</u>. "The gold fish died."

~어/아 버리다 can also signify a sense of relief. Consider the following two sentences:

숙제를 끝냈어요. "(I) finished (my) homework."
숙제를 <u>끝내 버렸어요</u>. "(I) finished (my) homework."

Notice that the referential messages of both sentences are the same. However, ~어/아 버리다 in the second sentence adds a sense of relief since the task (e.g., doing homework) has come to an end. Here are more examples that indicate a sense of relief:

아픈 기억을 <u>지워 버렸어요</u>. "(I) erased the painful memory (completely)."
신용 카드 빚을 다 <u>갚아 버렸어요</u>. "(I) paid all of (my) credit card debt."

~고 말다

The verb 말다 means "stop," as in 눈이 오다가 <u>말았어요</u> "(It) snowed but then (it) stopped." However, as an auxiliary verb, ~고 말다 means "end up (doing)," and it implies that the completed action is against the subject's intention or wish. It is used when the action is carried out despite the subject's previous effort or wishes against the completed action. Compare the following two sentences:

차 사고로 <u>죽었어요</u>. "(He) died because of the car accident."
차 사고로 <u>죽고 말았어요</u>. "(He) ended up dying because of the car accident."

Notice that the completed action (dying) is against the subject's will. Here are more examples:

누나는 한국에 <u>돌아가고 말았어요</u>. "As for (my) older sister, (she) ended up returning to Korea."
술에 <u>취하고 말았어요</u>. "(We) ended up drunk."
소파에 커피를 <u>쏟고 말았어요</u>. "(I) ended up spilling coffee on the sofa."
돌부리에 걸려 <u>넘어지고 말았어요</u>. "(I) ended up tripping on the jagged edge of a stone."
차 안에서 잠이 <u>들고 말았어요</u>. "(I) ended up falling asleep in the car."
전쟁이 결국 <u>터지고 말았습니다</u>. "The war finally broke out."
늦게 <u>자고 말았어요</u>. "(I) ended up going to bed late."

~어/아 주다

The verb 주다 means "give," as shown in the following examples:

조지한테 책을 <u>줬어요</u>. "(I) gave the book to George."
매달 여동생한테 용돈을 <u>줘요</u>. "(I) give pocket money to (my) younger sister every month."
스티븐이 리사한테 꽃을 <u>줄 거예요</u>. "Steven will give flowers to Lisa."

However, as an auxiliary verb, ~어/아 주다 means "do something as a favor (for someone)."

팔다 "sell"   팔아 주다 "sell (something for someone)"
가르치다 "teach"   가르쳐 주다 "teach (something for someone)"
믿다 "believe"   믿어 주다 "believe (something for someone)"

Compare the following two sentences:

데이빗이 파티에 <u>왔어요</u>. "David came to the party."
데이빗이 파티에 <u>와 줬어요</u>. "David came to the party" (lit. "David did a favor for somebody by coming to the party").

Notice that the first sentence simply expresses that David came to the party. On the other hand, the second sentence signifies that David came to the party for the benefit of the speaker or somebody. Here are more examples:

친구들이 음식을 맛있게 <u>먹어 줬어요</u>. "(My) friends ate the food with gusto (for me)."
앤서니가 선물을 <u>보내 줬어요</u>. "Anthony sent (her) the present (for me)."
제가 문을 <u>열어 줄게요</u>. "I will open the door (for you)."
로라가 시계를 <u>사 줄 거예요</u>. "Laura will buy (me) a bag (for me)."

However, one can optionally use 위해서 "on the behalf of" when wishing to explicitly state who the beneficiary was.

남자 친구를 <u>위해서</u> 맛있는 점심을 <u>만들어 줬어요</u>. "(She) made delicious lunch for (her) boyfriend."
우리를 <u>위해서</u> 병원에 <u>와 주셨어요</u>. "(He) came to the hospital for us."

~어/아 드리다 vs. ~어/아 주다

Meanwhile, if the beneficiary of the action is an esteemed person (e.g., a higher person in age or social status), ~어/아 드리다 is used instead of ~어/아 주다. Compare the following two sentences:

(O) 할머니께 시계를 <u>사 드렸어요</u>. "(I) bought a watch for (my) grandmother."
(X) 할머니께 시계를 <u>사 줬어요</u>. "(I) bought a watch for (my) grandmother."

The second sentence with ~어/아 주다 is inappropriate since the beneficiary of the action is an esteemed person (e.g., grandmother). Here are more examples:

아버지께 아침을 <u>만들어 드렸어요</u>. "(I) made breakfast for (my) father."
안마 <u>해 드릴게요</u>. "(I) will massage (your) back)."
와인을 <u>사 드리고</u> 싶어요. "(I) want to buy wine (for him)."

Requesting ~어/아 주세요

The verb 주시다 is the honorific form of 주다. ~어/아 주세요 is used when requesting something politely. It is equivalent to "please do (something for me/someone)." Compare the following two sentences:

잠깐 기다리세요. "Please wait a moment."
잠깐 <u>기다려 주세요</u>. "Please wait a moment (for me)."

Both sentences can be used for requesting. However, the second sentence with ~어/아 주세요 is more polite than the first sentence. Here are more examples:

다른 사이즈로 <u>바꿔 주세요</u>. "Please exchange (this) with a different size (for me)."
차를 앞으로 <u>움직여 주세요</u>. "Please move (your) car forward (for me)."
곧 일을 <u>끝내 주세요</u>. "Please finish (your) work soon (for me)."
책을 크게 <u>읽어 주세요</u>. "Please read the book aloud (for me)."

Exercises

Key vocabulary for Unit 5 exercises

가게 store
가다 to go
고기 meat
고장이 나다 to get out of order
구별하다 to distinguish
굽다 to roast
그리다 to paint/to draw
그림 painting/picture
금 gold
길 road/street
나오다 to come out
남자 man
노래 song
닫다 to close

또 again
만들다 to make
문 door
미끄러지다 to slide/to glide
바꾸다 to change
받다 to receive
부르다 to sing/to call out
비밀 secret
시키다 to order/to force (a person to do)
싸우다 to fight/to dispute (with)
쓰다 to write/to use
언니 older sister
열다 to open
옷 clothes
은 silver
읽다 to read

전등 electric lamp
전화기 telephone
점심 lunch
지우다 to erase
차 car
창문 window
책 book
친구 friend
캐다 to dig into/to unearth
켜다 to light/to switch on
파일 file
팔다 to sell
편지 letter
학교 school
헤어지다 to break up
형 older brother
화내다 to get angry

Exercise 5.1

Finish the following translation using ~어/아 내다 and the sentence cue provided in parenthesis, as shown in the example.

Example: "(He) extracted the tooth." (이를 뽑다)
= 이를 뽑아 냈어요.

1 (She) caught a big fish (큰 물고기를 낚다)
2 (They) dammed up the river (강물을 막다)
3 (We) got the project (프로젝트를 따다)
4 (He) received the money (돈을 받다)
5 (I) wrote the thesis (논문을 쓰다)

Exercise 5.2

Conjugate the predicate using ~어/아 내다, as shown in the example. Then translate the sentence.

Example: 일을 하다
= 일을 해 냈어요. "(He) did the work."

1 비밀을 캐다
2 전화기를 만들다
3 고기를 굽다
4 금하고 은을 구별하다
5 그림을 그리다

Exercise 5.3

Finish the following translation using ~어/아 버리다 and the sentence cue provided in parenthesis, as shown in the example.

Example: "(I) sold the house yesterday." (어제 집을 팔다)
= 어제 집을 팔아 버렸어요.

1 Andrew took pictures (앤드류가 사진을 찍다)
2 Sara borrowed the notebook (사라가 노트북을 빌리다)
3 (We) used all the money (돈을 다 쓰다)
4 Kevin watched the drama till the end (케빈이 드라마를 끝까지 보다)
5 Angie moved (her) job (앤지가 직장을 옮기다)

Auxiliary
verbs II

Exercise 5.4

Conjugate the predicate using ~어/아 버리다, as shown in the example.
Then translate the sentence.

> Example: 약속을 잊다
> = 약속을 잊어 버렸어요. "(I) forgot about the appointment."

1 차가 또 고장이 나다
2 가게 문을 닫다
3 파일을 지우다
4 친구가 뉴욕으로 떠나다
5 학교에서 나오다

Exercise 5.5

Finish the following translation using ~고 말다 and the sentence cue provided in parenthesis, as shown in the example.

> Example: "(I) ended up being late for school." (학교에 지각하다)
> = 학교에 지각하고 말았어요.

1 (He) ended up getting up late (늦게 일어나다)
2 (They) ended up drinking whisky (위스키를 마시다)
3 (He) ended up confessing (his) love to (his) girlfriend (여자 친구한테 사랑을 고백하다)
4 (He) finally ended up quitting (his) job (결국 일을 그만두다)
5 (My) car ended up being broken down (차가 고장이 나다)

Exercise 5.6

Conjugate the predicate using ~고 말다, as shown in the example. Then translate the sentence.

> Example: 조지가 시험에 떨어지다
> = 조지가 시험에 떨어지고 말았어요.
> "George ended up failing the test."

1 로날드가 형하고 싸우다
2 샐리가 남자 친구하고 헤어지다
3 테렌스가 노트북을 팔다
4 씬디가 길에서 미끄러지다
5 조앤이 언니한테 화내다

Exercise 5.7

Finish the following translation using ~어/아 주다 and the sentence cue provided in parenthesis, as shown in the example.

> Example: "Thomas bought an umbrella (for me)."
> (토마스가 우산을 사다)
> = 토마스가 우산을 사 줬어요.

1 Tina helped (my) project (for me) (티나가 프로젝트를 돕다)
2 (My) older brother bought (me) a bag (오빠가 가방을 사다)
3 John sold the car (for me) (존이 차를 팔다)
4 Megan will take pictures (for us) (메건이 사진을 찍다)
5 (My) older sister will wash dishes (for me) (언니가 설거지를 하다)
6 Please lend (me) the book (책을 빌리다)
7 Please repair the computer (for me) (컴퓨터를 고치다)
8 Please refund the dress (for me) (옷을 환불하다)
9 Please play the piano (for me) (피아노를 치다)
10 Please turn on the radio (for me) (라디오를 틀다)

Exercise 5.8

Conjugate the predicates using ~어/아 드렸어요, as shown in the example. Then translate the sentence.

> Example: 어머니를 돕다
> = 어머니를 도와 드렸어요. "(I) helped (my) mother."

1 책을 읽다
2 편지를 쓰다
3 전화를 받다
4 창문을 닫다
5 전등을 켜다
6 문을 열다
7 옷을 바꾸다
8 노래를 부르다
9 점심을 만들다
10 커피를 시키다

UNIT 6
Auxiliary verbs III

~어/아 놓다 (or ~어/아 두다)

The verb 놓다 means "release/place/put down," as in:

고양이를 <u>놓아 주세요</u>. "Let the cat go/loose."
접시를 식탁 위에 <u>놓았어요</u>. "(I) placed the plate on the dining table."
지갑을 어디에 <u>놓으셨어요</u>? "Where have (you) left the wallet?"

However, as an auxiliary verb, what ~어/아 놓다 can express is twofold. First, ~어/아 놓다 is used to indicate the continuation of a certain action or state after the completion of the action or state. For instance, compare the following sentences:

거실에 전등을 <u>켰어요</u>. "(I) turned on the electric lamp in the living room."
거실에 전등을 <u>켜 놓았어요</u>. "(I) turned on the electric lamp in the living room (and it is still on)."

The verb 켜다 means "turns on (an electric lamp)." Notice that the action of the main verb 켜다 is completed for both sentences, since they are marked by the past tense. However, while the first sentence simply indicates the past action (e.g., turned on the electric lamp), the second sentence with the auxiliary verb ~어/아 놓다 indicates the continuation of the completed action (e.g., the electric lamp continues to be on). Here are more examples:

피터가 문을 <u>열어 놓았어요</u>. "Peter opened the door (and it is still open)."
차에 시동을 <u>걸어 놓았어요</u>. "(I) started the car (and it is on)."
서랍을 <u>잠가 놓았아요</u>. "(I) locked the drawer (and it is still locked)."

Second, ~어/아 놓다 means "doing something for later (future use)." Compare the following two sentences:

조깅을 하기 전에 물을 많이 <u>마셨어요</u>. "(I) drank water a lot, before jogging."
조깅을 하기 전에 물을 많이 <u>마셔 놓았어요</u>. "(I) drank water a lot for later, before jogging."

Notice that the first sentence simply indicates the past action, 마셨어요 "drank." However, the auxiliary verb ~어/아 놓다 in the second sentence indicates that the past action (e.g., drinking) was done for later. Here are more examples:

연습을 많이 <u>해 놓았어요</u>. "(We) practiced a lot for later."
미리 열심히 <u>공부해 놓으세요</u>. "Study hard beforehand for later."
여행 계획을 <u>세워 놓을 거예요</u>. "(We) will make travel plans for later."
방을 <u>청소해 놓을 거예요</u>. "(They) will clean the room for later."

Alternatively, the verb 두다 can be used instead of 놓다. The verb 두다 means "place/keep," as shown in the following examples:

열쇠를 식탁 위에 <u>두십시오</u>. "Place the key on the dining table."
돈을 금고에 <u>두었어요</u>. "(I) kept the money in the safe."
생선은 냉장고에 <u>둘 거예요</u>. "As for the fish, (I) will keep (it) in the refrigerator."

As an auxiliary verb, the meaning of ~어/아 두다 is similar to that of ~어/아 놓다. In fact ~어/아 두다 and ~어/아 놓다 can be used interchangeably, as shown below:

누나가 아침을 <u>차려 두었어요/놓았어요</u>. "(My) older sister prepared breakfast (and it is still there/for later)."
그 일은 폴한테 <u>맡겨 두세요/놓으세요</u>. "As for that task, entrust (it) to Paul (for later)."
차를 서점 앞에 <u>주차해 뒀어요/놓았어요</u>. "(I) parked the car in front of the bookstore (and it is still there/for later use).
좌석을 <u>예약해 둘 거예요/놓을 거예요</u>. "(We) will reserve seats (for later)."

~어/아 있다

The verb 있다 means "exist/stay/have," as shown in the following examples:

로라가 서울에 <u>있어요</u>. "Laura is in Seoul."
평양이 북한에 <u>있어요</u>. "Pyongyang is in North Korea."

아이색은 애플 컴퓨터(가) 있<u>어요</u>. "As for Isaac, (he) has an Apple Computer."

As an auxiliary verb, ~어/아 있다 is mainly used with intransitive verbs and is used to indicate that the state brought about by the action of the main verb persists. Compare the following three sentences:

토미가 의자에 <u>앉아요</u>. "Tommy sits on the chair."
토미가 의자에 <u>앉고 있어요</u>. "Tommy is sitting on the chair."
토미가 의자에 <u>앉아 있어요</u>. "Tommy is seated on the chair."

The first sentence simply states what Tommy does. The second sentence indicates the progressive action of the main verb. On the other hand, ~어/아 있다 in the third sentence indicates that the state resulting from the main verb continues to exist. Consider another three sentences:

문이 <u>열려요</u>. "The door opens."
문이 <u>열리고 있어요</u>. "The door is being opened."
문이 <u>열려 있어요</u>. "The door is open."

The first sentence simply indicates that the door opens. The second sentence indicates the progressive action. The third sentence, however, indicates the continuous state, brought about by the main verb 열리다 "to be opened."
Here are more examples of ~어/아 있다:

아직 침대에 <u>누워 있어요</u>. "(He) is still lying down on the bed."
교실 앞에 <u>서 있어요</u>. "(They) are standing in front of the classroom."
문이 굳게 <u>닫혀 있어요</u>. "The door is closed firmly."
브라이언이 도서관에 <u>와 있어요</u>. "Brian is at the library (as a result of coming here)."
지금 로마에 <u>가 있어요</u>. "(They) are in Rome now (as a result of going there)."
가방 안에 책하고 지갑이 <u>들어 있습니다</u>. "(My) book and wallet are inside of the bag."

Meanwhile, a limited number of verbs of "wearing" (e.g., 입다, 쓰다, 끼다, and 매다) do not take the ~어/아 있다 pattern but the ~고 있다 pattern to indicate the resultant state. For instance, to say "(I) am wearing socks" is 양말을 신고 있어요 not 양말을 신어 있어요.

바지를 <u>입고 있어요</u>. "(I) am wearing pants."
안경을 <u>쓰고 있어요</u>. "(I) am wearing glasses."
반지를 <u>끼고 있어요</u>. "(I) am wearing a ring."
넥타이를 <u>매고 있어요</u>. "(I) am wearing a necktie."

~어/아하다

The aforementioned auxiliary verbs are all mainly used with verbs. However, Korean has a limited number of auxiliary verbs that are used primarily with adjectives, such as ~어/아하다 and ~어/아지다.

In English, one can state how another person feels, using emotion- or sense-related adjectives, such as "sad," "happy," and "cold." For instance, it is grammatically correct to say a sentence like "Lisa is sad" or "Peter is cold." However, in Korean, one cannot use adjectives to express how a third person or people feel or think. Since Korean emotive and/or sensory adjectives denote unobservable internal feelings, a speaker cannot speak for how other people feel or think. Consequently, a sentence like 리사가 슬퍼요 "Lisa is sad" is grammatically incorrect.

In order to speak for a third person's or people's feelings or emotions, one has to change an emotive or sensory adjective into a verb form, using the auxiliary verb construction ~어/아하다, as shown below:

Adjective	Adjective stem + 어/아하다
싫다 "unpleasant"	싫어하다 "dislike"
좋다 "good"	좋아하다 "like"
밉다 "detestable"	미워하다 "hate"
무섭다 "scary"	무서워하다 "fear"
괴롭다 "painful"	괴로워하다 "suffer (from)"
기쁘다 "glad"	기뻐하다 "rejoice"
슬프다 "sad"	슬퍼하다 "grieve"
부럽다 "enviable"	부러워하다 "envy"
피곤하다 "tired"	피곤해하다 "feel tired"
귀엽다 "cute"	귀여워하다 "hold (a person) dear"
가엽다 "pitiful"	가여워하다 "pity"
싶다 "desirous"	싶어하다 "want"
춥다 "cold"	추워하다 "feel cold"
덥다 "hot"	더워하다 "feel hot"

For instance, compare the following three sentences:

제가 피곤해요. "I am tired."
수잔, 피곤하세요? "Susan, are (you) tired?"
티모티가 피곤해해요. "Timothy feels tired."

Notice that when the subject of the sentence is the third person, a verb 피곤해하다 "feel tired" is used instead of the adjective 피곤하다 "be tired." In addition, note that unlike other auxiliary verb compounding structures that normally require a space between the main verb and the auxiliary verb, as in 열어 놓다 "open (for later)," ~어/아하다 does not leave a space between the main adjective and 하다 (e.g., 슬퍼하다 not 슬퍼 하다). This is due to the Korean spelling convention.

Meanwhile, when speaking of another person's emotion or feeling in the past tense, one can use an adjective (without using ~어/아하다). This is because the speaker could have information about the third person's internal feeling. Consider the following examples:

> (X) 리사가 슬퍼요. "Lisa is sad."
> (O) 리사가 <u>슬퍼해요</u>. "Lisa grieves."
> (O) 리사가 <u>슬펐어요</u>. "Lisa was sad."
> (O) 리사가 <u>슬퍼했어요</u>. "Lisa grieved."

Notice that 슬펐어요 as well as 슬퍼했어요 are both acceptable, since both refer to the third person's feeling in the past tense.

~어/아지다

The verb 지다 means "bear/owe," as shown in the following examples:

제가 책임을 <u>지겠습니다</u>. "I will take the responsibility."
그 친구한테 빚을 <u>졌었어요</u>. "(I) owed (money) to that friend."

However, as an auxiliary verb, ~어/아지다 is typically used with an adjective, and it is used to express a gradually intensified change that occurs in the meaning of the adjective. It can be translated as "become/begin to be/get to be" in English. For instance, compare the following two sentences:

날씨가 추워요. "The weather is cold."
날씨가 <u>추워져요</u>. "The weather becomes cold."

Notice in the second sentence that ~어/아지다 changes the adjective 춥다 "cold" into an intransitive verb, 추워지다 "becomes cold." In addition, the auxiliary verb ~어/아지다 adds the meaning of progressive change in the meaning of the adjective (e.g., "is cold" => "becomes cold"). Moreover, just like ~어/아하다, ~어/아지다 does not leave a space between the main adjective and 지다. Here are more examples:

가을에 날씨가 <u>서늘해져요</u>. "In autumn, the weather becomes cool."
여름에 낮이 <u>길어져요</u>. "In summer, the daytime becomes long."
미셸이 <u>예뻐졌어요</u>. "Michelle became pretty."
방이 <u>깨끗해질 거예요</u>. "The room will become clean."

Exercises

Key vocabulary for Unit 6 exercises

값 price/value
고맙다 to be thankful
궁금하다 to be curious
기억하다 to remember/to memorize
까맣다 to be black
꺼지다 to be extinguished/to die out
꽃 flowers
날씨 weather
눕다 to lie down
덥다 to be hot (the weather)
맑다 to be clear
번호 number
부럽다 to be envious
비싸다 to be expensive
신문 newspapers
씻다 to wash

아프다 to be sick
야채 vegetables
얼굴 face
예쁘다 to be pretty
예약하다 to reserve
오다 to come
음식 food
익히다 to make oneself familiar with
읽다 to read

좌석 seat
전등 electric lamp
전화 telephone
정원 garden
지리 geographical features
집 house
친구 friend
침대 bed
크다 to be big
키 height
피다 to bloom
환자 patient

Exercise 6.1

Finish the following translation using ~어/아 놓으세요 and the sentence cue provided in parenthesis, as shown in the example.

> Example: "Open the window for later." (창문을 열다)
> = 창문을 열어 놓으세요.

1 Finish (your) homework for later (숙제를 끝내다)
2 Draw a map for later (지도를 그리다)
3 Make a sauce for later (소스를 만들다)
4 Boil water for later (물을 끓이다)
5 Receive money for later (돈을 받다)

Exercise 6.2

Conjugate the predicate using ~어/아 두세요, as shown in the example. Then translate the sentence.

> Example: 저금하다
> = 저금해 두세요. "Save money for later."

1 전화 번호를 기억하다
2 신문을 읽다
3 좌석을 예약하다
4 지리를 익히다
5 야채를 씻다

Exercise 6.3

Finish the following translation using ~어/아 있다 and the sentence cue provided in parenthesis, as shown in the example.

> Example: "The dress is wet." (옷이 젖다)
> = 옷이 젖어 있어요.

1 The gate is close (문이 닫히다)
2 The picture is hung on the wall (사진이 벽에 걸리다)
3 The store is open (가게가 열리다)
4 The customer is seated on the sofa (손님이 소파에 앉다)
5 James is standing in front of the door (제임스가 문 앞에 서다)

Exercise 6.4

Conjugate the predicate with ~어/아 있다, as shown in the example. Then translate the sentence.

>   Example: 목이 붓다
>   = 목이 부어 있어요. "(My) throat is swollen."

1 버스가 오다
2 정원에 꽃이 피다
3 친구가 집에 오다
4 환자가 침대에 눕다
5 전등이 꺼지다

Exercise 6.5

Finish the following translation using ~어/아하다 and the sentence cue provided in parenthesis, as shown in the example.

>   Example: "(He) grieves." (슬프다)
>   = 슬퍼해요.

1 (She) feels happy (행복하다)
2 (He) rejoices (기쁘다)
3 (They) will feel bored (지루하다)
4 (She) felt depressed (우울하다)
5 (He) felt painful (괴롭다)

Exercise 6.6

Change the following adjective into a verb form, using ~어/아해요. Then translate the sentence.

>   Example: 외롭다
>   = 외로워해요. "(He) feels lonely."

1 덥다
2 아프다
3 고맙다
4 궁금하다
5 부럽다

Exercise 6.7

Finish the following translation using ~어/아지다 and the sentence cue provided in parenthesis, as shown in the example.

    Example: "The house has become quiet." (집이 조용하다)
              = 집이 조용해졌어요.

1 (My) head has become dizzy (머리가 어지럽다)
2 (Her) personality has become calm (성격이 차분하다)
3 (Your) voice has become soft (목소리가 부드럽다)
4 (His) body has become strong (몸이 튼튼하다)
5 (Your) car will become dirty (차가 더럽다)

Exercise 6.8

Conjugate the predicate using ~어/아지다, as shown in the example. Then translate the sentence.

    Example: 방이 깨끗하다
              = 방이 깨끗해졌어요. "The room has become clean."

1 아이의 키가 크다
2 제시카가 예쁘다
3 음식 값이 비싸다
4 날씨가 맑다
5 얼굴이 까맣다

UNIT 7
Clausal conjunctives (purpose or intention)

This unit discusses some major characteristics of Korean clausal conjunctives, and then introduces three clausal conjunctives, ~(으)러, ~(으)려고, and ~도록, that indicate the purpose or intention of the speaker.

Clausal conjunctives

Clausal conjunctives are used to link two or more clauses and to add special meanings, such as simultaneous actions, contrastive actions or states, paralleling actions, and so on. Examples of English clausal conjunctives include "and," "whereas," "while," and "though."

Korean has an extensive list of clausal conjunctives that indicate various meanings, such as "and (e.g., ~고)," "because/and then (e.g., ~어/아서)," "while (e.g., ~으면서)," "although (e.g., ~지만)," "in order to (e.g., ~도록)," and so forth. Korean clausal conjunctives are non-sentence-final endings, since they attach to the predicate stem of the preceding clause. Consider how the conjunctive ~(으)면서 "while" serves to connect two different clauses:

> [팝콘을 먹어요 "(I) eat popcorn"] + [영화를 봐요 "(I) see a movie"] = 팝콘을 <u>먹으면서</u> 영화를 봐요 "(I) see a movie, while eating popcorn."

In the example above, the conjunctive ~(으)면서 attaches to the verb stem of the first clause 먹 "eat" and indicates the new meaning "while" to the first clause: 팝콘을 먹어요 "(I) eat popcorn" changes to 팝콘을 먹으면서 "while eating popcorn." Notice that the conjunctive ~(으)면서 is not a sentence-final ending, since it does not end the sentence. Instead, ~어/아요 in the main clause (or the second clause) is the sentence-final ending since it attaches to the verb stem of the main clause 보 "see" and ends the whole sentence. Consider another example:

> 눈이 <u>내리고</u> 바람이 붑니다. "The snow falls and the wind blows."

The clausal conjunctive ~고 "and" links two clauses: 눈이 내리다 "Snow falls" and 바람이 불다 "Wind blows." Again, the conjunctive ~고 ends the verb stem of the first clause 내리다 "fall," while the deferential speech level ending ~습니다/ㅂ니다 ends both the verb stem of the main clause 불다 "blow" as well as the whole sentence.

Restrictions

Some Korean clausal conjunctives may be subject to various restrictions regarding how they are used in sentences.

Tense agreement

The first restriction concerns the tense agreement. Since a clausal conjunctive connects two different clauses, there are at least two predicates within a clausal-conjunctive sentence. In English, the tense of each clause embedded within the sentence must be the same. Consider the following example:

"I eat a pizza and watched TV."

The above sentence is grammatically incorrect because the tense of the two predicates is not the same. In contrast to English, the tense of each clause can be different in Korean. This is possible because some Korean conjunctives are not conjugated for the tense. Consider the following examples:

열심히 공부했지만 C 를 받았어요. "Although (I) studied hard, (I) received a C."
열심히 공부해서 A 를 받았어요. "Because (I) studied hard, (I) received an A."

Notice that both sentences are about past actions. In the first example, both the conjunctive ~지만 "although" in the first clause as well as the predicate of the main clause 받다 take the past tense marker. However, in the second example, the conjunctive ~어/아서 "because" of the first clause does not take the past tense marker but only the predicate of the main clause 받다.

Subject agreement

The second restriction concerns the subject agreement. Some conjunctives can have different subjects, while some cannot. In other words, for some conjunctives, the subject of the clauses within a sentence must be the same. Consider the following examples:

친구가 커피를 <u>마셨지만</u> 나는 우유를 마셨어요. "Although (my) friend drank coffee, as for me (I) drank milk."
의사가 <u>되려고</u> 열심히 공부했어요. "(I) studied hard in order to become a doctor."

In the first example, each clause has its own subject. However, in the second example, both clauses have the same subject.

Predicate types

The third restriction is about whether the conjunctive may be used with adjectives, copulas, and/or verbs. Some conjunctives must be used only with verbs, whereas some conjunctives may be used with verbs, adjectives, as well as copulas. For instance, the conjunctive ~지만 "although" can be attached to verb, adjective, and copula stems, as shown below:

열심히 <u>공부하지만</u> 어려워요. "Although (I) study hard, (it) is difficult."
학교가 <u>멀지만</u> 매일 가요. "Although the school is far, (I) go (there) everyday."
팀이 <u>한국 사람이지만</u> 한국 역사에 대해서 많이 몰라요. "Although Tim is a Korean, (he) does not know much about Korean history."

On the other hand, a certain conjunctive such as ~(으)려고 "in order to" must be used only with verb stems.

법대에 <u>들어가려고</u> 준비하고 있어요. "(I) am preparing to enter law school."

Sentence types

The fourth restriction is that there are conjunctives that can be used for all sentence types, such as declarative, interrogative, imperative, and propositive, while some conjunctives must be used only for certain sentence types. For instance, consider the conjunctive ~(으)니까 and ~어/아서, which both mean "because/since."

<u>추우니까</u> 창문을 닫습니다. "(I) close the window because (it) is cold."
<u>추우니까</u> 창문을 닫습니까? "Do (you) close the window because (it) is cold?"
<u>추우니까</u> 창문을 닫으십시오. "Close the window because (it) is cold."
<u>추우니까</u> 창문을 닫읍시다. "(Let us) close the window because (it) is cold."

추워서 창문을 닫습니다. "(I) close the window because (it) is cold."
추워서 창문을 닫습니까? "Do (you) close the window because (it) is cold?"
(X) 추워서 창문을 닫으십시오. "Close the window because (it) is cold."
(X) 추워서 창문을 닫읍시다. "(Let us) close the window because (it) is cold."

Notice that ~(으)니까 can be used for all sentence types, whereas ~어/아서 must be used only for declarative and interrogative sentences.

~(으)러

The clausal conjunctive ~(으)러 is used to express the purpose of the speaker's action. It is translated as "for the purpose of" or "to" in English. ~(으)러 is a two-form ending: ~으러 is used after a verb stem that ends in a consonant (e.g., 먹으러 "to eat"), while ~러 is used after a verb stem that ends in a vowel (e.g., 가르치러 "to teach").

~(으)러 is usually used with a motion verb, such as 가다 "to go" and 오다 "to come," to indicate the purpose of going or coming, as shown in the examples below:

편지를 부치러 우체국에 가요. "(I) go to the post office to send a letter."
여자 친구를 만나러 서울로 떠나세요? "(Do you) leave for Seoul to meet (your) girlfriend?"

~(으)러 is subject to some of the aforementioned restrictions. First, the subjects of both clauses must be the same. Second, it is not conjugated for the tense, as shown below:

책을 사러 서점에 갔어요. "(I) went to the bookstore to buy books."
(X) 책을 샀러 서점에 갔어요. "(I) went to the bookstore to buy books."

Third, it is used only with verbs.

한국어를 공부하러 서울에 왔습니다. "(I) came to Seoul to study the Korean language."
(X) 행복하러 결혼하고 싶어요. "(I) want to marry (her) to be happy."

However, there is no restriction regarding sentence type. For instance, it can be used with any of four sentence types as shown below:

친구를 <u>만나러</u> 기차역에 갑니다. "(I) go to the train station to meet (my) friends."
언제 책을 <u>사러</u> 서점에 갈 거예요? "When will (you) go to the book-store to buy books?"
점심 <u>먹으러</u> 아파트에 들르세요. "Stop by (my) apartment to have lunch."
커피를 <u>마시러</u> 스타벅스에 갑시다. "(Let us) go to Starbucks to drink coffee."

~(으)려고

The clausal conjunctive ~(으)려고 is used to express the speaker's intention or plan. It is a two-form ending: ~으려고 is used after a verb stem that ends in a consonant (e.g., 먹으려고 "intending to eat"), and ~려고 is used after a verb stem that ends in a vowel (e.g., 만나려고 "intending to meet").

The meaning of ~(으)려고 is similar to that of ~(으)러. However, in contrast to ~(으)러, which is normally collocated with motion verbs such as 가다 or 오다, ~(으)려고 can be used with any verb, as shown below:

영어 교사로 <u>일하려고</u> 학위를 땄어요. "(I) earned the degree (intend-ing) to work as an English teacher."
유럽을 <u>여행하려고</u> 돈을 모으고 있어요. "(I) am saving money (intend-ing) to travel in Europe."
A 를 <u>받으려고</u> 열심히 공부했어요. "(I) studied hard (intending) to receive an A."
내년에 새 차를 <u>사려고</u> 해요. "(I) intend to buy a new car next year."
대신 집에서 <u>공부하려고</u> 도서관에 안 갔어요. "(I) did not go to the library, intending to study at home instead."
좋은 학교에 <u>들어가려고</u> 열심히 공부했습니다. "(I) studied hard (intend-ing) to enter a good school."

~(으)려고 is subject to the following restrictions: (1) it is not conjugated for the tense; (2) the subject of the clauses must be the same; (3) it is used only with verbs; (4) it is used only for declarative and interrogative sentences.

제이슨을 <u>만나려고</u> 회사에 갔어요. "(I) went to the company to meet Jason."
언제 책을 <u>사려고</u> 서점에 갈 거예요? "When will (you) go to the bookstore to buy the book?"
(X) 저녁을 <u>먹으려고</u> 가십시오. "Go (intending to) have dinner."
(X) 커피를 <u>마시려고</u> 스타벅스에 갑시다. "(Let us) go to Starbucks to drink coffee."

~도록

The clausal conjunctive ~도록 is used to express "so that" or "to the point where."

나무가 잘 <u>자라도록</u> 돌봐 주셨어요. "(He) took care of (the tree), so that the tree would grow better."

병이 빨리 <u>낫도록</u> 기도했어요? "Did (you) pray so that the illness would be healed soon?"

톰이 제니퍼를 <u>죽도록</u> 사랑했어요. "Tom loved Jennifer to death."

우리는 눈물이 <u>나도록</u> 웃었어요. "As for us, (we) laughed till tears ran down our faces."

~도록 is subject to only one restriction: It is not conjugated for the tense. However, it can be used with any sentence type; it can be used with any predicate type; its subject does not have to be the same as that of the main clause.

감기 <u>안 걸리도록</u> 조심했습니다. "(I) was careful so that (I) would not catch a cold."

우리 팀이 게임을 <u>이기도록</u> 열심히 응원하고 있습니까? "Are (they) cheering (for our team) enthusiastically, so that our team may win?"

목이 <u>아프도록</u> 소리를 지르십시오. "Shout to the extent (your) throat hurts."

수잔이 뉴욕으로 <u>떠날 수 있도록</u> 수잔을 도웁시다. "(Let us) help Susan so that Susan can leave for New York."

Exercises

Key vocabulary for Unit 7 exercises

가다 to go
가족 family
같이 together
고르다 to select
공부하다 to study
공항 airport
기다리다 to wait
기차 train
길 road/street
남자 man
남편 husband
도서관 library

돈 money
떠나다 to leave/to depart

마시다 to drink
만나다 to meet
맞추다 to set/to put together
먹다 to eat
벌다 to earn
비키다 to get out of the way
빌리다 to borrow
빨리 fast/immediately
사다 to buy
생일 birthday
선물 present/gift
시험에 붙다 to pass a test
식당 restaurant
싸게 at a cheap price
씻다 to wash

아르바이트 a side job
아침 morning/breakfast
알람 alarm (clock)
앰블란스 ambulance
야채 vegetables
얼굴 face
여자 woman
역 station
열심히 eagerly/enthusiastically/hard
웃다 to smile
인상 impression
일어나다 to get up
일찍 early

잘 well/excellently
점심 lunch
주다 to give
중국 China
지나가다 to pass by
차 car
책 book
친구 friend
타다 to ride
학교 school
혼내다 to teach a lesson/to frighten (a person) out of his wits/to scare
화장실 toilet
흥정 buying and selling/making a deal (with)

Exercise 7.1

Complete the following translation using ~(으)러 and the sentence cues provided in parenthesis, as shown in the example.

> Example: "(I) will go to the office to send the fax."
> (팩스를 보내다 / 사무실로 갈 거예요)
> = 팩스를 보내러 사무실로 갈 거예요.

1 Come to the post office to get (your) package (소포를 받다 / 우체국에 오세요)
2 (They) are going to the service station to repair (their) car (차를 고치다 / 정비소에 가고 있어요)
3 (Let us) go to the beach to do fishing (낚시질 하다 / 바닷가로 갑시다)
4 (I) will go to the airport to catch the flight (비행기를 타다 / 공항에 갈 거예요)
5 Do (you) go to (your) friend's house often to play computer games? (컴퓨터 게임을 하다 / 친구 집에 자주 가세요?)

Exercise 7.2

Connect the following two sentences using ~(으)러. Then translate the sentence.

> Example: 양파를 사다 / 슈퍼마켓에 갔어요
> = 양파를 사러 슈퍼마켓에 갔어요.
> "(I) went to the supermarket to buy onions."

1 커피를 마시다 / 스타벅스에 갔어요
2 시험 공부하다 / 도서관에 가십시오
3 얼굴을 씻다 / 화장실에 가고 있어요
4 점심을 먹다 / 중국 식당에 갑시다
5 케이트를 만나다 / 공항에 갑니까?

Exercise 7.3

Complete the following translation using ~(으)려고 and the sentence cues provided in parenthesis, as shown in the example.

> Example: "(I) am studying hard to receive an A."
> (A 를 받다 / 열심히 공부하고 있어요)
> = A 를 받으려고 열심히 공부하고 있어요.

(I) exercise to lose weight (살을 빼다 / 운동해요)

(She) was waiting in the office to meet the teacher (선생님을 만나다 / 사무실에서 기다리고 있었어요)

(He) is studying hard intending to enter medical school (의과 대학에 들어가다 / 열심히 공부하고 있어요)

(I) reserved an airplane ticket intending to go to Korea this summer (이번 여름에 한국에 가다 / 비행기표를 예약했어요)

(She) was making efforts to get a job (취직하다 / 노력하고 있었어요)

Exercise 7.4

Connect the following two sentences using ~(으)려고. Then translate the sentence.

Example: 무역 회사에 취직하다 / 중국어를 배우고 있어요
= 무역 회사에 취직하려고 중국어를 배우고 있어요.
"(I) am learning Chinese intending to get a job at a trading company."

1 남편한테 생일 선물로 주다 / 선물을 고르고 있어요
2 파리로 떠나다 / 기차 역에 갔어요.
3 같이 점심을 먹다 / 로비에서 친구를 기다려요
4 싸게 차를 사다 / 흥정을 하고 있어요
5 돈을 벌다 / 아르바이트를 했어요

Exercise 7.5

Complete the following dialogue using the sentence cue provided in parenthesis, as shown in the example.

Example: A: 왜 여행사에 전화하세요?
B: 비행기표를 사려고 전화해요.
(비행기표를 사다)

1 A: 어디에 가세요?
B: _____ 도서관에 가요.
(책을 빌리다)
2 A: 어디 가세요?
B: _____ 슈퍼마켓에 가요.
(야채를 사다)
3 A: 왜 장미를 사세요?
B: _____ 사요.
(여자 친구한테 주다)

59

4 A: 왜 지하철을 탔어요?
   B: _____ 탔어요.
       (학교에 빨리 가다)
5 A: 서울에는 왠 일이세요?
   B: _____ 왔어요.
       (남자 친구의 가족을 만나다)

Exercise 7.6

Complete the following translation using ~도록 and the sentence cue
provided in parenthesis, as shown in the example.

Example: "Please prepare so that (we) can leave at 7 a.m."
          (오전 7 시에 떠날 수 있다 / 준비해 주세요)
          = 오전 7 시에 떠날 수 있도록 준비해 주세요.

1 Please turn on the radio, so that (we) can listen to the news (뉴스를 들
   을 수 있다 / 라디오를 켜 주세요)
2 Please allow (me) so that (I) can use (your) car (차를 쓸 수 있다 / 허
   락해 주세요)
3 Please help (him) so that (he) can recover (his) health (건강을 회복할
   수 있다 / 도와 주세요)
4 Please write (her) a recommendation letter so that (she) can get a job
   (취직할 수 있다 / 추천서를 써 주세요)
5 Please turn off the electric lamp so that (she) can sleep (잘 수 있다 /
   전등을 꺼 주세요)

Exercise 7.7

Connect the following two sentences using ~도록. Then translate the
sentence.

Example: 조용히 공부할 수 있다 / 텔레비전을 꺼 주세요
          = 조용히 공부할 수 있도록 텔레비전을 꺼 주세요.
          "Please turn off the TV so that (he) can study quietly."

1 앰블란스가 지나갈 수 있다 / 길을 비켜 주세요
2 좋은 인상을 줄 수 있다 / 웃어 주세요
3 시험에 붙다 / 열심히 공부하십시오
4 아침에 일찍 일어날 수 있다 / 알람을 맞추어 주세요
5 열심히 공부할 수 있다 / 혼내 주세요

UNIT 8
Clausal conjunctives (reasons and cause)

~어/아서

Functions

The clausal conjunctive ~어/아서 expresses two things. First, it indicates a cause-and-effect relation between two actions or states, equivalent to "so" or "because/since" in English. In other words, it is used when the action and/or state of the first clause provides a cause or reason for the action and/or state of the main clause. Consider the following example:

너무 기뻐서 메리한테 전화하고 있어요. "(I) am so glad, so (I) am making a phone call to Mary."

The state of the first clause 기쁘다 "glad" gives a reason for the action of the main clause 전화하다 "make a phone call." Consider another example:

요즈음 새벽에 조깅을 해서 아침에 바빠요. "(I) jog at dawn nowadays, so (I) am busy in the morning."

Notice that the action of the first clause (e.g., 조깅을 하다 "jog") is the reason for the state of the main clause (e.g., 바쁘다 "busy"). Here are more examples:

가격이 너무 비싸서 못 사요. "The price is too expensive, so (I) cannot buy (it)."
다음 주에 시험이 있어서 바빠요. "(I) have a test next week, so (I) am busy."

Second, ~어/아서 links two chronologically ordered actions or events without implying any cause-and-effect relation between them. Its English translation is equivalent to "and then."

학교에 <u>가서</u> 선생님을 만날 거예요. "(I) will go to school and then meet the teacher."

In the example above, ~어/아서 indicates that the action of the first clause 가다 "go" occurrs before the action of the main clause 만나다 "meet." Here are more examples:

백화점에 <u>가서</u> 생일 카드를 살 거예요? "Will (you) go to the department store and then buy a birthday card?"
사과를 <u>깍아서</u> 먹으십시오. "Eat the apple after peeling (it)."
오늘 피터 집에 <u>가서</u> 저녁을 먹읍시다. "Today, (let us) go to Peter's house and then eat dinner (there)."

Forms

~어/아서 is a two-form ending: ~아서 is used after a predicate stem that ends in 아 or 오, whereas ~어서 is used after a predicate stem that ends in all other vowels.

Verb	**~어/아서**
가다 "go"	가서 (contracted from 가 + 아서)
찾다 "find"	찾아서
가르치다 "teach"	가르쳐서 (contracted from 가르치 + 어서)
믿다 "believe"	믿어서

Adjective	**~어/아서**
좋다 "good"	좋아서
기쁘다 "happy"	기뻐서 (기쁘 + 어서)

Copula	**~어/아서**
이다 "to be"	이어서/(이)라서
아니다 "not be"	아니어서/아니라서

Notice that the combination of ~어/아서 with the copula 이다 has two forms: 이어서 and (이)라서. The negative copula, 아니다, also has two forms: 아니어서 and 아니라서. The use of (이)라서/아니라서 is more common than that of 이어서/아니어서.

한국 사람이라서/이어서	"since (I) am a Korean"
소고기라서/여서	"since (it) is beef"
한국 사람이 아니라서/아니어서	"because (I) am not a Korean"
소고기가 아니라서/아니어서	"because (it) is not beef"

Restrictions

~어/아서 is subject to two restrictions. First, it is not conjugated for the tense. Consider the following example:

저녁을 안 먹어서 배고팠어요. "(I) did not eat dinner, so (I) was hungry."

Notice that the past tense is not marked in the first clause (e.g., 안 먹어서) but in the main clause (e.g., 배고팠어요). Here are more examples:

공부를 많이 해서 A 를 받았어요. "(I) studied a lot, so (I) received an A."
바빠서 집에 못 갔어요. "(I) was busy, so (I) could not go home."
약국에 들러서 아스피린을 샀어요. "(I) bought aspirin after stopping at the pharmacy."
내일이 아버지 생신이라서 곧 집에 돌아올 거예요. "Tomorrow is (her) father's birthday, so (she) will return home soon."
돈이 없어서 파티에 안 갈 거예요. "(I) do not have money, so (I) will not go to the party."

Second, when ~어/아서 indicates a cause-and-effect relation, it cannot be used for the imperative and/or propositive sentences, as shown below:

(O) 머리가 아파서 약을 먹습니다. "(My) head aches, so (I) take medicines."
(O) 머리가 아파서 약을 먹습니까? "Do (you) take medicines, since (your) head aches?"
(X) 머리가 아파서 약을 먹으십시오. "Take medicines, since (your) head aches."
(X) 머리가 아파서 약을 먹읍시다. "(Let us) take medicines, since (our) heads ache."

However, when ~어/아서 is used to link two chronological actions or states, it can be used for any sentence type, as shown below:

맨하턴에 가서 브로드웨이 뮤지컬을 볼 거예요. "(We) will go to Manhattan and then see Broadway musicals."
슈퍼마켓에 가서 살 거예요? "Will (you) go to the supermarket and then buy (it)?"
오렌지를 씻어서 먹으십시오. "Wash the orange and then eat (it)."
집에 가서 이야기합시다. "(Let us) go home and then talk."

~(으)니까

The clausal conjunctive ~(으)니까 is used to specify a reason for the main clause, and it can be translated as "since," "so," and "because" in English. ~(으)니까 is a two-form ending: ~으니까 is used after a predicate stem that ends in a consonant, and ~니까 is used after a predicate stem that ends in a vowel.

Verb	**~(으)니까**
보다 "see"	보니까
배우다 "learn"	배우니까
잡다 "catch"	잡으니까
먹다 "eat"	먹으니까

Adjective	**~(으)니까**
싸다 "cheap"	싸니까
작다 "small"	작으니까

Copula	**~(으)니까**
이다 "to be"	이니까
아니다 "not be"	아니니까

The function of ~(으)니까 is similar to that of ~어/아서 since both provide a cause or reason for the action and/or state of the main clause. However, there are three differences between these two conjunctives.

First, the reason and/or cause provided by ~(으)니까 sounds more specific than those given by ~어/아서. Second, while ~어/아서 "because/since/so" must be used only for declarative and interrogative sentences, ~(으)니까 may be used for any sentence type, as shown below:

(O) 커피가 뜨거워서 천천히 마십니다. "Since the coffee is hot, (I) drink (it) slowly."
(O) 커피가 뜨거워서 천천히 마십니까? "Do (you) drink the coffee slowly because (it) is hot?"
(X) 커피가 뜨거워서 천천히 마시십시오. "Since the coffee is hot, drink (it) slowly."
(X) 커피가 뜨거워서 천천히 마십시다. "Since the coffee is hot, (let us) drink (it) slowly."
(O) 커피가 뜨거우니까 천천히 마십니다. "Since the coffee is hot, (I) drink (it) slowly."
(O) 커피가 뜨거우니까 천천히 마십니까? "Do (you) drink the coffee slowly because (it) is hot?"
(O) 커피가 뜨거우니까 천천히 마시십시오. "Since the coffee is hot, drink (it) slowly."
(O) 커피가 뜨거우니까 천천히 마십시다. "Since the coffee is hot, (let us) drink (it) slowly."

Third, ~(으)니까 is conjugated for the tense, while ~어/아서 is not, as shown below:

(O) 어제 내가 설거지 <u>했으니까</u> 오늘 네가 해. "Since I washed dishes yesterday, you do (it) today."
(X) 어제 내가 설거지 <u>했어서</u> 오늘 네가 해. "Since I washed dishes yesterday, you do (it) today."
(O) 내일 아침 일찍 보스톤으로 <u>떠날 거니까</u> 일찍 잡시다. "(Let us) sleep early, since (we) will leave for Boston tomorrow early morning."
(X) 내일 아침 일찍 보스톤으로 <u>떠날 거어서</u> 일찍 잡시다. "(Let us) sleep early, since (we) will leave for Boston tomorrow early morning."

~느라고

The clausal conjunctive ~느라고 is a one-form ending, and it means "as a result of/because of." Similar to ~어/아서 and ~(으)니까, ~느라고 expresses that the action of the first clause is the reason or cause for the main clause.

However, there is a subtle meaning difference between ~느라고 and ~어/아서 (or ~(으)니까). The clause with ~느라고 generates a negative implication that the action of the main clause is performed at the expense of the action of the first clause. In other words, it indicates that the action of the first clause leads to the undesirable action of the main clause. Consider the following example:

밤 새 컴퓨터 게임을 <u>하느라고</u> 학교에 못 갔어요. "(I) could not go to school because of playing computer games all night."

Notice that the action of the first clause with ~느라고 contributes to the undesirable action of the main clause (e.g., could not go to school).
~느라고 is subject to more restrictions than ~어/아서 and ~(으)니까. First ~느라고 cannot be used for imperative and/or propositive sentences. Second, it must be used only with verbs. Third, it is not conjugated for the tense. Finally, the subject of the ~느라고 clause must be the same with that of the main clause.

늦게 <u>일어나느라고</u> 아침을 못 먹어요. "(I) cannot eat breakfast because of getting up late."
텔레비전을 <u>보느라고</u> 전화 못 했어요. "(I) could not make a phone call, because of watching TV."
너무 빨리 <u>걷느라고</u> 지갑을 떨어뜨렸어요. "(I) dropped (my) wallet because of walking too fast."

Exercises

Key vocabulary for Unit 8 exercises

가다 to go
감기 걸리다 to catch (a cold)
곧 soon
기다리다 to wait
나가다 to go out
내일 tomorrow
넣다 to insert/to put (something) in
놀다 to play/to enjoy (oneself)
눈 snow/eyes
늦다 to be late
다이어트 diet
더 more
덥다 to be hot/to be warm
도서관 library
도착하다 to arrive
돕다 to help
듣다 to listen
뜨겁다 to be hot/to be heated
라디오 radio

마시다 to drink
많이 a lot/plenty
맛있다 to be delicious
머리 head
먹다 to eat
모래 the day after tomorrow
물어보다 to ask (a person about something)
뮤지컬 musical
미안하다 to be sorry
바쁘다 to be busy
밖 outside
밤 night
보다 to see/to watch/to read

사다 to buy
사람들 people
새우다 to stay up all night
생일 birthday
선물 present/gift
소금 salt

소리 sound
숙제 homework
시간 hour/time
식당 restaurant
싱겁다 to be watery/to be insipid

아침 morning/breakfast
아프다 to be painful/to be sore
약 medicine
약속 appointment
어제 yesterday
에어콘 air conditioner
여기 here
오다 to come
오전 a.m.
요리하다 to cook
운동하다 to do (physical) exercise/sports
은행 bank
음식 food
음악 music
이사 moving (housing)
이야기하다 to talk
이제 now
일어나다 to get up
일찍 early

자주 often
재미있게 interestingly
저녁 dinner/evening
전화 telephone
조금 little
좋다 to be good
주다 to give
집 house
찾다 to look for/to seek for
천천히 slowly
초인종 doorbell
친구 friend
크게 greatly/loudly
틀다 to switch on
파티 party
포장하다 to pack/to wrap
학교 school
흥겹게 merrily/pleasantly

Exercise 8.1

Finish the following translation using ~어/아서 "and then" and the sentence
cues provided in parenthesis, as shown in the example.

Example: "(I) went to Hawaii and then met (his) parents."
(하와이에 가다 / 부모님을 만났어요)
= 하와이에 가서 부모님을 만났어요.

1 (I) will call the travel agency and then ask about the airfare (여행사에
전화하다 / 항공 요금에 대해서 물어 볼 거예요)
2 (We) went to school and then met the professor (학교에 가다 / 교수님
을 만났어요)
3 Did (she) wash the strawberry and then eat (it)? (딸기를 씻다 / 먹었
어요?)
4 Buy that ring and then give (it) to (your) girlfriend (그 반지를 사다 /
여자 친구한테 주세요)
5 (Let us) learn the Korean language and then get a job in Seoul (한국
어를 배우다 / 서울에서 취직합시다)

Exercise 8.2

Connect the following two sentences using ~어/아서 "and then." Then
translate the sentence.

Example: 슈퍼마켓에 가다 / 돼지고기를 삽시다
= 슈퍼마켓에 가서 돼지고기를 삽시다.
"(Let us) go the supermarket and then buy (some) pork."

1 아침에 일찍 일어나다 / 운동할래요
2 친구 집에 가다 / 요리하십시오
3 언제 뉴욕에 가다 / 뮤시컬을 볼 거예요?
4 선물을 포장하다 / 생일 파티 때 줬어요.
5 파티에 가다 / 흥겹게 놉시다

Exercise 8.3

Finish the following translation using ~어/아서 "because/since" and the sentence cues provided in parenthesis, as shown in the example.

Example: "Since (it) is too expensive, (I) will not buy (it)."
(너무 비싸다 / 안 살 거예요)
= 너무 비싸서 안 살 거예요.

1 Since traffic was held up, (I) was late for the class (교통이 막히다 / 수업에 늦었어요)
2 Since (I) ate breakfast late, (I) have not had lunch yet (아침을 늦게 먹다 / 아직 점심을 안 먹었어요)
3 Since (my) stomach hurts, (I) want to go home early (배가 아프다 / 집에 일찍 가고 싶어요)
4 Since the room is too dirty, (we) will clean (it up) today (방이 너무 더럽다 / 오늘 청소할 거예요)
5 Since (it) was (her) birthday, (he) went home early (생일이다 / 일찍 집에 갔어요)

Exercise 8.4

Connect the following two sentences using ~어/아서 "because/since." Then translate the sentence.

Example: 날씨가 좋다 / 산책했어요
= 날씨가 좋아서 산책했어요.
"Since the weather was nice, (we) took a walk."

1 어제가 친구 생일이다 / 생일 파티에 갔습니다.
2 이 식당 음식이 맛있다 / 자주 와요.
3 눈이 많이 오다 / 학교에 못 갈 것 같아요.
4 감기 걸리다 / 약을 먹고 있어요.
5 약속 시간에 늦다 / 미안합니다.

Exercise 8.5

Finish the following translation using ~(으)니까 and the sentence cues provided in parenthesis, as shown in the example.

Example: "Since (it) is late night, (let us) call (him) tomorrow."
(늦은 밤이다 / 내일 전화합시다)
= 늦은 밤이니까 내일 전화합시다.

1 Since (she) does not drink coffee, (let us) buy green tea instead (커피
   를 못 마시다 / 대신 녹차를 삽시다)
2 Since (it) is the closing hour, traffic is held up (퇴근 시간이다 / 교통이
   막힙니다)
3 Since (I) don't have time, tell (me) only the main points (시간이 없다
   / 용건만 말하십시오)
4 Since (my) back hurts, (I) do not want to meet anyone (허리가 아프다
   / 누구도 만나고 싶지 않습니다)
5 Since (it) is cold, close the window (춥다 / 창문을 닫으십시오)

Exercise 8.6

Connect the following two sentences using ~(으)니까. Then translate the
sentence.

> Example: 방이 어둡다 / 전등을 켜 주세요.
> = 방이 어두우니까 전등을 켜 주세요.
> "Since (my) room is dark, turn the light on."

1 내일 바쁘다 / 모래 전화할게요.
2 도서관이다 / 크게 이야기하지 마십시오.
3 머리가 아프다 / 약을 사 주세요.
4 내일 아침에 이사하다 / 오전 8 시까지 오세요.
5 음식이 싱겁다 / 소금을 넣으십시오.
6 덥다 / 에어콘을 틀어 주세요.
7 이제 곧 피자가 도착하다 / 조금 더 기다립시다.

Exercise 8.7

Finish the following translation using ~느라고 and the sentence cues
provided in parenthesis, as shown in the example.

> Example: "(I) could not sleep because of preparing for the interview."
> (인터뷰를 준비하다 / 못 잤어요)
> = 인터뷰를 준비하느라고 못 잤어요.

1 (I) spent all of (my) money because of buying beer (맥주를 사다 /
   돈을 다 썼어요)
2 (I) could not leave (my) office yet because of repairing the computer
   (컴퓨터를 고치다 / 아직 퇴근을 못 했어요).
3 (I) could not eat dinner together because of talking over the phone for
   a long time (오래 통화하다 / 저녁을 같이 못 먹었어요)

4 (I) dropped (my) wallet as a result of inserting coins (동전을 넣다 / 지갑을 떨어뜨렸어요)
5 (I) was late because of looking for keys (열쇠를 찾다 / 늦었어요)

Exercise 8.8

Connect the following two sentences using ~느라고. Then translate the sentence.

Example: TV 를 보다 / 전화를 못 했어요
= TV 를 보느라고 전화를 못 했어요.
"(I) could not make a phone call because of watching TV."

1 숙제를 하다 / 밤을 새웠어요.
2 라디오를 듣다 / 초인종 소리를 못 들었어요.
3 사라를 기다리다 / 늦었어요?
4 다이어트를 하다 / 저녁을 많이 안 먹습니다.
5 은행을 찾다 / 사람들한테 물어보고 있었어요.

UNIT 9
Clausal conjunctives (conditions)

~(으)면

The clausal conjunctive ~(으)면 is used to express that the first clause is the condition of the main clause. It is equivalent to "if" and/or "when" in English. It is a two-form ending: ~으면 is used after a stem that ends in a consonant (e.g., 먹으면 "if I eat"); ~면 is used after a stem that ends in a vowel (e.g., 보면 "if I see").

오늘 저녁으로 한국 음식을 먹으면 연락하세요. "If (you) eat Korean food for dinner tonight, contact (us)."
다음 학기에 변교수님이 한국어 수업을 가르치시면 들을 거예요. "If Professor Byon teaches the Korean language class next semester, (I) will take (it)."
룸메이트가 집에 돌아오면 나갈게요. "When (my) roommate returns home, (I) will go out."

The conjugation of ~(으)면 with the copula 이다 has two forms: ~(이)면 and ~(이)라면. ~면/라면 is used after a noun that ends in a vowel (e.g., 의사면 "if he is a doctor"), whereas ~이면/이라면 is used after a noun that ends in a consonant (e.g., 미국 사람이면 "if (he) is an American").

학생이면/이라면 제 방으로 보내세요. "If (they) are students, send (them) to my room."
커피면/라면 마실 거예요. "If (it) is coffee, (I) will drink (it)."

When ~(이)면/(이)라면 occurs after a time word, it means "in" or "at the end of," as shown below:

한 학기면 졸업해요. "In one semester, (I will) graduate."
세 시면 영화가 끝날 거예요. "By three o'clock, the movie will end" (lit. "When it is three o'clock, the movie will end").

~(으)면 is not subject to any restriction. For instance, it is conjugated for the tense, as shown below:

겨울이 되면 스키 타러 갑시다. "When (it) becomes winter, (let us) go for skiing."
수잔이 한국에 갔으면 나한테 전화했을 거예요. "If Susan went to Korea, (she) would have given me a call."
생일 파티를 할 거면 집에서 하세요. "If (you) will host a birthday party, do (it) at home."

Second, it can be used with any predicate type.

열심히 공부하면 A 를 받을 수 있어요. "If (you) study hard, (you) can receive an A."
날씨가 너무 추우면 나가지 맙시다. "If the weather is too cold, (let us) not go out."
다음 손님도 한국 사람이(라)면 전화해 주십시오. "If the next customer is also a Korean, please call (me)."

Third, there is no restriction regarding subject agreement.

대학을 졸업하면 한국에 가고 싶어요. "When (I) graduate from college, (I) want to go to Korea."
토마스가 커피를 시키면 제가 콜라를 시킬게요. "If Thomas orders coffee, I will order cola."

Finally, ~(으)면 may be used with any sentence type.

겨울이 되면 눈대신 비가 와요. "When (it) becomes winter, rain falls instead of snow."
새 차를 사면 먼저 어디에 가고 싶어요? "When (you) buy a new car, where do (you) want to go first?"
집에 도착하면 나한테 전화하세요. "When (you) arrive at home, call me."
안 바쁘면 내일 만납시다. "If (you) are not busy, (let us) meet tomorrow."

~(으)면 하다/좋겠다 *"wish/hope"*

The combination of ~(으)면 and the verb 하다 "do" or the adjective 좋겠다 "would/will be nice" expresses the speaker's wish or hope. ~(으)면 하다 sounds slightly more polite than ~(으)면 좋겠다. However, both can be translated as "wish/hope" in English.

이번 크리스마스에 눈이 많이 <u>오면</u> 해요. "(I) wish that (it) snows a lot this Christmas."

빨리 봄이 <u>되면</u> 좋겠어요. "(I) wish spring comes early (lit. It would be nice, if it would become spring soon)."

내년에 새 컴퓨터를 <u>사면</u> 좋겠어요. "(I) wish that (I) buy a new computer next year."

Adding the past tense marker 었/았 to ~(으)면 하다/좋겠다 makes the speaker's desire or wish sound more assertive or emphatic.

이제부터 돈 걱정을 <u>안 했으면</u> 해요. "(I) wish that (I) would not worry about money from now on."

수요일에 시험을 <u>봤으면</u> 합니다. "(I) wish that (I) would take the test on Wednesday."

서울에 갈 때 동경에 <u>들렀으면</u> 합니다. "(I) wish that (I) would stop by Tokyo on my way to Seoul."

이번 여름에 일본을 <u>여행했으면</u> 좋겠어요. "(I) wish that (I) would travel in Japan this summer."

한국이 빨리 통일이 <u>됐으면</u> 좋겠어요. "(I) wish that Korea would be unified immediately."

~(으)려면

The clausal conjunctive ~(으)려면 "if one intends to do" is the combination of ~(으)려고 "intending to" with the conjunctive ~(으)면 "if/when." It is a two-form ending: ~려면 is used after a stem that ends in a vowel (e.g., 배우려면 "if you intend to learn"), and ~으려면 is used after a stem that ends in a consonant (e.g., 먹으려면 "if you intend to eat").

한국어를 잘 <u>하려면</u> 한국인 친구들을 사귀어야 해요. "If (you) intend to speak Korean well, (you) need to make Korean friends."

이 양복을 <u>입으려면</u> 살을 빼야 해요. "If (you) intend to wear this suit, (you) should lose weight."

학교에 <u>다니려면</u> 먼저 등록금을 내세요. "If (you) intend to attend the school, pay the tuition first."

교수님을 <u>만나려면</u> 미리 전화해야 돼요. "If (you) intend to meet the professor, (you) must call in advance."

프로같이 피아노를 잘 <u>치려면</u> 열심히 연습해야 돼요. "If (you) intend to play the piano like a professional, (you) need to practice hard."

좋고 싼 물건을 <u>사려면</u> 어디로 가야 해요? "If (we) intend to buy good and cheap items, where should (we) go?"

<u>퇴근하려면</u> 30 분 더 기다리세요. "If (you) intend to leave office, wait 30 more minutes."

~(으)ㄹ수록

The clausal conjunctive ~(으)ㄹ수록 expresses continuous increase in the nature of an action or state. It can be translated as "the more...the more" in English. ~(으)ㄹ수록 is a two-form ending: ~을수록 is used after a stem that ends in a consonant (e.g., 믿을수록 "the more I believe"), while ~ㄹ수록 is used after a stem that ends in a vowel (e.g., 마실수록 "the more I drink").

김치가 <u>먹을수록</u> 맛있어요. "The more (I) eat kimchi, the more tasty (it) is."
태권도는 <u>배울수록</u> 재미있어요. "As for Taekwondo, the more (I) learn (it), the more interesting (it) is."

In addition, ~(으)면 "if/when" can be optionally used along with ~(으)ㄹ수록, as shown below:

골프는 <u>치면 칠수록</u> 어려워요. "As for golf, the more (you) play (it), the more difficult (it) is."
강아지를 <u>보면 볼수록</u> 귀여워요. "The more (I) look at the puppy, the more cute (it) is."
사랑은 시간이 <u>지나면 지날수록</u> 소중해져요. "As for love, the more time passes, the more precious (it) becomes."
<u>자면 잘수록</u> 피곤해요. "The more (you) sleep, the more tired (you) are."
노트북은 <u>작으면 작을수록</u> 비싸요. "As for notebook, the smaller (it) is, the more expensive (it) is."

~어/아야

The clausal conjunctive ~어/아야 indicates that the ~어/아야 ending clause is a prerequisite or necessary condition of the main clause. It is corresponding to "only if" in English. Consider the following example:

학교에 <u>가야</u> 교수님을 만날 수 있어요. "Only if (you) go to school, (you) can meet the professor."

Notice that the action of the first clause "going to school" is the necessity for the action of the main clause "meeting the professor."
~어/아야 is a two-form ending: ~아야 is used after a stem that ends in either 아 or 오, whereas ~어야 is used after a stem that ends in all other vowels.

75

Verb	**Verb stem + 어/아야**
오다 "see"	와야 (contracted from 오 + 아야)
잡다 "catch"	잡아야
배우다 "learn"	배워야 (contracted from 배우 + 어야)
믿다 "believe"	믿어야

Adjective	**Adjective stem + 어/아야**
싸다 "cheap"	싸야
작다 "small"	작아야
슬프다 "sad"	슬퍼야 (슬프 + 어야)
어렵다 "difficult"	어려워야 (어려우 + 어야)

Copula	**Copula stem + 어/아야**
이다 "to be"	이어야/이라야
아니다 "not be"	아니어야/아니라야

To add an emphatic meaning, one can use the particle 만 "only" along with ~어/아야, as shown below:

앤드류를 만나야만 데니엘에대해 들을 수 있어요. "Only if (you) meet Andrew, (you) can hear about Daniel."

의과 대학을 졸업해야만 의사가 될 수 있어요. "Only if (you) graduate from a medical school, (you) can become a doctor."

열쇠를 찾아야만 집에 갈 수 있어요. "Only if (we) find the key, (we) can go home."

~거든

The clausal conjunctive ~거든 is used to indicate that the ~거든 ending clause is the condition for the main clause. It is equivalent to "if" in English. ~거든 is subject to one restriction: It must be used only with imperative and/or propositive sentences, as shown in the following examples:

할 말이 있거든 하십시오. "If (you) have something to say, say (it)."

바쁘지 않거든 연락해요. "If (you) are not busy, contact (me)."

편지가 도착하거든 매튜한테 전화하십시오. "If the letter arrives, give Matthew a phone call."

앨리스가 한국에 가거든 우리도 갑시다. "If Alice goes to Korea, (let us) go (there) as well."

시험이 끝나거든 같이 저녁 먹읍시다. "If the test ends, (let us) have dinner together."

Meanwhile, in spoken communication, ~거든 (or ~거든요) is often used as a sentence ending. The sentence ending ~거든요 expresses an emphatic meaning, and it can be translated as "you know," "you see (because)," and "indeed" in English. Consider the following dialogue:

A: 일요일인데 도서관에 어떻게 오셨어요?
   "(It) is Sunday, but what brought you to the library?"
B: 내일 시험이 있거든요.
   "(I) have a test tomorrow, you know."

Notice that B's response ends with ~거든요. By using ~거든요, B offers a kind of follow-up explanation (e.g., having a test tomorrow) to what has been implied (e.g., to be in the library on Sunday). Here are more examples:

A: 또 한 잔 시키세요?
   "(You) order a cup again?"
B: 제가 여기 커피를 좋아하거든요.
   "I like the coffee of this place, you know."
A: 피곤해 보여요.
   "(You) look tired."
B: 어제 밤 늦게까지 일했거든요.
   "(I) worked late last night, you know."
A: 어제 먹은 음식을 또 시킬 거예요?
   "Will (you) order the food (you) ate yesterday, again?"
B: 아주 맛있었거든요.
   "(It) was really delicious, you know."

Exercises

Key vocabulary for Unit 9 exercises

가다 to go
가깝다 to be near
가르치다 to teach
건강 health
걱정거리 source of anxiety
공 ball
끊다 to quit
끓이다 to boil
남자 man
남편 husband
날씨 weather
내다 to pay
내일 tomorrow
냄비 pot
너무 too (much)
노래 song

노트북 notebook
놀다 to play
누구 who
늦게 late

다음 next
담배 cigarette
대학 college
덥다 to be hot (the weather)
도움 help
드시다 to eat
들어가다 to enter
따뜻하다 to be warm/to be mild
룸메이트 roommate
말하다 to speak
만나다 to meet
많이 a lot
머리 head/hair (of one's head)
먹다 to eat
모르다 do not know
모자라다 to be short of
목 throat
묻다 to ask
물 water
미국 U.S.A.

바꾸다 to change
바쁘다 to be busy
받다 to receive
배 stomach
배우다 to learn
법대 law school
병원 hospital
보다 to see/to watch/to read
비자 visa

사다 to buy
사람 person/people
사용하다 to use
사이즈 size
살다 to live
생일 birthday
선물 present/gift
소파 sofas
시험을 보다 to take tests/exams
식당 restaurant

식사 meal
심심하다 to be bored
쓰다 to use

아르바이트 a side job
아프다 to be sore
어제 yesterday
약 medicine
여행 trip/travel
연락하다 to contact
열다 to open
예약하다 to make a reservation
오다 to come
요금 fee
유학가다 to go abroad for study
입국하다 to enter a country
일찍 early

자다 to sleep
작다 to be small
잘 well/expertly
저금 saving
저녁 dinner/evening
전화 telephone
제출하다 to submit
조금 little
조심하다 to be careful/to take care of
졸업장 diploma
주일 week (day)
지하철 subway
직장 one's place of work
집 house

창문 window
책 book
추천서 recommendation letter
춥다 to be cold
취직 getting employment
치다 to play/to strike
친구 friend
켜다 to switch on
타다 to ride
피곤하다 to be tired
필요하다 to be in need of
학기 semester
한국 Korea

화장실 toilet
회사 company
히터 heater

Exercise 9.1

Finish the following translation using ~(으)면 and the sentence cues provided in parenthesis, as shown in the example.

> Example: "If (it) is cold outside, (let us) not go out." (밖이 춥다 / 나가지 맙시다)
> = 밖이 추우면 나가지 맙시다.

1 When (I) have time, (I) will make a phone call to Bill (시간이 있다 / 빌한테 전화할 거예요)
2 If the road is congested, (let us) take a subway (길이 막히다 / 지하철을 탑시다)
3 If (it) is expensive, will (you) buy (it)? (비싸다 / 사겠어요?)
4 If (you) get up early tomorrow morning, wake (me) up (내일 아침 일찍 일어나다 / 깨워 주세요)
5 If (I) told (him), (he) probably would get angry (이야기했다 / 화냈을 거예요)

Exercise 9.2

Connect the following two sentences using ~(으)면. Then translate the sentence.

> Example: 가격이 싸다 / 사세요
> = 가격이 싸면 사세요. "If (its) price is cheap, buy (it)."

1 배가 아프다 / 병원에 가세요
2 날씨가 너무 춥다 / 히터를 켜겠어요
3 모르다 / 물어 보세요
4 덥다 / 창문을 엽시다
5 도움이 필요하다 / 누구한테 전화하세요?

Exercise 9.3

Finish the following translation using ~(으)면 좋겠다 and the sentence cue provided in parenthesis, as shown in the example.

Example: "(I) wish that (it) snows tomorrow." (내일 눈이 오다)
= 내일 눈이 오면 좋겠어요.

1 (I) wish that (we) meet at the airport (공항에서 만나다)
2 (I) wish that (I) receive a watch for (my) birthday present (생일 선물
로 시계를 받다)
3 (I) wish that (we) order red wine (레드 와인을 시키다)
4 (I) wish that (we) have Korean food for dinner (저녁으로 한국음식을
먹다)
5 (I) wish that (I) make a lot of money (돈을 많이 벌다)

Exercise 9.4

Conjugate the following predicate using ~(으)면 좋겠다. Then translate
the sentence.

Example: 빨리 차를 팔다
= 빨리 차를 팔면 좋겠어요.
"(I) wish that (I) sell (my) car immediately."

1 룸메이트가 한국 사람이다
2 캐나다로 유학가다
3 직장이 집에서 가깝다
4 내일 날씨가 따뜻하다
5 남편이 일찍 자다
6 다음 학기에 김교수님이 가르치시다
7 남자 친구가 담배를 끊다
8 노트북을 생일 선물로 받다

Exercise 9.5

Connect the following two sentences using ~(으)려면. Then translate the
sentence.

Example: 김치를 만들다 / 배추가 필요해요
= 김치를 만들려면 배추가 필요해요.
"If (you) intend to make kimchi, (you) need Chinese
cabbage."

1 물을 끓이다 / 냄비가 필요해요
2 이 식당에서 저녁을 먹다 / 예약하십시오
3 병원에 가다 / 지하철을 타세요

4 미국에 입국하다 / 비자를 받아야 해요
5 이 회사에 취직하다 / 대학 졸업장을 제출하세요
6 브로드웨이 쇼를 보다 / 뉴욕에 가야 돼요
7 테니스를 치다 / 공하고 라켓이 필요해요
8 화장실을 사용하다 / 요금을 내세요

Exercise 9.6

Finish the following translation using the ~(으)면 ~(으)ㄹ수록 pattern and the sentence cues provided in parenthesis, as shown in the example.

> Example: "The more (I) meet that friend, the more (I) want to meet (him)."
> (그 친구를 만나다 / 더 만나고 싶어요)
> = 그 친구를 만나면 만날수록 더 만나고 싶어요.

1 The more (I) read the letter, the angrier (I) am (편지를 읽다 / 화나 요)
2 The cloudier the weather is, the colder (it) is (날씨가 흐리다 / 추워 요)
3 The more time passes, the more (I) long for old days (시간이 지나다 / 옛날이 그리워요)
4 The bigger (it) was, the more expensive (it) was (크다 / 비쌌어요)
5 The more (I) read that book, the more interesting (it) was (그 책을 읽 다 / 재미있었어요)

Exercise 9.7

Connect the following sentences using the ~(으)면 ~(으)ㄹ수록 pattern. Then translate the sentence.

> Example: 담배를 피우다 / 중독돼요
> = 담배를 피우면 피울수록 중독돼요.
> "The more (you) smoke, the more (you) become addicted to (it)."

1 한국에서 살다 / 좋아요
2 사람들을 만나다 / 피곤합니다
3 돈을 쓰다 / 필요합니다
4 여행을 하다 / 많이 배울 거예요
5 바쁘다 / 건강 조심하세요

Exercise 9.8

Finish the following translation using ~거든 and the sentence cues provided in parenthesis, as shown in the example.

Example: "Do not call (me) if (you) are busy." (바쁘다 / 전화 하지 마세요)
= 바쁘거든 전화하지 마세요.

1 Hug the baby if the baby cries (아기가 울다 / 아기를 안아 주세요)
2 If (it) is tasty, (let us) order (it) more (맛있다 / 더 시킵시다)
3 If (you) make a Christmas tree, take a picture (크리스마스 트리를 만들다 / 사진을 찍으세요)
4 If (you) work this weekend, do not come to the party (이번 주말에 일하다 / 파티에 오지 마세요)
5 If (we) meet Mary later, (let us) convey the message (나중에 메리를 만나다 / 메세지를 전해 줍시다)

Exercise 9.9

Connect the following two sentences using ~거든. Then translate the sentence.

Example: 집에 도착하다 / 전화하세요
= 집에 도착하거든 전화하세요.
"If (you) arrive at home, please call (me)."

1 추천서가 필요하다 / 저한테 연락하세요
2 또 머리가 아프다 / 약을 드세요
3 걱정거리가 있다 / 말하세요
4 심심하다 / TV 보세요
5 병원에 가다 / 박선생님을 만나세요

Exercise 9.10

Answer to the following question using ~거든요 and the sentence cue provided in parenthesis, as shown in the example. Then translate the answer.

Example: 왜 파티에 안 가세요? (약속이 있다)
= 약속이 있거든요. "(I) have an appointment, you know."

1 왜 저녁 식사를 안 하세요? (점심을 늦게 먹었다)
2 왜 노래 안 하세요? (목이 아프다)
3 왜 조금 드세요? (다이어트를 하고 있다)
4 왜 안 사세요? (돈이 없다)
5 왜 안 마시세요? (술을 못 마시다)
6 왜 옷을 바꾸셨어요? (사이즈가 작았다)

Exercise 9.11

Finish the following translation using ~어/아야 and the sentence cues
provided in parenthesis, as shown in the example.

Example: "Only if (we) have money, (we) can go to Hawaii."
(돈이 있다 / 하와이에 갈 수 있어요)
= 돈이 있어야 하와이에 갈 수 있어요.

1 Only if (my) girlfriend is happy, (I) am also happy (여자 친구가 행복
하다 / 저도 행복해요)
2 Only if (it) is on sale, (I) can buy (it) (세일을 하다 / 살 수 있어요)
3 Only if (you) study hard, (you) can become a doctor (열심히 공부하다
/ 의사가 될 수 있어요)
4 Only if (he) quits (his) work, (he) can travel (일을 그만두다 / 여행을
할 수 있어요)
5 Only if (she) quits smoking, (her) illness can be cured (담배를 끊다 /
병이 나을 수 있어요)

Exercise 9.12

Connect the following two sentences using ~어/아야. Then translate the
sentence.

Example: 매일 운동을 하다 / 건강해질 수 있어요
= 매일 운동을 해야 건강해질 수 있어요.
"Only if (you) exercise everyday, (you) can become healthy."

1 시험을 잘 보다 / 법대에 들어갈 수 있어요
2 아르바이트를 하다 / 학비를 낼 수 있어요
3 저금을 하다 / 새 소파를 살 수 있어요
4 파리에 가다 / 에펠타워를 볼 수 있어요
5 크리스틴을 만나다 / 책을 받을 수 있어요

UNIT 10
Clausal conjunctives (listing and choice)

~고

The function of the clausal conjunctive ~고 is twofold. First, it simply connects two different clauses, regardless of their sequence. It corresponds to "and" in English. Consider the following examples:

제니퍼가 청소하고 매튜가 요리해요. "Jennifer cleans up, and Matthew cooks."
매튜가 요리하고 제니퍼가 청소해요. "Matthew cooks, and Jennifer cleans up."

Notice that the meanings of the sentences above are the same, even if the sequences of the clauses are different. Here are more examples:

존은 신문을 읽고 수잔은 텔레비전을 봐요. "As for John, (he) reads newspaper, and as for Susan, (she) watches TV."
앤이 일본으로 가고 톰이 한국으로 가요. "Ann goes to Japan, and Tom goes to Korea."
머리가 아프고 졸려요. "(My) head aches, and (I) am sleepy."
앤드류가 스페인어를 전공하고 이사벨이 프랑스어를 전공해요. "Andrew majors in Spanish, and Isabel majors in French."

Second, ~고 links two sequential actions or events, equivalent to "and then" in English. Consider the following examples:

숙제를 하고 점심을 먹어요. "(I) do the homework and then eat lunch."
점심을 먹고 숙제를 해요. "(I) eat lunch and then do the homework."

Notice that ~고 indicates the order of the action. In other words, the change in the sequence of the clauses generates a different meaning. Here are more examples:

저녁을 <u>먹고</u> 서점에 갑니다. "(I) eat dinner and then go to a bookstore."
샤워를 <u>하고</u> 자요? "Do (you) take a shower and then go to bed?"
손을 <u>씻고</u> 요리하십시오. "Wash (your) hands and then cook."
친구를 <u>만나고</u> 집에 갑시다. "(Let us) meet (our) friends and then go
home."

~고 is subject to one restriction: It is not conjugated for the tense.
Consider the following examples:

아침을 <u>먹고</u> 우체국에 <u>갔어요</u>. "(I) ate breakfast and then went to the
post office."
어제는 날씨가 <u>흐리고</u> <u>추웠어요</u>. "As for yesterday, the weather was
cloudy and cold."

Notice that both sentences are about the past action and state. However,
the past tense is not marked by the ~고 ending clauses but by the main
clauses.

~(으)며

The clausal conjunctive ~(으)며 means "and" or "while." It is a two-form
ending: ~으며 is used when the preceding stem ends in a consonant (e.g.,
먹으며 "eat and"); ~며 is used when the preceding stem ends in a vowel
(e.g., 가르치며 "teach and").

Verbs/adjectives	Stem + (으)며
먹다 "eat"	먹으며
믿다 "believe"	믿으며
잡다 "catch"	잡으며
좋다 "good"	좋으며
많다 "many"	많으며
가르치다 "teach"	가르치며
가다 "go"	가며
보다 "see"	보며
기쁘다 "glad"	기쁘며
크다 "big"	크며

The meaning of ~(으)며 is similar to that of ~고 since both connect two
actions or states. However, while ~고 can indicate both the non-sequential
as well as sequential actions/states (e.g., "and" and "and then"), ~(으)며
indicates only non-sequential actions/states. In addition, while ~고 is widely
used both in spoken and written communication, ~(으)며 tends to be used
only in writing. Consider the following sentences:

필립은 경제학을 <u>전공하며</u> 찰스는 <u>심리학을</u> 전공합니다. "As for Philip, (he) majors in economics, and as for Charles, (he) majors in psychology." 리사는 재즈를 <u>좋아하며</u> 제임스는 클래식을 좋아해요. "As for Lisa, (she) likes jazz, and as for James, (he) likes classic."

오늘은 바람이 많이 <u>불며</u> 춥겠습니다. "As for today, (it) will be very windy and cold." 이 옷은 옷감이 <u>좋으며</u> 디자인이 예쁩니다. "As for this dress, the fabric is good, and the design is pretty." 우체국이 왼쪽에 <u>있으며</u> 공원이 오른쪽에 있어요. "The post office is on the left side, and the park is on the right side." 에드워드는 캐나다 사람이며 마리오는 멕시코 사람이에요. "As for Edward, (he) is a Canadian, and as for Mario, (he) is a Mexican."

Notice in the examples above that ~(으)며 simply links two separate and/or non-sequential actions or states.

When the subjects of both clauses are the same, ~(으)며 indicates that two or more actions or events occur simultaneously. Consider the following examples:

맥주를 <u>마시며</u> 이야기해요. "(We) talk while drinking beer." 그레이스가 음악을 <u>들으며</u> 조깅을 해요. "Grace jogs, while listening to music."

Note in the above examples that ~(으)며 is translated as "while" rather than "and" in English.

~(으)며 is subject to one restriction: It is not conjugated for the tense, as shown below:

교수님의 강의를 <u>들으며</u> 노트를 적었어요. "While listening to the professor's lecture, (I) took notes." 춤을 <u>추며</u> 노래를 불렀어요? "Did (you) sing, dancing?"

Notice in the examples that only the main clauses are conjugated for the past tense.

~거나

The clausal conjunctive ~거나 is used to list two or more actions/states. It is equivalent to "or" in English, as shown in the following examples:

토요일에는 보통 친구들하고 영화를 <u>보거나</u> 집에서 쉬어요. "As for Saturday, (I) normally see a movie with (my) friends or take a rest at home."

아프거나 피곤할 때 집 생각해요? "When (you) are sick or tired, do (you) think about (your) home?"

피터의 아버지가 선생님이거나 공무원일 거예요. "(I guess that) Peter's father is either a teacher or a government officer."

이메일을 보내거나 전화를 하세요. "Send (him) an e-mail or give (him) a call."

도서관에 가거나 커피숍에 갑시다. "(Let us) go to the library or the coffee shop."

~거나 may imply that the actions or states listed by the conjunctive are trivial, while the predicate or the content of the main clause is essential. In such case, ~거나 is translated as "whether...or" in English. Consider the following example:

날씨가 춥거나 덥거나 매일 뛰어요. "Whether the weather is cold or hot, (I) run everyday."

Notice that the two states denoted by two adjectives, 춥다 "cold" and 덥다 "hot," are trivial, whereas the predicate of the main clause, 뛰다 "run" is important. Here are more examples:

맛있거나 맛없거나 배 고프면 아무거나 먹어요. "Whether (it) is delicious or not, (we) eat anything if (we) are hungry."

어렵거나 쉽거나 열심히 배울래요? "Whether (it) is hard or easy, will (you) learn (it) enthusiastically?"

TV를 보거나 자거나 오후 7 시까지 집에 있으십시오. "Stay home until 7 p.m., whether (you) watch TV or sleep."

슬프거나 기쁘거나 언제나 전화하십시오. "Whether (you) are sad or happy, call (me) anytime."

비가 오거나 눈이 오거나 매일 운동합시다. "Whether (it) rains or snows, (let us) exercise everyday."

~든지

The clausal conjunctive ~든지 is used to list a series of selections or to imply an unenthusiastic or indifferent attitude toward the selections. It can be translated in English as "or," "no matter," and/or "regardless." Consider the following example:

커피를 마시든지 아이스크림을 먹든지 뭔가 시킵시다. "(Let us) order something, whether (we) drink coffee or eat ice creams."

Notice in the example above that ~든지 enumerates two activities (e.g., drinking coffee and eating ice creams). However, it also implies that the speaker is not enthusiastic about these activities. Here are more examples:

내일 비가 <u>오든지</u> 눈이 <u>오든지</u> 예정대로 진행하겠습니다. "(We) will proceed (the event) according to the schedule, regardless (it) rains or snows tomorrow."
그 옷이 <u>바싸든지</u> <u>싸든지</u> 꼭 사 주세요. "Please buy (me) that dress whether (it) is expensive or inexpensive."
그 아이들은 옆에 사람이 <u>있든지</u> <u>없든지</u> 항상 시끄러워요. "As for those kids, (they) are always noisy, whether people are around or not."
어디를 <u>가든지</u> 무엇을 <u>하든지</u> 건강하십시오. "Wherever (you) go and whatever (you) do, be healthy."

Exercises

Key vocabulary for Unit 10 exercises

가다 to go
갈아입다 to change (clothes)
길다 to be long
꽃 flowers
날씬하다 to be slim
날씨 weather
내다 to pay out
돼지고기 pork
땀 sweat
마시다 to drink
만들다 to make
맛없다 to be tasteless
머리 head/hair (of the head)
먹다 to eat

바닷가 beach
방 room
보다 to see/to watch/to read
보통 usually
비 rain
사다 to buy
산 mountain
살 age
성격 personality

세수 face washing
소고기 beef
소리 sound/noise
숙제 homework
시원하다 to be cool/to be refreshing
신문 newspapers
싸다 to be cheap
쓰다 to use

아침 morning/breakfast
언제 when
얼굴 face
영화 movie
예쁘다 to be pretty
옷 clothes
외식 dining out
울다 to cry
의사 doctor
인터넷 internet
읽다 to read

작다 to be small
저녁 dinner/evening
좋다 to be good
지르다 to cry out
지불하다 to pay
착하다 to be good/to be kindhearted
춥다 to be cold
치다 to play/to strike
친절하다 to be kind
크다 to be big
키 height
현금 cash
흐리다 to be cloudy
흘리다 to spill/to drop

Exercise 10.1

Complete the following translation using ~고 and the sentence cues provided in parenthesis, as shown in the example.

Example: "(I) will listen to (my) friend's story and then decide."
(제 친구의 이야기를 듣다 / 결정하겠습니다)
= 제 친구의 이야기를 듣고 결정하겠습니다.

(I) eat breakfast and then exercise (아침을 먹다 / 운동합니다)

Brush (your) teeth and then go to bed (이를 닦다 / 자요)

Do (you) ask the teacher first and then go to the restroom? (선생님 한테 먼저 물어 보다 / 화장실에 갑니까?)

(Let us) leave after making a reservation (예약을 하다 / 떠납시다)

(I) want to get a job after graduating from college (대학교를 졸업하다 / 취직하고 싶어요)

As for Susan, (her) eyes are big and (she) is quiet (수잔은 눈이 크다 / 조용해요)

As for Tim, (his) voice is good and (he) has humor (팀은 목소리가 좋다 / 유머가 있어요)

As for Andrew, (he) is humble and diligent (앤드류는 겸손하다 / 부지런해요)

Exercise 10.2

Connect the following two sentences using ~고. Then translate the sentence.

Example: 저녁을 먼저 먹다 / 숙제를 할 거예요?
= 저녁을 먼저 먹고 숙제를 할 거예요?
"Will (you) eat dinner first and then do (your) homework?"

1 세수를 하다 / 옷을 갈아 입으세요
2 숙제를 하다 / 인터넷을 쓰겠어요
3 샤워를 하다 / 저녁을 먹읍시다
4 키가 크다 / 얼굴이 작았어요
5 존이 31 살이다 / 의사입니다

Exercise 10.3

Complete the following translation using ~(으)며 and the sentence cues provided in parenthesis, as shown in the example.

Example: "The subway is convenient and fast." (지하철이 편하다 / 빠릅니다)
= 지하철이 편하며 빠릅니다.

1 Paul's voice is loud and soft (폴의 목소리가 크다 / 부드럽습니다)
2 James is a scientist and an inventor (제임스가 과학자이다 / 발명가입니다)
3 Wendy is an actress and a singer (웬디가 배우이다 / 가수입니다)

4 Today's weather is clear and cool (오늘 날씨가 맑다 / 선선합니다)
5 That school is good and famous (그 학교가 좋다 / 유명합니다)
6 Train is safe and convenient (기차가 안전하다 / 편합니다)

Exercise 10.4

Connect the following two sentences using ~(으)며. Then translate the
sentence.

> Example: 헬렌이 웃다 / 이야기했어요
> = 헐렌이 웃으며 이야기했어요. "Helen talked, smiling."

1 테렌스가 커피를 마시다 / 신문을 읽고 있어요
2 그레이스가 텔레비전을 보다 / 저녁을 먹었어요
3 리처드가 팝콘을 먹다 / 영화를 봐요
4 에스더가 땀을 흘리다 / 테니스를 치고 있어요
5 로버트가 울다 / 소리 질렀어요
6 니콜이 날씬하다 / 착해요
7 클라라가 예쁘다 / 성격이 좋아요
8 로라는 머리가 길다 / 친절했어요
9 서울은 날씨가 흐리다 / 비가 오겠어요
10 이 방이 크다 / 시원해요

Exercise 10.5

Complete the following translation using ~거나 and the sentence cues
provided in parenthesis, as shown in the example.

> Example: "(I) will buy (it) whether (it) is cheap or expensive."
> (싸다 / 비싸다 / 살 거예요)
> = 싸거나 비싸거나 살 거예요.

1 (He) is (my) older brother whether (he) is a rich man or a beggar
(부자이다 / 거지이다 / 제 형이에요)
2 (I) want to study Korean whether (it) is difficult or easy (어렵다 /
쉽다 / 한국어를 공부하고 싶어요)
3 (I) will wait (for her), whether (she) comes or not (오다 / 안 오다 /
기다릴 거예요)
4 (I) will try asking (him), whether (he will) lend (it to me) or not (빌려
주다 / 안 빌려주다 / 물어 볼 거예요)
5 Watch that drama again whether (it) is interesting or dull (재미있다 /
재미없다 / 그 드라마를 다시 보십시오)

Exercise 10.6

Connect the following two sentences using ~거나. Then translate the sentence.

Example: TV 를 보다 / 컴퓨터를 쓸 거예요
= TV 를 보거나 컴퓨터를 쓸 거예요.
"(I) will watch TV or use the computer."

1 보통 언제 영화를 보다 / 외식을 합니까?
2 꽃을 사다 / 케이크를 만드십시오
3 아침에 조깅을 하다 / 요가를 해요
4 현금으로 내다 / 카드로 지불할 거예요
5 산으로 가다 / 바닷가로 갑시다

Exercise 10.7

Complete the following translation using ~든지 and the sentence cues provided in parenthesis, as shown in the example.

Example: "(Let us) clean the room or do the laundry."
(방을 청소하다 / 빨래를 합시다)
= 방을 청소하든지 빨래를 합시다.

1 (We) will eat lunch or drink coffee (점심을 먹다 / 커피를 마실 거예요)
2 (Let us) go home or a coffee shop (집에 가다 / 커피숍에 갑시다)
3 Drink apple juice or tomato juice (사과 주스를 마시다 / 토마토 주스를 마시세요)
4 (Let us) see an action movie or a horror movie (액션 영화를 보다 / 공포 영화를 봅시다)
5 (We) will play tennis whether (it) is cold or hot (춥다 / 덥다 / 테니스를 칠 거예요)

Exercise 10.8

Connect the following two sentences using ~든지. Then translate the sentence.

Example: 은행에 가다 / 우체국에 갈 거예요.
= 은행에 가든지 우체국에 갈 거예요.
"(I) will go to the bank or the post office."

10

Clausal conjunctives (listing and choice)

1 콜라를 사다 / 주스를 사겠어요.
2 소고기를 먹다 / 돼지고기를 먹읍시다.
3 커피를 마시다 / 케이크를 먹어요.
4 날씨가 흐리다 / 추울 거예요.
5 신문을 읽다 / TV를 볼 거예요.

UNIT 11
Clausal conjunctives (time)

~(으)면서

The clausal conjunctive ~(으)면서 is used when two actions (or states) are carried out simultaneously by the same subject. It corresponds to "while" in English. ~(으)면서 is a two-form ending: ~으면서 is used after a stem that ends in a consonant (e.g., 먹으면서 "while eating"); ~면서 is used after a stem that ends in a vowel (e.g., 마시면서 "while drinking").

팝콘을 먹으면서 영화를 보고 있어요. "(He) is seeing a movie, eating popcorn."
운전하면서 전화하고 있어요? "Are (you) calling (someone), while driving?"
커피를 마시면서 이야기하십시오. "Talk, drinking coffee."
한국 노래를 부르면서 같이 걸으십시다. "(Let us) walk together, singing Korean songs."

디자인이 예쁘면서 값이 싸요. "While the design is pretty, the price is inexpensive."
이 집이 크면서 학교에서도 가까워요. "While this house is big, (it) is also near from school."
음식이 비싸면서 서비스도 나빠요. "While (their) food is expensive, (their) service is also bad."
군인이면서 학생이에요. "While (he) is a military man, (he) is a student."

~(으)면서 is not conjugated for the tense. Consider the following examples:

돈을 벌면서 대학에 다녔어요. "(I) attended the college, while earning money."
편지를 읽으면서 울었어요? "Did (she) cry, while reading the letter?"
그 친구를 생각하면서 이 사진들을 보고 있었어요. "(I) was looking at these pictures, while thinking about that friend."

Notice in the examples above that only the predicates of the main clauses are conjugated for the tense.

~(으)면서 is often used for disapproving, criticizing or complaining. This is when two simultaneous actions or states, connected by ~(으)면서, are disagreeing or inconsonant each other. Consider the following example:

공부를 안 하면서 A 를 받고 싶어해요. "While (he) does not study, (he) wants to receive an A."

Notice that the action of the first clause (e.g., not studying) and that of the main clause (want to receive an A) are inconsonant each other. In addition, the sentence is a speech act of complaining or disapproving. Here are more examples:

제일 높은 봉급을 받으면서 실력이 없어요. "While (he) receives the highest salary, (he) does not have any merit."
직업도 없으면서 비싼 차만 찾아요. "While (he) does not even have a job, (he) only looks for expensive cars."

~자마자

The clausal conjunctive ~자마자 means "as soon as" or "immediately after." ~자마자 is subject to the following restrictions. First, it must be used only with verbs, as shown below:

일을 마치자마자 집에 갈 거예요. "(I) will go home as soon as (I) finish with (my) work."
일어나자마자 샤워할 거예요? "Will (you) take a shower as soon as (you) get up?"
공항에 도착하자마자 연락하세요. "Contact (them) as soon as (you) arrive in the airport."

Second, it is not conjugated for the tense.

유니스가 방에 들어오자마자 피터가 전등을 켰어요. "Peter turned the electric lamp on as soon as Eunice entered the room."
편지를 읽자마자 울었어요. "(She) cried as soon as (she) read the letter."
소식을 듣자마자 밖으로 나갔어요. "(He) went outside as soon as (he) heard the news."

Notice in the examples above that only the main clauses are conjugated for the tense.

~다가

The clausal conjunctive ~다가 is used to express the shift in action or state. When it is attached to a verb stem, it indicates that the subject shifts his/her action to another. Consider the following examples:

책을 읽다가 잤어요. "As (I) read the book, (I) slept."
학교에 가다가 슈퍼마켓에 들렀어요. "On my way to school, (I) stopped by the supermarket."

Notice in the examples above that the subjects shifted certain actions (e.g., reading, going to school) to another actions (e.g., sleeping, stopping by the supermarket). Here are more examples:

10 분 전까지 그 친구를 기다리다가 집에 갔어요. "(He) waited for that friend until 10 minutes ago and then went home."
커피를 마시다가 친구를 만났어요. "While drinking coffee, (I) met (my) friends."
우체국에 가다가 무엇을 샀어요? "What did (you) buy on (your) way to the post office?"
뛰다가 10 분 정도 쉬세요. "Run and then rest about 10 minutes."
메뉴를 보다가 음식을 시킵시다. "(Let us) look at the menu and then order food."

When ~다가 is attached to an adjective stem, it indicates the shift in state to another. Consider the following example:

맛이 싱겁다가 짜요. "The taste was watery and then (it) is salty (now)."

Notice in the example above that there was a shift in the state (e.g., from "being watery" to "being salty"). The first state is no longer in effect in favor of the second state. Here are more examples:

오전까지 날씨가 좋다가 지금은 흐립니다. "The weather was good until a.m. and then (it) is cloudy now."
크리스마스 전까지 비싸다가 12 월 26 일부터는 싸졌어요. "(They) were expensive before Christmas but then (they) became inexpensive (starting) from December 26."

The use of the past tense marker 었/았 is optional for ~다가. If the speaker wishes to highlight the past action rather than the shift in the action, he/she can optionally use the past tense marker. Compare the following two sentenes:

학교에 <u>가다가</u> 친구들을 만났어요. "On (my) way to school, (I) met
(my) friends."
학교에 <u>갔다가</u> 친구들을 만났어요. "(I) went to school and then met
(my) friends."

Notice that there is a subtle meaning difference between the two sentences.
While the first sentence simply indicates the shift in the action, the second
sentence highlights the completed past action that took place before the
shift of the action took place. Here are more examples:

약속을 <u>했다가</u> 취소했어요. "(I) made a promise and then (I) cancelled
(it)."
어디 <u>갔다가</u> 오셨어요? "Where did you go and come back?"
컴퓨터를 <u>샀다가</u> 팔았어요. "(We) bought the computer and then sold
(it)."
전등을 <u>켰다가</u> <u>껐다가</u> 그래요. "(They) do things like turning the electric lamp on and off."
언제 대사관에 <u>갔다가</u> 왔어요? "When did (you) go to the embassy and
come back?"

~다가는

The topic particle 는 can be optionally attached to the conjunctive ~다가.
~다가는 is used to warn about the action or state of the prior clause.
Consider the following examples:

매일 술을 <u>마시다가는</u> 건강을 해칠 수 있어요. "If (you) drink alcohol
everyday, (you) can harm (your) health."
추운 날씨에 밖에서 오래 <u>운동하다가는</u> 감기 걸릴 수 있어요. "If (you)
exercise for a long time under the cold weather outside, (you) can catch
a cold."

Notice in the examples above that ~다가는 indicates that the continual
action of the first clause may generate an unpleasant or troublesome
consequence.

~(으)려다가

The combination of ~(으)려고 "intending to" with ~다가 creates a new
clausal conjunctive ~(으)려다가. The conjunctive ~(으)려다가 is used when
one tries to do something but comes across another situation. It indicates
that the intentional action of the first clause was never actualized, but the
action of the main clause was realized instead. Consider the following
example:

집에 <u>가려다가</u> 서점에 갔습니다. "As (I) intended to go home, (I) went to a bookstore."

Notice that the action of the first clause (e.g., going home) was never actualized. Instead, the action of the main clause was realized. Here are more examples:

개를 <u>잡으려다가</u> 넘어졌어요. "As (I) intended to catch the dog, (I) fell (on the ground)."
도서관에 <u>가려다가</u> 길에서 제임스를 만나서 같이 저녁을 먹었어요. "As (I) intended to go to the library, (I) met James on the street and had dinner together."
프린터를 <u>사려다가</u> 대신 컴퓨터를 샀어요. "As (we) intended to buy a printer, (we) bought a computer instead."
무엇을 <u>팔려다가</u> 못 팔았어요? "What did (you) intend to sell, but could not sell?"

Exercises

Key vocabulary for Unit 11 exercises

가다 to go
거지 beggar
걷다 to walk
계단 stairs
계속 continually
골다 to snore
길 road
깨다 to break/to smash
넘어지다 to fall (down over)
노래 song
놀다 to play/to amuse
대학 college
돈 money
되다 to become/to get to/to elapse
떨어지다 to fall/to drop

많이 a lot
먹다 to eat
멈추다 to stop
무언가 something
바꾸다 to change
배탈나다 to have a stomachache

보다 to see/to watch/to read
사다 to buy
살찌다 to gain weight
세수 face washing
시키다 to order
시험 test/exam
신문 newspapers
쓰다 to use

양치질 brushing teeth
열심히 hard/earnestly/enthusiastically
영화 movie
오른쪽 right side
올라가다 to climb/to go up
요리 cooking
울다 to cry
웃다 to smile
이사 (house) moving
이야기하다 to talk
일하다 to work
일어나다 to get up
읽다 to read

자다 to sleep
전에 before
점심 lunch
접시 dish
졸다 to doze off
졸업하다 to graduate
주소 address
중얼거리다 to mutter/to murmur
쫓겨나다 to be expelled
차 car
찾다 to look for/to seek for
책 book
혼자 alone
회사 company/firm

Exercise 11.1

Finish the following translation using ~(으)면서 and the sentence cues
provided in parenthesis, as shown in the example.

Example: "Do not chew a gum, while working."
(일하다 / 껌을 씹지 마세요)
= 일하면서 껌을 씹지 마세요.

1 (She) is calling (someone), crying (울다 / 전화를 하고 있어요)
2 Will (you) make friends while traveling? (여행을 하다 / 친구를 사귈 거예요?)
3 Do not fall from the bed, while getting up (일어나다 / 침대에서 떨어지지 마십시오)
4 (Let us) not break dishes while cooking (요리하다 / 접시를 깨뜨리지 맙시다)
5 Did (you) fall, while riding a bike? (자전거를 타다 / 넘어졌습니까?)

Exercise 11.2

Connect the following two sentences using ~(으)면서 as shown in the example. Then translate the sentence.

Example: 커피를 마시다 / 운전을 하고 있어요
= 커피를 마시면서 운전을 하고 있어요.
"(I) am driving, while drinking coffee."

1 톰하고 제리가 웃다 / 이야기하고 있어요
2 스티브가 책을 읽다 / 혼자 중얼거려요
3 루이스가 자다 / 코를 골았어요
4 해리가 노래를 하다 / 샤워를 해요
5 조디가 길을 걷다 / 무언가 찾고 있었어요

Exercise 11.3

Finish the following translation using ~자마자 and the sentence cues provided in parenthesis, as shown in the example.

Example: "(He) danced as soon as (he) wore shoes."
(신발을 신다 / 춤을 췄어요)
= 신발을 신자마자 춤을 췄어요.

1 (I) want to get married as soon as (I) get a job (취직하다 / 결혼하고 싶습니다)
2 (She) cried as soon as (she) met (her) boyfriend (남자 친구를 만나다 / 울었어요)

3 (He) will snore as soon as (he) lies down on the bed (침대에 눕다 / 코를 골 거예요)
4 What do (you) want to do as soon as (you) graduate from college? (대학을 졸업하다 / 무엇을 하고 싶어요?)
5 Call (your) older sister as soon as (you) arrive in London (런던에 도착하다 / 누나한테 전화하십시오)
6 (Let us) buy (some) popcorn as soon as (we) enter the theatre (영화관에 들어가다 / 팝콘을 삽시다)

Exercise 11.4

Connect the following two sentences using ~자마자. Then translate the sentence.

> Example: 커피를 마시다 / 사무실로 돌아갔어요
> = 커피를 마시자마자 사무실로 돌아갔어요.
> "(He) returned to the office, as soon as (he) drank coffee."

1 일어나다 / 세수를 합니다
2 새 집으로 이사를 하다 / 주소를 바꿨어요
3 대학을 졸업하다 / 차를 살 거예요?
4 점심을 먹다 / 커피를 시킵시다
5 세수를 하다 / 양치질을 하십시오

Exercise 11.5

Finish the following translation using ~다가 and the sentence cues provided in parenthesis, as shown in the example.

> Example: "As (I) did laundry, (I) answered the phone."
> (빨래를 하다 / 전화를 받았어요)
> = 빨래를 하다가 전화를 받았어요.

1 (I) watched TV and then slept (텔레비전을 보다 / 잤어요)
2 As (he) bought vegetables in the supermarket and (he) ran into (his) friend (슈퍼마켓에서 야채를 사다 / 친구와 마주쳤어요)
3 As (she) opened the door, (she) got (her) wrist injured (문을 열다 / 손목을 다쳤어요)
4 As (he) played basketball, (he) sprained (his) ankle (농구를 하다 / 발목을 삐었어요)
5 (I) wrote a letter and then went to the restroom (편지를 쓰다 / 화장실에 갔어요)

Exercise 11.6

Connect the following two sentences using ~다가. Then translate the sentence.

> Example: 점심을 먹다 / 전화를 받았어요.
> = 점심을 먹다가 전화를 받았어요.
> "As (he) ate lunch, (he) answered the phone."

1 신문을 읽다 / 졸았어요
2 영화를 보다 / 울었어요
3 오른쪽으로 가다 / 멈추세요
4 계단을 올라가다 / 넘어졌어요?
5 누가 요리를 하다 / 접시를 깼어요?

Exercise 11.7

Finish the following translation using ~다가는 and the sentence cues provided in parenthesis, as shown in the example.

> Example: "If (you) leave late, (you) can miss the bus."
> (늦게 떠나다 / 버스를 놓칠 수 있어요)
> = 늦게 떠나다가는 버스를 놓칠 수 있어요.

1 If (you) do not study hard, (you) cannot enter college (열심히 공부를 안 하다 / 대학에 못 들어가요)
2 If (you) continue to smoke, (you) can get a cancer (담배를 계속 피우다 / 암에 걸릴 수 있어요)
3 If (you) overspeed, an accident may occur (과속을 하다 / 사고가 날 거예요)
4 If (you) do not contact (each other), (you) can end up forgetting each other (연락을 안 하다 / 서로 잊어 버릴 수 있어요)
5 If (you) continue to turn down, (you) can miss an opportunity (계속 거절하다 / 기회를 놓칠 수 있어요)
6 If (he) drinks whisky everyday, (he) may become an alcoholic (매일 위스키를 마시다 / 알콜 중독자가 될 거예요)

Exercise 11.8

Connect the following two sentences using ~다가는. Then translate the
sentence.

Example: 텔레비전을 오래 보다 / 시력이 나빠질 수 있어요
= 텔레비전을 오래 보다가는 시력이 나빠질 수 있어요.
"If (you) watch TV for a long time, (your) vision can become
worse."

1 자기 전에 많이 먹다 / 살찔 거예요
2 계속 놀다 / 시험에 떨어질 수 있어요.
3 돈만 쓰다 / 거지가 될 거예요.
4 열심히 일을 안 하다 / 회사에서 쫓겨날 수 있어요.
5 많이 먹다 / 배탈날 거예요

UNIT 12
Clausal conjunctives (background)

~는/(으)ㄴ데

Function

The clausal conjunctive ~는 /(으)ㄴ데 is used to provide background information for the main clause. Consider the following example:

한국어를 <u>공부하는데</u> 재미있어요. "(I) study Korean, and (it) is interesting."

In this example, the first clause 한국어를 공부하다 "(I) study Korean" is the background information for the main clause 재미있다 "(it) is interesting." Here are more examples:

오늘 밤 날씨가 <u>추운데</u> 밖에 나가지 마세요. "The weather is cold tonight, so do not go outside."
점심 때가 <u>됐는데</u> 어디 가서 뭔가 먹읍시다. "(It) has become lunchtime, so (let us) go somewhere and eat something."
이번 주에 약속이 <u>있는데</u> 다음 주가 어때요? "(I) have an appointment this week, so how about next week?"
내일까지 일을 <u>마쳐야 하는데</u> 하나도 안 했어요. "(I) have to finish the work by tomorrow, but (I) have not done anything."
오늘은 <u>바쁜데</u> 내일 만납시다. "As for today, (I) am busy, so (let us) meet tomorrow."

How it is conjugated

~는데 is used after a verb stem.

Verb	Verb stem + 는데
가다 "go"	가는데
배우다 "learn"	배우는데
가르치다 "teach"	가르치는데
요리하다 "cook"	요리하는데

Verb	Verb stem + 는데
공부하다 "study"	공부하는데
먹다 "eat"	먹는데
찾다 "find"	찾는데
있다 "have/exist"	있는데
없다 "not have/exist"	없는데

As for adjectives and copulas, ~은데 is used after a stem that ends in a consonant, and ~ㄴ데 is used after a stem that ends in a vowel, as shown below:

Adjective	Adjective stem + (으)ㄴ데
작다 "small"	작은데
좋다 "good"	좋은데
맑다 "clear"	맑은데
춥다 "cold"	추운데
싸다 "cheap"	싼데
행복하다 "happy"	행복한데
이상하다 "strange"	이상한데

Copula	Copula stem + (으)ㄴ데
이다 "be"	인데
아니다 "be not"	아닌데

As for an adjective that is made of 있다/없다, such as 재미있다 "interesting" and 맛없다 "tasteless," ~는데 is used.

Adjective	Adjective stem + 는데
재미없다 "uninteresting"	재미없는데
맛있다 "delicious"	맛있는데
멋있다 "stylish"	멋있는데

As for the past tense, ~는데 is used after the past tense marker 었/았, and this applies to any predicate type, as shown below:

Verb stem + Past tense marker + 는데: 어제 한국 식당에 <u>갔는데</u> 손님 이 많았어요. "(I) went to the Korean restaurant yesterday, and there were many customers."

Adjective stem + Past tense marker + 는데: 어제 <u>추웠는데</u> 사람이 많 았어요. "(It) was cold yesterday, but there were many people."

Copula stem + Past tense marker + 는데: 작년까지 고등 학생<u>이었는데</u> 이제 대학생이에요. "Until last year, (she) was a high school student, but (she) is a college student now."

~는/(으)ㄴ데요 as a sentence ender

In spoken communication, conjunctives often end a sentence. For instance, in a delicate or face-threatening communicative situation, such as expressing disagreement, requesting, complaining, and refusing, people often opt out of saying the main clause as a strategy to be indirect and polite (e.g., so that they may reduce the degree of imposition when requesting or they may not hurt the addressee's feeling when refusing or complaining). For instance, consider the following dialogue:

A: Can you come to my birthday party tonight?
B: I have a test tomorrow so…(I will not be able to make it).

Notice that the speaker B uses the ellipsis, leaving the main clause out.

In a similar manner the English conjunctive "so" ends the first clause in the example above, ~는/(으)ㄴ데 may be used as a sentence ender. The politeness ending 요 is optionally attached to ~는/(으)ㄴ데, as in ~는/(으)ㄴ데요, to sound more polite. Consider the following dialogue:

A: 내일 파티에 같이 갈래요?
  "Would (you) like to go to the party together tomorrow?"
B: 이번 주는 바쁜데요.
  "(I) am busy this week (so)."

Notice that the speaker B just provides background information (e.g., he/she is busy), and opts out saying the main clause. In this way, the speaker B makes the speaker A figures out the implicit message (e.g., so I can't go to the party tomorrow).

~는/(으)ㄴ데도

The combination of the conjunctive ~는/(으)ㄴ데 and the particle 도 "even/also" is a new conjunctive ~는/(으)ㄴ데도 "although/despite (the fact that)/even if." Consider the following examples:

작은데도 방세가 비싸요. "Although (it) is small, the room rent is expensive."
주말인데도 손님이 별로 없어요. "Although (it) is a weekend, there are not many customers."
많이 잤는데도 아직도 피곤해요. "Although (I) slept a lot, (I) am still tired."
약을 먹었는데도 배가 여전히 아파요. "Although (I) took the medicine, (my) stomach still aches."

Exercises

Key vocabulary for Unit 12 exercises

가다 to go
가방 bag/suitcase
같이 together
금방 just now/at once
기다리다 to wait
기타 guitar
끓이다 to boil
내일 tomorrow
너무 too much
다음 next
도착하다 to arrive
돕다 to help

마시다 to drink
많다 to be many/to be much
머리 head/hair (of one's head)
먹다 to eat
목마르다 to be thirsty
무겁다 to be heavy
무척 very much/extremely
물 water
미국 U.S.A.
미안하다 to be sorry
바쁘다 to be busy
방 room
배우다 to learn
백화점 department store
부엌 kitchen
부치다 to send/to mail
비싸다 to be expensive
빌리다 to borrow

사다 to buy
사람 person/people
소리 sound/noise
소포 parcel/package
수리하다 to fix/to repair
시끄럽다 to be noisy
아프다 to be sore
약 medicine
없다 do not have/do not exist

연락 contact
요즈음 nowadays
음식 food
있다 to have/to exist

좀 a little/please
주 week
주다 to give
줄이다 to reduce
지금 now
지난 last
차 car/tea
켜다 to switch on
춥다 to be cold
친구 friend
학교 school
한국 Korea
히터 heater

Exercise 12.1

Finish the following translation using ~는데 and the sentence cues provided in parenthesis, as shown in the example.

　　Example: "(We) saw the movie, and (it) was really interesting."
　　　　　　(영화를 봤다 / 아주 재미있었어요)
　　　　　　= 영화를 봤는데 아주 재미있었어요.

1 (I) am chewing a gum, but (my) tooth aches (껌을 씹고 있다 / 이가 아파요)
2 (I) am sweeping the street, and will (you) help (me)? (길을 청소하고 있다 / 도와 줄래요?)
3 (I) have to buy a gift, and (let us) go to the department store together (선물을 사야 하다 / 백화점에 같이 갑시다)
4 (We) met Eric yesterday, but (he) was exactly the same as before (어제 에릭을 만났다 / 전하고 똑같았어요)
5 (He) studied hard but (he) failed the exam (공부를 열심히 했다 / 시험에 떨어졌어요)

Exercise 12.2

Connect the following two sentences using ~는데. Then translate the sentence.

Example: 지금 아침을 먹고 있다 / 기다려 주세요.
          = 지금 아침을 먹고 있는데 기다려 주세요.
          "(She) is eating breakfast now, so please wait."

1 부엌을 수리하고 있다 / 비싸요
2 지금 학교에 가다 / 같이 갑시다
3 물을 끓이고 있다 / 마실래요?
4 백화점에 갔다 / 사람들이 너무 많았어요
5 지난 주에 소포를 부쳤다 / 도착했어요?

Exercise 12.3

Finish the following translation using ~었/았는데 and the sentence cues
provided in parenthesis, as shown in the example.

Example: "(I) was hungry, but (I) could not eat lunch."
          (배가 고프다 / 점심을 못 먹었어요)
          = 배가 고팠는데 점심을 못 먹었어요.

1 (She) was a student last year, but (she) is a teacher now (작년에 학생
  이었다 / 이제 선생님이에요)
2 There were many people before, but there are not many now. (전에
  사람들이 많았다 / 이제 별로 없어요)
3 As for yesterday, (it) was hot, but as for today, (it) is cool (어제는
  더웠다 / 오늘은 선선해요)
4 As for the price, (it) was cheap, but the quantity was small (값은
  쌌다 / 양이 적었어요)
5 The weather was bad, but there were many customers (날씨가 나빴
  다 / 손님이 많았어요)

Exercise 12.4

Connect the following two sentences using ~(으)ㄴ데. Then translate the
sentence.

Example: 날씨가 좋다 / 산책할까요?
          = 날씨가 좋은데 산책할까요?
          "The weather is good, so shall (we) take a walk?"

1 기타를 배우고 싶다 / 같이 배웁시다
2 머리가 아프다 / 약 있어요?
3 가방이 무겁다 / 도와 주실래요?

4 앤드류는 미국 사람이다 / 스페인어도 잘 해요
5 요즈음 무척 바쁘다 / 다음 주에 연락주세요

Exercise 12.5

Complete the following dialogue using the sentence cue provided in parenthesis and ~는/(으)ㄴ데요, as shown in the example.

> Example: A: 오늘 저녁 시간 있으세요?
> B: _____ (저녁에 일하다)
> = 저녁에 일하는데요

1 A: 내일 파티에 같이 갈까요?
  B: 미안해요. _____ (내일은 좀 바쁘다)

2 A: 뭐 먹을까요?
  B: _____ (한국 음식이 먹고 싶다)

3 A: 10 달라만 빌려 줄래요?
  B: _____ (5 달라밖에 없다)

4 A: _____ (아직 음식이 안 나왔다)
  B: 죄송합니다. 금방 나올 거예요.

5 A: 좀 _____ (시끄럽다)
  B: 미안합니다. 소리를 줄이겠습니다.

Exercise 12.6

Finish the following translation using ~는/(으)ㄴ데도 and the sentence
cues provided in parenthesis, as shown in the example.

> Example: "Although the house is big, the house rent is inexpensive."
> (집이 크다 / 집세가 싸요)
> = 집이 큰데도 집세가 싸요.

1 Although (he) is an English teacher, (he) can't speak English well
  (영어 선생님이다 / 영어를 잘 못해요)
2 Although the quantity is small, (it) is delicious (양이 적다 / 맛있어요)
3 Although the salary is much, (I) will quit (it) (월급이 많다 / 그만둘
  거예요)
4 Although the test was hard, (he) passed (the test) (시험이 어려웠다 /
  합격했어요)
5 Although (they) were poor, (they) were happy (가난했다 / 행복했
  어요)

Exercise 12.7

Connect the following two sentences using ~는/(으)ㄴ데도. Then translate
the sentence.

> Example: 날씨가 좋다 / 집에 있을 거예요?
> = 날씨가 좋은데도 집에 있을 거예요?
> "Although the weather is nice, will (you) stay home?"

1 약을 먹었다 / 머리가 아파요
2 물을 두 컵이나 마셨다 / 목말라요?
3 그 차가 비싸다 / 살 거예요
4 히터를 켰다 / 방이 추웠어요
5 돈이 없었다 / 서울에 가고 싶었어요

UNIT 13
Clausal conjunctives (although)

~지만

The clausal conjunctive ~지만 is used to acknowledge the action and/or state of the first clause but to indicate something contrary or opposite to that of the main clause. It is equivalent to "but" or "although" in English.

눈이 많이 오지만 안 추워요. "(It) snows a lot, but (it) is not cold."
집이 학교에서 멀지만 교통이 편해요. "Although the house is far from school, the traffic is convenient."

~지만 is not subject to any restriction. For instance, it is conjugated for the tense, as shown below:

한국에 가고 싶지만 돈이 없어요. "Although (I) want to go to Korea, (I) do not have money."
일본어를 배웠지만 잘 못 읽었어요. "(I) learned Japanese, but (I) could not read (it) well."

Second, there is no subject agreement restriction.

열심히 공부하지만 잘 모르겠어요. "(I) study hard, but (I) do not understand (it) well."
언니는 노래를 잘 하지만, 저는 잘 못 해요. "As for my older sister, (she) sings well, but as for me (I) cannot sing well."

Third, it may be used with any predicate type.

김치를 먹지만 좋아하지 않아요. "(I) eat Kimchi, but (I) do not like (it)."
몸이 피곤하지만 행복해요. "Although (my) body is tired, (I) am happy."

형은 경찰관이지만 형의 여자 친구는 선생님이에요. "As for my older brother, (he) is a policeman, but as for his girlfriend, (she) is a teacher."

Finally, it can be used for all sentence types, as shown below:

열심히 <u>공부했지만</u> A 를 못 받았어요. "Although (I) studied hard, (I) could not receive an A."
곧 기차가 <u>도착할 거지만</u> 안 기다릴 거예요? "The train will arrive (here) soon, but won't (you) wait?"
값은 <u>비싸지만</u> 빨리 사세요. "As for the price, (it) is expensive, but buy (it) immediately."
밖에 비가 <u>오지만</u> 나갑시다! "Although (it) rains outside, (let us) go out!"

~(으)나

The clausal conjunctive ~(으)나 is used to indicate that the content of the first clause does not comply with that of the main clause. It is also equivalent to "but/although" in English. ~(으)나 is a two-form conjunctive: ~으나 is used after a stem that ends in a consonant (e.g., 읽으나 "read but"), and ~나 is used after a stem that ends in a vowel (e.g., 배우나 "learn but"). In addition, just like ~지만, ~(으)나 is not subject to any restriction.

가격은 <u>비싸나</u> 기능이 많아요. "As for the price, (it) is expensive, but (it) has many functions."
골프를 치고 <u>싶으나</u> 시간이 없어요. "Although (I) want to play golf, (I) do not have time."
아침을 <u>먹었으나</u> 여전히 배가 고팠어요. "Although (I) ate breakfast, (I) was still hungry."

~(으)나 may be used with two or more clauses, before the main clause (e.g., ~으나 ~으나). In such cases ~(으)나 is used to list selections of actions or states that have opposite meanings and to indicate that the content of the main clause happens regardless of the selections indicated by ~(으)나. Consider the following example:

<u>이기나 지나</u> 열심히 할 거예요. "Whether (we) win or lose, (we) will do (our) best."

Notice that ~(으)나 lists two activities that have opposite meanings (e.g., winning or losing), while the main clause occurs anyway regardless of the activities of the previous clauses. Here are more examples:

즐거우나 슬프나 부인을 사랑하시겠습니까? "Will (you) love (your) wife, whether (you) are happy or sad?"
앉으나 서나 당신만을 생각할 거예요. "Whether (I) sit or stand, (I) will think only of you."

~어/아도

The clausal conjunctive ~어/아도 is also equivalent to "but/although" in English. In addition, it is not subject to any restriction. ~아도 is used after a stem that ends in 아 or 오, whereas ~어도 is used after a stem that ends in all other vowels.

매일 연습해도 실력이 안 늘어요. "Although (I) practice (it) everyday, (my) skill does not make any progress."
커피를 많이 마셔도 졸려요? "(You) drink coffee a lot, but do (you) feel drowsy?"
늦게 일어나도 꼭 오십시오. "Come by all means, even if (you) get up late."
돈이 있어도 사지 맙시다. "Although (we) have money, (let us) not buy (it)."
몸이 피곤해도 행복해요. "Although my body is exhausted, (I) am happy."
커피라도 좋아요. "Even if (it) be coffee, (it) is fine."
아침을 많이 먹었어도 여전히 배고팠어요. "Although (I) ate breakfast a lot, (I) was still hungry."
집이 회사에서 멀었어도 저는 괜찮았어요. "Although the house was far from the company, (it) was fine with me."

Exercises

Key vocabulary for Unit 13 exercises

가깝다 to be near
가다 to go
걱정되다 to be anxious/to feel uneasy
게으르다 to be lazy
고기 meat
귀엽다 to be cute
길다 to be long
나쁘다 to be bad/to be wrong
내성적 introvert
다리 legs/bridge

115

등록금 tuition
똑똑하다 to be smart
뚱뚱하다 to be chubby
맛있다 to be delicious
맵다 to be spicy
먹다 to eat
멀다 to be far
미국 U.S.A.

보내다 to send
백화점 department store
비싸다 to be expensive
사다 to buy
싸다 to be cheap
어렵다 to be difficult
어리다 to be young/to be juvenile/to be immature
역 station
영문학 English literature
영어 English
오다 to come
옷 clothes
유학 studying abroad
음식 food
자주 often
작다 to be small
잘 well
재미있다 to be interesting
전공하다 to major in
좋아하다 to like
지하철 subway
초대장 invitation
키가 크다 to be tall
편하다 to be convenient
한국어 the Korean language
활발하다 to be active

Exercise 13.1

Finish the following translation using ~지만 and the sentence cues provided
in parenthesis, as shown in the example.

Example: "Although (it) is expensive, (it) is delicious." (비싸다 / 맛있
어요)
= 비싸지만 맛있어요.

1 Although Dave is in Seoul, (he) calls Barbara everyday (데이브가 서울에 있다 / 바바라한테 매일 전화해요)
2 Although the bag is big, (it) is light (가방이 크다 / 가벼워요)
3 Although (I) want to go (there) together, (I) have an appointment (같이 가고 싶다 / 약속이 있어요)
4 Although (I) will take an exam tomorrow, (I) did not study (내일 시험을 볼 거다 / 공부를 안 했어요)
5 Although (it) was hot in summer, (it) was cold in winter (여름에 덥웠다 / 겨울에 추웠어요)

Exercise 13.2

Exercise 13.2

Connect the following two sentences using ~지만. Then translate the sentence.

Example: 중국 음식을 먹다 / 좋아하지 않아요
중국 음식을 먹지만 좋아하지 않아요.
"Although (I) eat Chinese food, (I) do not like (it)."

1 한국어는 어렵다 / 재미있어요
2 미국으로 유학을 가고 싶다 / 등록금때문에 걱정돼요
3 고기를 좋아하다 / 자주 먹지 못 해요
4 영문학을 전공했다 / 영어를 잘 못해요
5 초대장을 보냈다 / 안 올 것 같아요

Exercise 13.3

Finish the following translation using ~(으)나 and the sentence cues provided in parenthesis, as shown in the example.

Example: "(I) slipped in the bathroom, but (I) was fine."
(화장실에서 미끄러지다 / 괜찮았어요)
= 화장실에서 미끄러졌으나 괜찮았어요.

1 (I) learned the Korean language for a year, but (it) is still difficult (한국어를 일년 배우다 / 아직 어려워요)
2 (They) waited for one hour, but (she) did not come (한 시간 기다리다 / 안 왔어요)
3 (I) argued with (my) older brother, but (I) reconciled with (him) at once (오빠하고 다투다 / 금방 화해 했어요)
4 The living room is spacious but the kitchen is small (거실이 넓다 / 부엌이 좁아요)
5 The room is clean but noisy (방이 깨끗하다 / 시끄러워요)

Exercise 13.4

Connect the following two sentences using ~(으)나. Then translate the sentence.

> Example: 커피를 가끔 마시다 / 안 좋아해요
> = 커피를 가끔 마시나 안 좋아해요.
> "Although (I) drink coffee sometimes, (I) do not like (it)."

1 레이먼드는 키가 크다 / 뚱뚱해요
2 조지는 활발하다 / 데이빗은 내성적이에요
3 백화점이 가깝다 / 지하철 역이 멀어요
4 택시는 편하다 / 비싸요
5 음식은 쌌다 / 서비스가 나빴어요

Exercise 13.5

Finish the following translation using the [~(으)나…~(으)나] pattern and the sentence cues provided in parenthesis, as shown in the example.

> Example: "Whether (it) is cold or hot, (let us) go outside."
> (춥다 / 덥다 / 밖으로 나갑시다)
> = 추우나 더우나 밖으로 나갑시다.

1 Whether the food is delicious or not, (let us) eat (it) all (음식이 맛있다 / 맛없다 / 다 먹읍시다)
2 Whether the test is easy or difficult, (I) must take (it) (시험이 쉽다 / 어렵다 / 봐야 해요)
3 Whether (you) jog or do yoga, do (it) everyday (조깅을 하다 / 요가를 하다 / 매일 하십시오)
4 Whether (you) go to Korea or Japan, (you) need a visa (한국으로 가다 / 일본으로 가다 / 비자가 필요해요)
5 Whether (it) is pork or beef, (they) are all expensive (돼지고기이다 / 소고기이다 / 다 비싸요)

Exercise 13.6

Finish the following translation using ~어/아도 and the sentence cues provided in parenthesis, as shown in the example.

Example: "Even if (I) drink water, (I) am still thirsty."
(물을 마시다/ 목이 여전히 말라요)
= 물을 마셔도 목이 여전히 말라요.

1 Even if (I) turn the heater on, (it) is still cold (히터를 켜다 / 여전히 추워요)
2 Even if (he) smoked, (he) was healthy (담배를 피우다 / 건강했어요)
3 Even if (she) eats a lot, (she) does not gain weight (많이 먹다 / 살이 안 쪄요)
4 Even if (I) waited two hours, there was no contact (두 시간을 기다리다 / 연락이 없었어요)
5 Even if (I) am sick, (I) will go to school (아프다 / 학교에 갈 거예요)

Exercise 13.7

Connect the following two sentences using ~어/아도. Then translate the sentence.

Example: 피곤하다 / 매일 조깅해요
= 피곤해도 매일 조깅해요.
"Even if (I) am tired, (I) jog everyday."

1 에밀리가 어리다 / 키가 커요
2 한국 음식이 맵다 / 맛있어요
3 로버트가 게으르다 / 똑똑해요
4 옷이 비싸다 / 사고 싶었어요
5 사이즈가 작다 / 귀여웠어요

UNIT 14
Permission, prohibition, and obligation

Permission

Seeking and/or giving permission in Korean is typically carried out by the form ~어/아도 되다. This form is constructed from ~어/아도 "even if" and the verb 되다 "become/get/turn into." Some other adjectives, such as 괜찮다 "be fine" or 좋다 "be good," can be used instead of 되다 to indicate the similar meaning. Consequently, the construction ~어/아도 되다 (or 괜찮다/좋다) literally means "it is all right even if…"

The selection between ~어도 and ~아도 depends on the same principle of choosing between ~어요 and ~아요, the informal polite speech level endings. ~아도 is used after a stem that ends in 아 or 오 (e.g., 가도 "even if I go"), whereas ~어도 is used after a stem that ends in all other vowels (e.g., 배워도 "even if I learn").

~어/아도 되다 in an interrogative sentence is used to ask for permission. On the other hand, ~어/아도 되다 in a declarative sentence is used to give permission, as shown in the examples below.

Asking for permission

이제 집에 <u>가도 돼요</u>? "May (I) go home now (lit. Is it all right even if I go home now)?"
물을 <u>마셔도 돼요</u>? "May (I) drink water?"
먼저 <u>먹어도 괜찮아요</u>? "May (I) eat first?"
<u>매워도 괜찮아요</u>? "Is (it) okay even if (it) is spicy?"
긴 <u>여행이라도 좋아요</u>? "Is (it) all right even if (it) is a long trip?"

Giving permission

텔레비전을 <u>봐도 돼요</u>. "(You) may watch TV (lit. It is okay even if you watch TV)."
이제 차를 <u>팔아도 돼요</u>. "(You) may sell the car now."
먼저 <u>시켜도 괜찮아요</u>. "(You) may order (it) first."

좀 더 <u>비싸도</u> 괜찮아요. "(It) is fine even if (it) is a little more expensive."
물이 <u>아니라도</u> 좋아요. "(It) is fine even if (it) is not water."

~어/아도 되다 in a negative sentence means "…do not have to…" as shown in the examples below:

바쁘면 <u>안 가도</u> 좋아요. "If (you) are busy, (you) do not have go (lit. If you are busy, it is all right, even if you do not go)."
불편하면 양복을 <u>입지 않아도</u> 괜찮아요. "If (you) feel uncomfortable, (you) do not have to put on a suit."
너무 비싸면 그 책을 <u>안 사도</u> 돼요. "If (it) is too expensive, (you) do not have to buy that book."

Prohibition

For denying permission, prohibiting some action, or giving a warning, the form ~(으)면 안 되다 is used. This form is the combination of ~(으)면 "if," the negative 안 "not," and the verb 되다 "become/get/turn into." It can be translated as "(it) would not be all right if…" or "you should/must not" in English.

거짓말 <u>하면 안 돼요</u>. "(You) should not lie."
결혼식 때 <u>울면 안 돼요</u>. "(You) should not cry during the wedding ceremony."
먼저 <u>떠나면 안 돼요</u>. "(You) should not leave first."
여기서 담배를 <u>피우면 안 됩니다</u>. "(You) should not smoke here."
여기에 쓰레기를 <u>버리면 안 됩니다</u>. "(You) should not throw garbage away here."
옷이 너무 <u>비싸면 안 돼요</u>. "(It) would not be all right if the dress is too expensive."
날씨가 <u>흐리면 안 돼요</u>. "(It) would not be all right if the weather is cloudy."
수업에 <u>늦으면 안 돼요</u>. "(It) would not be all right if (you) are late for the class."
룸메이트가 <u>남학생이면 안 돼요</u>. "(It) would not be all right if the roommate is a male student."

Meanwhile, the non-negating form of ~(으)면 안 되다 would be ~(으)면 되다. Note that ~(으)면 되다 means literally "it would be all right if…" or "it would do if." ~(으)면 되다 is typically used when one wishes to stress what is minimally necessary or required. It is equivalent to "all one has to do is…" Consider the following examples:

열심히 <u>공부하면 돼요</u>. "(It) would do if (you) study hard."
한국에 <u>가면 돼요</u>. "All (you) have to do is to go to Korea."
디자인이 <u>예쁘면 돼요</u>. "(It) would do if the design is pretty."
날씨가 <u>좋으면 돼요</u>. "(It) would do if the weather is good."
한국 사람<u>이면 돼요</u>. "(It) would do if (they) are Koreans."
목적지가 <u>런던이면 돼요</u>. "(It) would do if the destination is London."

Obligation

In English, a sense of obligation or necessity is expressed by various
auxiliary verbs, such as "should," "must," "ought to," "need to," and "have
to." In Korean, a sense of obligation can be expressed by the following
two constructions: (1) 안 ~(으)면 안 되다/~지 않으면 안 되다 and (2)
~어/아야 되다.

안 ~(으)면 안 되다/ ~지 않으면 안 되다

Previously, it was noted that ~(으)면 안 되다 is used to express "prohibi-
tion" or "warning." Notice that 안 ~(으)면 안 되다 or ~지 않으면 안 되다
are the combinations of ~(으)면 안 되다 and the negative form. Consider
the following examples:

[안 ~(으)면 안 되다]
물을 <u>안 마시면 안 돼요</u>. "(You) must drink water."

[~지 않으면 안 되다]
물을 <u>마시지 않으면 안 돼요</u>. "(You) must drink water."

Notice that the meanings of both sentences are the same. The difference
between 안 ~(으)면 안 되다 and ~지 않으면 안 되다 is that while the first
is the short-form negation, the second is the long-form negation. Here are
more examples:

아침에 일찍 <u>안 일어나면 안 돼요</u>.
아침에 일찍 <u>일어나지 않으면 안 돼요</u>.
"(You) must get up early in the morning."

토요일에 시카고에 <u>안 가면 안 돼요</u>.
토요일에 시카고에 <u>가지 않으면 안 돼요</u>.
"(We) must go to Chicago on Saturday."

시험 공부를 <u>안 하면 안 돼요</u>.
시험 공부를 <u>하지 않으면 안 돼요</u>.
"(I) must study for the test."

~어/아야 되다

The idea of obligation or necessity can be also expressed by ~어/아야 되다 (or ~어/아야 하다 for more formal usage).

내일 서울에 <u>가야 돼요</u>. "(I) must go to Seoul tomorrow."
매일 밤 약을 <u>먹어야 돼요</u>. "(I) must take medicines every night."
크리스마스 전까지 카드를 <u>보내야 합니다</u>. "(I) must send the card before Christmas."
성능이 <u>좋아야 돼요</u>. "The function has to be good."
꼭 <u>행복해야 돼요</u>. "(You) must be happy by all means."
집이 <u>커야 합니다</u>. "The house has to be big."
한국 사람<u>이라야 돼요</u>. "(He) has to be a Korean."
어른<u>이라야 돼요</u>. "(They) must be adults."
아버지의 <u>사인이라야 합니다</u>. "(It) must be (your) father's signature."

Exercises

Key vocabulary for Unit 14 exercises

가게 store
가격 price
가방 bag
고등학생 high-school student
공부 study
국 soup
길 road/street
날씨 weather
내다 to pay
내일 tomorrow
눈 snow/eyes

닫다 to close
도서관 library
따다 to obtain
뜨다 to open (one's eyes)
먹다 to eat
반찬 side dishes
방 room
손 hands
시작하다 to begin
시험 test/examination/experiment
싱겁다 to be watery
싸다 to pack/to be cheap

쓰다 to use
씻다 to wash

아직 yet/even now
아침 morning/breakfast
얼굴 face
여행 traveling
영화 movie
운전면허 driving license
위험하다 to be dangerous
이제 now/this time
일 work/matter/affair
일어나다 to get up
일찍 early

작다 to be small
잡다 to hold/to capture
재미없다 to be uninteresting/to be dull
전기세 electricity usage bill
점심 lunch
좁다 to be narrow/to be small
좋다 to be good
집 house
짜다 to be salty
청소 cleaning
타다 to ride
퇴근하다 to leave one's office/to go home

Exercise 14.1

Finish the following translation using ~어/아도 되다 and the sentence cue
provided in parenthesis, as shown in the example.

Example: "(You) may leave tomorrow." (내일 떠나다)
= 내일 떠나도 돼요.

1 (You) may trust Peter's story (피터의 이야기를 믿다)
2 (You) may use my computer (내 컴퓨터를 쓰다)
3 (You) may turn on the air conditioner (에어콘을 틀다)
4 (You) may turn off the electric lamp (전등을 끄다)
5 (You) may close the door (문을 닫다)

Exercise 14.2

Conjugate the following using ~어/아도 되다. Then translate the sentence.

Example: 피아노를 치다
= 피아노를 쳐도 돼요. "(You) may play the piano."

1 이제 퇴근하다
2 눈을 뜨다
3 얼굴을 씻다
4 손을 잡다
5 샤워를 하다

Exercise 14.3

Finish the following translation using ~(으)면 안 되다 and the sentence cue provided in parenthesis, as shown in the example.

Example: "(You) should not leave tomorrow." (내일 떠나다)
= 내일 떠나면 안 돼요.

1 (You) should not lose the key (열쇠를 잃어 버리다)
2 (You) should not cross the bridge (다리를 건너다)
3 (You) should not drink beer (맥주를 마시다)
4 (You) should not dump refuse (쓰레기를 버리다)
5 (You) should not smoke here (여기서 담배를 피우다)

Exercise 14.4

Conjugate the following using ~(으)면 안 되다. Then translate the sentence.

Example: 날씨가 춥다
= 날씨가 추우면 안 돼요.
"It would not be all right if the weather is cold."

1 국이 싱겁다
2 반찬이 짜다
3 영화가 재미없다
4 방이 작다
5 길이 좁다

Exercise 14.5

Finish the following translation using ~지 않으면 안 되다 and the sentence
cue provided in parenthesis, as shown in the example.

Example: "(You) must hurry." (서두르다)
= 서두르지 않으면 안 돼요.

1 (You) must study hard (열심히 공부하다)
2 (I) must clean up the office (사무실을 청소하다)
3 (He) must do the dishes (설거지를 하다)
4 (They) must go outside (밖에 나가다)
5 (She) must stay home (집에 있다)

Exercise 14.6

Conjugate the following using ~지 않으면 안 되다. Then translate the
sentence.

Example: 약을 먹다
= 약을 먹지 않으면 안 돼요. "(You) must take the
medicine."

1 시험 공부를 하다
2 일을 시작하다
3 손을 씻다
4 내일 아침 일찍 일어나다
5 운전면허를 따다

Exercise 14.7

Finish the following translation using ~어/아야 되다 and the sentence cue
provided in parenthesis, as shown in the example.

Example: "(You) must tie a necktie." (넥타이를 매다)
= 넥타이를 매야 돼요.

1 (He) has to be a doctor (의사이다)
2 (You) must wear a uniform (유니폼을 입다)
3 (We) must make money (돈을 벌다)
4 (You) must wash (your) face (얼굴을 씻다)
5 (I) must go to the hospital (병원에 가다)

Exercise 14.8

Conjugate the following using ~어/아야 되다. Then translate the sentence.

Example: 공항에 가다
= 공항에 가야 됩니다. "(I) must go to the airport."

1 여행 가방을 싸다
2 전기세를 내다
3 날씨가 좋다
4 가격이 싸다
5 고등학생이다

Exercise 14.9

Complete the following dialogue, as shown in the example.

Example: A: 오렌지 주스를 마셔도 돼요? "May (I) drink orange juice?"
B: 아니오, _____ "No, (you) should not drink (it)."
= 마시면 안 돼요.

1 A: 컴퓨터를 써도 돼요? "May (I) use (your) computer?"
B: 아니오, _____. "No, (you) should not use (it)."

2 A: 이제 퇴근해도 될까요? "May (I) leave the office?"
B: 네, _____. Yes, (you) may leave the office."

3 A: 창문을 닫아도 돼요? "May (I) close the window?"
B: 네, _____. "Yes, (you) may close the window."

4 A: 오토바이를 타도 돼요? "May (I) ride (your) motorcycle?"
B: 아니오, _____. No, (you) should not ride (it)."

Exercise 14.10

Finish the following translation using the sentence cues provided in parenthesis, as shown in the example.

Example: "(You) should not do laundry here."
(여기서 빨래를 하다 / ~(으)면 안 되다)
= 여기서 빨래를 하면 안 돼요.

1 (You) may smoke there (저기서 담배를 피우다 / ~어/아도 되다)
2 (You) may take pictures in the room (방에서 사진을 찍다 / ~어/아도 되다)
3 (I) must take a Korean language class (한국어 수업을 듣다 / 안 ~(으)면 안 되다)
4 (You) must buy a coat (코트를 사다 / 안 ~(으)면 안 되다)
5 (I) must talk in a loud voice (큰소리로 말하다 / ~지 않으면 안 되다)
6 (You) must wear seat belts (안전 벨트를 매다 / ~지 않으면 안 되다)
7 (You) must park (your car) here (여기에 주차하다 / ~어/아야 되다)
8 (I) must leave Paris (파리를 떠나다 / ~어/아야 되다)
9 (You) should not open the refrigerator (냉장고를 열다 / ~(으)면 안 되다)
10 (You) should not touch the painting (그림을 만지다 / ~(으)면 안 되다)

Passives and causatives

Passives

A sentence can be said either in the active voice or the passive voice. In the active sentence, the subject is the "doer" of the action. For instance, consider the following two sentences:

"John opens the door." (active)
"The door is opened by John." (passive)

In the first sentence, John is the doer, and the situation is depicted from the doer's standpoint. However, in the second sentence, the situation is depicted from the standpoint of the object (e.g., the door) instead. In this passive sentence, the focus is not on the doer but on the object of the action.

In English, one can change a verb into a passive form by using the copula "to be" along with the past particle of the verb (e.g., ~ed), as in "the door was opened." In Korean, one can change a verb into a passive verb by attaching the suffix ~이, ~히, ~리, or ~기 to the stem of verbs:

Suffix 이

보다 "to see"	보이다 "to be seen"
쓰다 "to use"	쓰이다 "to be used"
놓다 "to place"	놓이다 "to be placed"
섞다 "to mix"	섞이다 "to be mixed"
쌓다 "to pile up"	쌓이다 "to be piled up"

Suffix 히

닫다 "to close"	닫히다 "to be closed"
막다 "to block"	막히다 "to be blocked"
잡다 "to catch"	잡히다 "to be caught"
걷다 "to lift"	걷히다 "to be lifted"
밟다 "to step on"	밟히다 "to be stepped on"

Suffix 리

물다 "to bite"   물리다 "to be bitten"
열다 "to open"   열리다 "to be opened"
듣다 "to hear"   들리다 "to be heard"
팔다 "to sell"   팔리다 "to be sold"
밀다 "to push"   밀리다 "to be pushed"

Suffix 기

뺏다 "to take away"   뺏기다 "to be taken away"
안다 "to hold"   안기다 "to be held"
쫓다 "to chase"   쫓기다 "to be chased"
뜯다 "to tear out"   뜯기다 "to be torn out"
끊다 "to disconnect"   끊기다 "to be disconnected"

The use of passives is more common in English than in Korean. For instance, most English transitive verbs can be changed into passives (e.g. "I placed the book on the desk" vs. "The book was placed on the desk by me"). However, in Korean, there is only a limited set of transitive verbs that can be made passive (like the verbs listed above). One has to memorize both the verbs that can be changed into a passive verb as well as the suffix each verb takes.

When an active sentence is changed into a passive sentence, the subject and object relationship changes. For instance, the object of the active sentence becomes the subject of the passive sentence. Consider the following two sentences.

한국 학생들이 이 책을 읽는다. "Korean students read this book."
이 책이 한국 학생들한테 (or 에게) 읽힌다. "This book is read by Korean students."

In the first sentence, the subject is 한국 학생들, whereas the subject is 책 in the second sentence. In addition, notice in the second sentence that 한국 학생들 is marked by 한테. When the object is an animate noun (e.g. human or animals), 한테 (or 에게) marks the object. However, when it is an inanimate noun (e.g., wind, car), 에 marks the object.

존이 애기를 안아요. "John holds the baby."
애기가 존한테 (에게) 안겨요. "The baby is held by John."

태풍이 길을 막았어요. "The storm blocks the road."
길이 태풍에 막혔어요. "The road was blocked by the storm."

Causatives

The function of a causative is to (i) make someone or something to do something or (ii) to cause a change of state. In Korean, one can change a verb or adjective into a causative by attaching a causative suffix to the stem of verbs and/or adjectives. There are seven suffixes: ~이, ~히, ~리, ~기, ~우, ~구, and ~추.

Suffix 이
먹다 "to eat"	먹이다 "to feed someone"
보다 "to see"	보이다 "to show"
죽다 "to die"	죽이다 "to kill someone"
끓다 "to boil"	끓이다 "to boil something"

Suffix 히
입다 "to wear"	입히다 "to dress someone"
눕다 "to lie down"	눕히다 "to lay someone down"
앉다 "to sit"	앉히다 "to put someone into a seat"
넓다 "to be wide"	넓히다 "to widen"
좁다 "to be narrow"	좁히다 "to narrow"

Suffix 리
울다 "to cry"	울리다 "to make someone cry"
얼다 "to freeze"	얼리다 "to freeze something"
날다 "to fly"	날리다 "to let something fly"
알다 "to know"	알리다 "to inform"

Suffix 기
벗다 "to take off"	벗기다 "to undress someone"
웃다 "to laugh"	웃기다 "to make someone laugh"
신다 "to wear"	신기다 "to put shoes on someone"
남다 "to remain"	남기다 "to leave something behind"

Suffix 우
자다 "to sleep"	재우다 "to put someone to sleep"
타다 "to burn"	태우다 "to burn something"
깨다 "to wake"	깨우다 "to wake someone up"
끼다 "to join in"	끼우다 "to put in"

Suffix 구/추
돋다 "to rise"	돋구다 "to make higher"
맞다 "to be suited"	맞추다 "to make fit"
낮다 "to be low"	낮추다 "to lower"

There are some similarities between the causatives and passives. First, you may notice that both passive and causative suffixes contain ~이, ~히,

~리, and ~기. In fact, some verbs such as 보이다, 업히다 and 안기다 can function both as causatives as well as passives. For example, consider the following two sentences:

아이가 리사한테 업혔어요. "The child was put on Lisa's back."
어머니가 리사한테 아이를 업혔어요. "The mother put the child on Lisa's back."

In such cases, one can only tell whether 업혔어요 is a causative or a passive verb by its context.

In addition, as with passives, only a restricted number of verbs and adjectives (e.g., like the verbs and adjectives listed above) can take the suffixes and be changed into causative verbs.

Since there is no rule that specifies which verb/adjective can take which causative suffix, one has to learn both the verb/adjective that can be changed into a causative as well as the suffix each verb/adjective takes.

The long-form causative construction ~게 하다

Besides changing verbs/adjectives into causatives by adding the suffixes, there is one more way to change verbs/adjectives into causative constructions. One can add the causative meaning to the verbs and/or adjectives by attaching ~게 하다 after their stems.

가다 "to go"	가게 하다 "to make someone go"
먹다 "to eat"	먹게 하다 "to make someone eat"
배우다 "to learn"	배우게 하다 "to make someone learn"
보다 "to watch"	보게 하다 "to make someone watch"
따뜻하다 "to be warm"	따뜻하게 하다 "to make something warm"
맛있다 "to be delicious"	맛있게 하다 "to make something delicious"
기쁘다 "to be happy"	기쁘게 하다 "to make someone happy"
쉽다 "to be easy"	쉽게 하다 "to make something easy"

The ~게 하다 construction is a much more productive means to indicate causative function than the adding the causative suffix, since its usage is not restricted to the certain verbs and adjectives.

Exercises

Key vocabulary for Unit 15 exercises

고양이 cat
곰 bear
길다 to be long
껌 chewing gum
누나 older sister
다행히 fortunately
더 more
덥다 to be hot
뒤 back
마시다 to drink
맛있다 to be delicious
매일 everyday
먹다 to eat
먼저 first
모기 mosquito
물고기 fish

발표 presentation
밥 meal
보통 usually
비 rain
빨래 laundry
빨래줄 clothes-line
서재 a study/library
스웨터 sweater
시험 test/exam
싸다 to be cheap
씹다 to chew

아이 child
안개 fog
앞줄 front row
오늘 today
자주 often
재킷 jacket
저녁 evening/dinner
전기 electricity
전화 telephone
책 book
청바지 jeans
춥다 to be cold

133

Exercise 15.1

Complete each sentence with an appropriate active or passive form of the
verb indicated.

1 To sell (팔다 / 팔리다)
 a 그 가게가 I-Pods 를 _____. "That store sells I-Pods."
 b I-Pods 때문에 CD Player 는 많이 안 _____. "Because of
 I-Pods, CD players are not sold much."

2 To listen (듣다 / 들리다)
 a 전화 벨 소리를 못 _____. "(I) could not hear the phone ring."
 b 음악 소리가 안 _____. "Music is not heard."

3 To place (놓다 / 놓이다)
 a 컴퓨터를 어디에 _____? "Where should (I) place the computer?"
 b 컴퓨터가 책상 위에 _____. "The computer is placed on the table."

Exercise 15.2

Finish the following translation using the cues provided in parenthesis.

 Example: "The mountain is seen." (산 / 보이다)
 = 산이 보여요.

1 (I) only use olive oil (올리브 기름 / 쓰다)
2 This balloon is used for the birthday party (이 풍선 / 생일 파티 /
 쓰이다)
3 What time do (you) close the store? (몇 시 / 가게 / 닫다)
4 The door was closed by the wind (문 / 바람 / 닫히다)
5 (I) caught a mouse (쥐 / 잡다)
6 The thief was caught by the police (도둑 / 경찰 / 잡히다)
7 Mosquitoes bite (모기 / 물다)
8 John was bitten by mosquitoes a lot (존 / 모기 / 많이 물리다)
9 If the baby cries, please hug (him) (아기 / 울다 / 안다)
10 The baby was held by (her) dad (아기 / 아빠 / 안기다)

Exercise 15.3

Translate the following sentences into English.

 Example: 방문이 굳게 닫혀 있어요.
 = "The door is firmly closed."

1 책상에 책을 쌓아요.
2 시험때문에 스트레스가 쌓여요.
3 빨래를 빨래줄에서 걷었어요.
4 다행히 안개가 걷혔어요.
5 곰이 물고기를 물었어요.
6 모기한테 물렸어요.
7 싸게 파세요.
8 스웨터가 잘 팔려요.
9 먼저 전화 끊으세요.
10 비때문에 전기가 끊겼어요.

Exercise 15.4

Complete the following sentences, as shown in the example. Pay special
attentions to the causative form.

Example: 어머니는 아이에게 밥을 _____ (to feed)
= 어머니는 아이에게 밥을 먹입니다.

1 아침 7 시에 아이를 _____ (to wake)
2 아이에게 옷을 _____ (to dress)
3 아이에게 새 신발을 _____ (to put shoes on)
4 아이를 의자에 _____ (to put someone into a seat)
5 저녁 8 시에 아이를 _____ (to put someone to sleep)

Exercise 15.5

Finish the following translation using the cues provided in parenthesis.

Example: "(I) lowered the radio volume." (라디오 볼륨 / 낮추다)
= 라디오 볼륨을 낮췄어요.

1 Don't make the child cry (아이 / 울리다).
2 Did (you) dress (him) the uniform? (유니폼 / 입히다)
3 Please make the students laugh (학생들 / 웃기다).
4 Please wake me up at 6 o'clock (저 / 6 시에 깨우다).
5 Please boil the water (for me) (물 / 끓이다).
6 Please lay the baby on the bed (아기 / 눕히다).
7 Please do not burn the meat (고기 / 태우다).

Exercise 15.6

Translate the following into English.

> Example: 침대에 아이를 눕혔어요.
> = "(We) laid the child on the bed."

1 오늘 뭘 먹을까요?
2 수잔이 고양이에게 밥을 먹여요.
3 피터가 매일 7 시간 정도 자요.
4 누나가 보통 8 시 쯤에 아이를 재웁니다.
5 크리스는 청바지를 자주 입어요.
6 티셔츠를 입히세요.
7 뒤에 앉으세요.
8 앤드류를 앞 줄에 앉히세요.
9 스웨터를 벗지 마세요.
10 재킷을 벗겨 주세요.

Exercise 15.7

Finish the following translation using ~게 해 주세요 and the cues provided in parenthesis.

> Example: "Please make the hair short." (머리 / 짧다)
> = 머리를 짧게 해 주세요.

1 Please make the soup spicy (국 / 맵다).
2 Please make the room warm (방 / 따뜻하다).
3 Please make the surrounding dark (주위 / 어둡다).
4 Please make Lisa happy (리사 / 행복하다).
5 Please make (your) wife joyful (부인 / 기쁘다).

Exercise 15.8

Translate the following expressions into English.

> Example: 제니퍼를 행복하게 해 주세요.
> = "Please make Jennifer happy (for me)."

1 발표를 더 길게 하세요.
2 맛있게 해 주세요.
3 싸게 해 주세요.
4 커피를 마시게 하세요.
5 껌을 씹게 하세요.

UNIT 16
The noun-modifying endings

Modifier clauses

The typical examples of English modifiers are adjectives and relative clauses. The English modifiers can occur before the word they modify (e.g., in case of adjectives, as in "smart John") and/or after the word (e.g., in case of relative clauses, as in "John who is smart" or "John who studies history").

However, in Korean, modifiers (or modifying clauses) always come before the word they modify. Moreover, any predicate can be changed into a modifier by attaching a noun-modifying ending to the predicate stem. This unit introduces three Korean noun-modifying endings: ~는, ~(으)ㄴ, and ~(으)ㄹ.

The noun-modifying ending ~는

The noun-modifying ending ~는 is used with verbs, and it carries the present meaning. Consider the following examples:

Verb	Verb stem + 는
자다 "sleep"	집에서 <u>자는</u> 학생 "the student who sleeps at home"
마시다 "drink"	커피를 <u>마시는</u> 학생 "the student who drinks coffee"
오다 "come"	매일 여기에 <u>오는</u> 손님 "the customer who comes here everyday"
만나다 "meet"	존을 <u>만나는</u> 사람 "the person who meets John"
일하다 "work"	한국에서 <u>일하는</u> 리사 "Lisa who works in Korea"
찾다 "find"	내가 <u>찾는</u> 색 "the color I look for"
먹다 "eat"	톰이 <u>먹는</u> 음식 "the food that Tom eats"
만나다 "meet"	리사가 <u>만나는</u> 사람 "the person whom Lisa meets"
읽다 "read"	형이 <u>읽는</u> 책 "the book that (my) older brother reads"
다니다 "attend"	제시카가 <u>다니는</u> 대학교 "the college that Jessica attends"

Notice in the examples above that ~는 attaches to the verb stem and changes the predicate into the present form of a relative clause.

Although ~는 is primarily used with verbs, few adjectives that end with 있다/없다 take ~는, as shown below:

맛있다 "delicious"	맛있는 음식 "delicious food"
맛없다 "tasteless"	맛없는 점심 "tasteless lunch"
멋있다 "stylish"	멋있는 모자 "fanciful hat"
재미있다 "interesting"	재미있는 영화 "interesting movie"

The noun-modifying ending ~(으)ㄴ

The noun-modifying ending ~(으)ㄴ is used with adjectives, copulas, as well as verbs. When ~(으)ㄴ is used with adjectives or copulas, it indicates the present meaning; when it is used with verbs, it carries the past meaning.

~(으)ㄴ with adjectives and copulas

One can change an adjective and/or a copula into a noun-modifying unit by attaching ~(으)ㄴ to their stems: ~은 is used after a stem that ends in a consonant; ~ㄴ is used after a stem that ends in a vowel, as shown below:

Adjective	**Adjective stem + (으)ㄴ**
작다 "small"	작은 책상 "small desk"
좋다 "good"	좋은 사람 "good person"
많다 "many"	많은 돈 "a lot of money"
예쁘다 "pretty"	예쁜 꽃 "pretty flower"
바쁘다 "busy"	바쁜 스케줄 "busy schedule"
조용하다 "quiet"	조용한 방 "quiet room"
유명하다 "famous"	유명한 노래 "famous song"
어렵다 "difficult"	어려운 시험 "difficult test"

Copula	**Copula stem + (으)ㄴ**
이다 "be"	의사인 매튜 "Matthew who is a doctor"
아니다 "not be"	학생이 아닌 사람 "the person who is not a student"

~(으)ㄴ with verbs

When ~(으)ㄴ is attached to a verb stem, it changes the predicate into the past form of a relative clause, as shown in the following examples:

Verb	Verb stem + (으)ㄴ
먹다 "eat"	저녁을 먹은 사람 "the person who ate dinner"
찾다 "find"	내가 찾은 열쇠 "the key that I found"
읽다 "read"	이사벨이 읽은 책 "the book that Isabel read"
보다 "see"	내가 본 영화 "the movie that I saw"
배우다 "learn"	많이 배운 학생 "the students who learned a lot"
떠나다 "leave"	어제 떠난 남자 "the man who left yesterday"
공부하다 "study"	한국어를 공부한 사람 "the person who studied Korean"

Since ~(으)ㄴ denotes the past meaning, the use of past tense marker 었/았 along with ~(으)ㄴ is grammatically incorrect. For instance, saying a phrase like "the food that I ate" in Korean should be "내가 먹은 음식" not "내가 먹었은 음식."

The noun-modifying ending ~(으)ㄹ

The noun-modifying ending ~(으)ㄹ indicates that the action or state denoted by the predicate has not yet been actualized. ~을 is attached to a stem that ends in a consonant (e.g., 리처드가 먹을 음식 "the food that Richard will eat"); ~ㄹ is attached to a stem that ends in a vowel (e.g., 리사가 볼 영화 "the movie that Lisa will see").

공부하다	오늘 공부할 내용 "the content that (I) will study today"
읽다	내일 읽을 책 "the book (I) will read tomorrow"
가르치다	한국어를 가르칠 선생님 "the teacher who will teach Korean"
무겁다	무거울 가방 "the bag that will be heavy"
좋다	성격이 좋을 사람 "the person whose personality will be nice"
어렵다	어려울 시험 "the test that will be difficult"

As shown above, ~(으)ㄹ mainly indicates the prospective meaning. However, since the action or state has not been realized, the ending can also imply the meaning of intention or conjecture. This is particularly true when the ending is used with the past tense. Compare the following examples:

샐러드를 먹은 사람 "the person who ate salad"
샐러드를 먹는 사람 "the person who eats salad"
샐러드를 먹을 사람 "the person who will eat salad"
샐러드를 먹었을 사람 "the person who might have eaten salad"

The first sentence is the past form of a relative clause as indicated by ~은; the second sentence indicates the present action as indicated by ~는; the third sentence is about a prospective action as indicated by ~을. However, notice that the predicate of the fourth sentence has the past tense marker ~었 and ~(으)ㄹ (e.g., 먹 + 었 + 을). The ~(으)ㄹ ending in the fourth sentence does not indicate the prospective meaning but conjecture. Here are more examples:

어제 도착했을 편지 "the letter that might have arrived (there) yesterday"
한국으로 떠났을 톰 "Tom who might have left for Korea"
내가 만났을 사람 "the person that I might have met"
지난 월요일에 도서관에 갔을 사람 "the person who might have gone to the library last Monday"

Placing a noun-modifying unit in a sentence

When a predicate is changed into a noun-modifying unit, it becomes part of a new noun phrase, as shown in the following examples:

스파게티를 먹어요. "(I) eat spaghetti."
스파게티를 먹은 사람 "the person who ate spaghetti"
스파게티를 먹는 사람 "the person who eats spaghetti"
스파게티를 먹을 사람 "the person who will eat spaghetti"
스파게티를 먹었을 사람 "the person who might have eaten spaghetti"

These newly transformed noun phrases (or noun-modifying clauses) can be used as a subject, object, or indirect object, depending on the particle that attaches to them, as shown below:

스파게티를 먹은 사람이 존이에요. "The person who ate spaghetti is John."
스파게티를 먹은 사람을 좋아해요. "(I) like the person who ate spaghetti."
스파게티를 먹은 사람한테 전화했어요. "(I) made a phone call to the person who ate spaghetti."

Exercises

Key vocabulary for Unit 16 exercises

가다 to go
갈아타다 to change (car/train)/to transfer
결혼하다 to marry (a person)
과일 fruits
기차 train
내일 tomorrow
내 I/my
네 you
노래 song
높다 to be high
누나 older sister
다음 next
동료 colleague
듣다 to listen

만나다 to meet
만들다 to make
미국 U.S.A.
받다 to receive
방 room
버리다 to throw away
빌리다 to borrow
사다 to buy
사람 person/people
산 mountain
살다 to live
선물 gift/present
섬 island
싸다 to be cheap/to wrap up
쓰다 to use
쓰레기 trash

아름답다 to be beautiful
아침 morning/breakfast
아파트 apartment
양복 suit/dress
어제 yesterday
옷 clothes
음식 food
이사가다 to move (into a new address)

일하다 to work
입다 to wear (a dress)
작년 last year
제일 the first/most
조용하다 to be quiet
주 week
지난 last
집 house
책 book
친구 friend
학교 school
형 older brother
회사 company

Exercise 16.1

Finish the following translation using ~(으)ㄴ and the cues provided in parenthesis, as shown in the example.

> Example: "Yellow cab" (노랗다 / 택시)
> = 노란 택시

1 Pretty designs (예쁘다 / 디자인)
2 The most famous tourist attraction in Korea (한국에서 제일 유명하다 / 관광지)
3 The most popular actor in Korea (한국에서 제일 인기있다 / 배우)
4 The most expensive watch (제일 비싸다 / 시계)
5 Long hair (길다 / 머리)

Exercise 16.2

Change the following into a noun-modifying form using ~(으)ㄴ, as shown in the example. Then translate the phrase.

> Example: 맵다 / 김치
> = 매운 김치 "spicy kimchi"

1 이 집에서 제일 조용하다 / 방
2 데니엘이 가고 싶다 / 학교
3 제일 아름답다 / 섬
4 미국에서 제일 높다 / 산
5 제일 싸다 / 옷

Exercise 16.3

Finish the following translation using ~는 and the cues provided in parenthesis, as shown in the example.

Example: "The bus that I ride everyday" (내가 매일 타다 / 버스)
= 내가 매일 타는 버스

1 The book that Peter reads nowadays (피터가 요즈음 읽다 / 책)
2 The sports (we) enjoy during winter (겨울에 즐기다 / 스포츠)
3 The food that Korean people eat everyday (한국 사람이 매일 먹다 /
음식)
4 The store where Jessica works (제시카가 일하다 / 가게)
5 The man whom (my) older sister dates with (언니가 사귀다 / 남자)

Exercise 16.4

Change the following into a noun-modifying form using ~는, as shown in
the example. Then translate the phrase.

Example: 매일 걷다 / 거리
= 매일 걷는 거리 "The street that (I) walk everyday"

1 친구가 사다 / 과일
2 시카고에서 갈아타다 / 기차
3 형이 살다 / 아파트
4 누나가 쓰다 / 컴퓨터
5 내가 같이 일하다 / 사람

Exercise 16.5

Finish the following translation using ~(으)ㄴ and the cues provided in
parenthesis, as shown in the example.

Example: "The high school that I graduated from" (내가 졸업하다 /
고등학교)
= 내가 졸업한 고등학교

1 The picture that (we) took together (같이 찍다 / 사진)
2 The movie that (I) saw last month (지난 달에 보다 / 영화)
3 The dress that (she) exchanged yesterday (어제 바꾸다 / 옷)
4 The milk that (I) drank in the morning (아침에 마시다 / 우유)
5 The item that (I) sold in the afternoon (오후에 팔다 / 물건)

Exercise 16.6

Change the following into a noun-modifying form using ~(으)ㄴ, as shown in the example. Then translate the phrase.

> Example: 그저께 마시다 / 커피
> = 그저께 마신 커피 "The coffee that (I) drank the day before yesterday"

1 어제 부르다 / 노래
2 작년에 만나다 / 사람
3 지난 주에 받다 / 선물
4 아침에 버리다 / 쓰레기
5 내가 만들다 / 음식

Exercise 16.7

Finish the following translation using ~(으)ㄹ and the cues provided in parenthesis, as shown in the example.

> Example: "The tree that we will plant tomorrow" (우리가 내일 심다 / 나무)
> = 우리가 내일 심을 나무

1 The food that I will cook tomorrow (내가 내일 요리하다 / 음식)
2 The bottle that (I) will fill with milk (우유를 담다 / 병)
3 The water that the patient will drink (환자가 마시다 / 물)
4 The book that (we) will borrow from the library (도서관에서 빌리다 / 책)
5 The package which (you) will mail at the post office (우체국에서 부치다 / 소포)

Exercise 16.8

Change the following into a noun-modifying form using ~(으)ㄹ, as shown in the example. Then translate the phrase.

> Example: 월요일에 만나다 / 손님
> = 월요일에 만날 손님 "The customer that (I) will meet on Monday"

1 제이슨이 입다 / 양복
2 누나가 결혼하다 / 사람
3 우리가 다음 주에 이사가다 / 집
4 네가 내일 빌리다 / 책
5 제임스가 앉다 / 자리

Exercise 16.9

Finish the following translation using the cues provided in parenthesis, as shown in the example.

    Example: "John who studies Korean" (한국어를 공부하다 / 존)
                = 한국어를 공부하는 존

1 Maria who plays a guitar (기타를 치다 / 마리아)
2 The person who will leave for Japan tomorrow (내일 일본으로 떠나다 / 사람)
3 The woman who made a cake (케이크를 만들다 / 여자)
4 The season that I like (내가 좋아하다 / 계절)
5 The child who threw the ball (공을 던지다 / 아이)
6 The student who has an Apple computer (애플 컴퓨터가 있다 / 학생)
7 The man who will meet Laura on Tuesday (화요일에 로라를 만나다 / 남자)
8 Tom who has an expensive car (비싼 차가 있다 / 톰)
9 Dave who is a policeman (경찰관이다 / 데이브)
10 The customer who sent the letter yesterday (어제 편지를 보내다 / 손님)

UNIT 17
Describing the appearance of actions or states of affair

This unit introduces several expressions that are used to describe the appearance of actions or states of affair and to express the speaker's conjecture.

~는/(으)ㄴ/(으)ㄹ 것 같다

The construction ~는/(으)ㄴ/(으)ㄹ 것 같다 "(it) seems/looks like" is the combination of one of three noun-modifying endings (e.g., ~는, ~(으)ㄴ, and ~(으)ㄹ), the dependent noun 것 "the fact/the one/the being" (or 거 for colloquial settings), and the adjective 같다 "be the same." The selection of ~는, ~(으)ㄴ, and ~(으)ㄹ follows the same mechanism of the noun-modifying patterns: ~는 is used after a verb stem for the present meaning; ~(으)ㄴ is used after a verb stem for the past meaning or after an adjective/copula stem for the present meaning; ~(으)ㄹ is used after a verb or adjective stem for the prospective meaning.

~는 것 같다

요즈음 매일 아침 조깅을 하는 것 같아요. "(It) seems that (she) jogs every morning nowadays."
버스가 곧 도착하는 것 같아요. "(It) looks like the bus arrives soon."
매튜가 영어를 가르치는 것 같아요. "(It) seems that Matthew teaches English."

~(으)ㄴ 것 같다

폴이 모두에게 친절한 것 같아요. "Paul seems to be nice to everyone."
찰스가 영국 사람인 것 같아요. "Charles seems to be British."
이 차가 더 좋은 것 같아요. "This car seems to be better."
어제 맥주를 많이 마신 것 같아요. "(It) seems that (they) drank beer a lot yesterday."
토니가 도서관에 간 것 같아요. "(It) seems that Tony went to the library."

시험 공부를 많이 <u>한 것 같아요</u>. "(It) seems that (he) studied a lot for the test."

~(으)ㄹ 것 같다

내년에 한국에 <u>갈 것 같아요</u>. "(It) seems that (they) will go to Korea next year."
내일은 눈이 <u>올 것 같아요</u>. "As for tomorrow, (it) seems that snow will fall."
친구가 파티에 <u>안 올 것 같아요</u>. "(It) seems that (my) friend will not come to the party."
화요일이 <u>추울 것 같아요</u>. "(It) seems that Tuesday will be cold."
시험이 <u>어려울 것 같아요</u>. "(It) seems that the test will be difficult."

For the past tense, the past tense marker 었/았 is used after 같다. Consider the following examples:

방에서 <u>자고 있는 것 같았어요</u>. "(It) seemed that (he) was sleeping in the room."
제임스가 감기에 <u>걸린 것 같았어요</u>. "(It) seemed that James caught a cold."
소고기를 <u>안 먹을 것 같았어요</u>. "(It) seemed that (he) would not eat beef."
이 영화가 <u>재미있을 것 같았어요</u>. "(It) seemed that this movie would be interesting."
어머니가 일본 사람<u>인 것 같았어요</u>. "(It) seemed that (her) mother was a Japanese person."

~는/(으)ㄴ/(으)ㄹ 모양이다

~는/(으)ㄴ/(으)ㄹ 모양이다 "appears/looks like" consists of one of three noun-modifying endings, the noun 모양 "appearance/form/sign," and the copula 이다.

~는 모양이다

팝콘을 <u>만드는 모양이에요</u>. "(It) appears that (he) makes (some) popcorn."
한국어를 <u>배우는 모양이에요</u>. "(It) appears that (she) learns the Korean language."
열쇠가 <u>없는 모양이에요</u>. "(It) appears that (she) does not have the key."
영화가 <u>재미있는 모양이에요</u>. "(It) appears that the movie is interesting."

147

17
Describing
the
appearance
of actions or
states of
affair

~(으)ㄴ 모양이다

아침을 못 먹은 모양이에요. "(It) appears that (they) could not eat breakfast."
일본에서 고등학교를 다닌 모양이에요. "(It) appears that (he) attended a high school in Japan."
친구가 그리운 모양이에요. "(It) appears that (he) longs for a friend."

~(으)ㄹ 모양이다

담배를 끊을 모양이에요. "(It) appears that (he) will quit smoking."
디저트를 안 먹을 모양이에요. "(It) looks like (they) will not eat dessert."
오늘 집에 안 올 모양이에요. "(It) appears that (he) will not come home today."

~는/(으)ㄴ/(으)ㄹ 듯하다

~는/(으)ㄴ/ (으)ㄹ 듯하다 "seems/appears/looks like" is the combination of one of the noun-modifying endings, the dependent noun 듯 "seeming appearance," and the dependent adjective 하다 "really/indeed."

여름이 온 듯해요. "(It) seems that the summer has come."
자고 있는 듯합니다. "(He) seems to be asleep."
아직 살아 있는 듯합니다. "(He) seems to be alive still."
성실한 사람인 듯해요. "(He) appears to be a diligent person."
그 소문이 사실인 듯해요. "That rumor seems to be true."

For the past tense, the past tense marker 었/았 is used after 듯하다, as shown in the following examples:

재즈를 좋아하는 듯했어요. "(They) seemed to like jazz."
중국 역사를 전공한 듯했어요. "(It) seemed that (he) majored in Chinese history."
음식이 매운 듯했어요. "The food appeared to be spicy."

~나/(으)ㄴ가 보다

~나/(으)ㄴ가 보다 "guess/seem" is used to express the speaker's inferential judgment. It is corresponding to English expressions, such as "(I) guess that," and "(it) appears that." For verb stems, ~나 보다 is used, as shown below:

제시카가 태권도를 <u>배우나 봐요</u>. "(I) guess that Jessica learns Taekwondo/ (It) seems that Jessica learns Taekwondo."
커피를 많이 <u>마시나 봐요</u>. "(I) guess that (she) drinks coffee a lot."
한국 역사를 <u>전공하나 봐요</u>. "(I) guess that (he) majors in Korean history."
일요일마다 교회에 <u>가나 봐요</u>. "(I) guess that (they) go to church every Sunday."
돈이 많이 <u>있나 봐요</u>. "(I) guess that (he) has a lot of money."

For adjectives and copulas, ~(으)ㄴ가 보다 is used: ~은가 보다 is used after a stem that ends in a consonant, and ~ㄴ가 보다 is used after a stem that ends in a vowel.

에드워드가 기분이 <u>좋은가 봐요</u>. "(I) guess that Edward is in a good mood."
가방이 <u>작은가 봐요</u>. "(I) guess that (her) bag is small."
집이 아주 <u>비싼가 봐요</u>. "(I) guess that the house is very expensive."
밖이 <u>추운가 봐요</u>. "(I) guess that the outside is cold."
시험때문에 많이 <u>바쁜가 봐요</u>. "(I) guess that (they) are very busy because of the test."
가방이 <u>가벼운가 봐요</u>. "(I) guess that the bag is light."
한국 <u>사람인가 봐요</u>. "(I) guess that (he) is Korean."

For the past tense, ~나 보다 is used after the past tense marker 었/았: with verbs, adjectives, and copulas. Consider the following examples:

지난 달에 돈을 많이 <u>썼나 봐요</u>. "(I) guess that (they) spent money a lot last month."
저녁을 아직 안 <u>먹었나 봐요</u>. "(I) guess that (they) have not eaten dinner yet."
음식이 좀 <u>짰나 봐요</u>. "(I) guess that the food was a bit salty."
시험이 <u>쉬웠나 봐요</u>. "(I) guess that the test was easy."
음식이 너무 <u>달았나 봐요</u>. "(I) guess that the food was too sweet."
어제 많이 <u>피곤했나 봐요</u>. "(I) guess that (he) was very tired yesterday."
매우 배가 <u>고팠나 봐요</u>. "(I) guess that (they) were very hungry."
중국 <u>사람이었나 봐요</u>. "(I) guess that (he) was Chinese."
피터의 생일이 <u>어제였나 봐요</u>. "(I) guess that Peter's birthday was yesterday."

Note that the main verb 보다 does not take the tense marker. It is not grammatically incorrect to add the past tense marker to 보다. However, adding the past tense to the main verb generates a different meaning, as shown in the following examples:

149

17

Describing
the
appearance
of actions or
states of
affair

토마스가 학교에 <u>가나 봐요</u>. "(I) guess that Thomas goes to school."
토마스가 학교에 <u>갔나 봐요</u>. "(I) guess that Thomas went to school."
토마스가 학교에 <u>가나 봤어요</u>. "(I) checked whether Thomas goes to school."
토마스가 학교에 <u>갔나 봤어요</u>. "(I) checked whether Thomas went to school."

~어/아 보이다

~어/아 보이다 is used when the speaker expresses his/her opinion regarding the appearance of something. It is only used with adjectives, and it corresponds to "(it) looks/appears to be" in English.

옷이 비싸 <u>보여요</u>. "The dress looks expensive."
커피가 맛있어 <u>보입니다</u>. "The coffee looks delicious."
부엌이 커 <u>보여요</u>. "The kitchen appears to be big."

For the past tense, the auxiliary verb 보이다 takes the tense marker, while the ~어/아 ending adjective stem does not, as shown below:

기분이 나빠 <u>보였어요</u>. "(Her) mood appeared to be bad."
존이 어제 바빠 <u>보였어요</u>. "John looked busy yesterday."
얼굴이 늙어 <u>보였어요</u>. "(His) face looked old."

Exercises

Key vocabulary for Unit 17 exercises

가격 price
가난하다 to be poor
가다 to go
가르치다 to teach
가볍다 to be light
건너다 to cross/to go over
결혼하다 to marry
겸손하다 to be humble
고치다 to fix/to repair
공항 airport
귀걸이 earring
기다리다 to wait
기숙사 dormitory
김치 kimchi

깨끗하다 to be clean
끊다 to quit

날씨 weather
노래 song
노트북 notebook
눈 snow/eyes
다리 bridge/leg
다음 next
달 month
담배 cigarette
대학원생 graduate student
덥다 to be hot
도착하다 to arrive
돈 money
돌아가다 to return
돕다 to help
똑똑하다 to be smart
많다 to be many/to be much
맛없다 to be tasteless
맛있다 to be delicious
매일 everyday
머리 head/hair (of one's head)

바쁘다 to be busy
별로 not in particular
병원 hospital
봄 spring
부르다 to sing/to call out
부엌 kitchen
부지런하다 to be diligent
부치다 to send
비싸다 to be expensive
빌리다 to borrow
사다 to buy
사람 person/people
살다 to live
성실하다 to be earnest
수요일 Wednesday
슬프다 to be sad
시키다 to order (something)/to force (a person to do)
신혼여행 honeymoon
싱겁다 to be watery
싸다 to be cheap/to be inexpensive

17

Describing
the
appearance
of actions or
states of
affair

아프다 to be sore
안 inside
안경 glasses
애플파이 apple pie
없다 not have/not exist
영어 English
예쁘다 to be pretty
오다 to come/to precipitate/to drop
오후 afternoon/p.m.
요리하다 to cook
음식 food
인기 popularity
일본 Japan
일하다 to work

잘 well/expertly/nicely
젊다 to be young
좋아하다 to like
지갑 wallet
집 house
짜다 to be salty
찌개 pot stew
차 car
출발하다 to depart
춥다 to be cold
친구 friends
편지 letter
학기 semester
한국 Korea
형 older brother
흐리다 to be cloudy

Exercise 17.1

Conjugate the predicate using ~는 것 같다 (for verbs) and ~(으)ㄴ 것
같다 (for adjectives). Then translate the sentence.

> Example: 브라이언이 태권도를 배우다
> = 브라이언이 태권도를 배우는 것 같아요.
> "(It) seems that Brian learns Taekwondo."

1 와싱턴에서 출발하다
2 오후에 도착하다
3 친구를 기다리다

4 돈이 별로 없다
5 서울에 친구가 많다
6 찌개가 짜다
7 앤드류가 성실하고 똑똑하다
8 날씨가 춥고 흐리다
9 친구가 부지런하다
10 가격이 싸다

Exercise 17.2

Conjugate the predicate using ~(으)ㄹ 것 같다. Then translate the sentence.

> Example: 서비스가 좋다
> = 서비스가 좋을 것 같아요. "(It) seems that service will be nice."

1 신혼 여행은 라스베가스로 가다
2 폴이 담배를 끊다
3 다음 수요일에 집에 돌아가다
4 형이 돈을 빌려 주다
5 다음 학기부터 기숙사에서 살다
6 제인이 노래를 잘 하다
7 음식이 맛없다
8 매일 바쁘다
9 날씨가 덥다
10 존이 겸손하다

Exercise 17.3

Conjugate the predicate using ~는 모양이다 (for verbs) and ~(으)ㄴ 모양이다 (for adjectives). Then translate the sentence.

> Example: 에밀리가 일본어를 공부하다
> = 에밀리가 일본어를 공부하는 모양이에요.
> "(It) appears that Emily studies Japanese."

1 제임스가 한국에서 영어를 가르치다
2 토마스가 부엌에서 요리하다
3 존이 다리를 건너다
4 샌디가 친구를 기다리다
5 앤서니가 차를 고치다

153

17

Describing
the
appearance
of actions or
states of
affair

6 사라가 편지를 부치다
7 찰스가 커피를 시키다
8 웬디가 가난하다
9 케이트가 부지런하다
10 샐리가 인기가 많다

Exercise 17.4

Finish the following translation using ~는/(으)ㄴ/(으)ㄹ 듯하다 and the sentence cue provided in parenthesis, as shown in the example.

Example: "(It) seems that flowers are blooming." (꽃이 피고 있다)
= 꽃이 피고 있는 듯합니다.

1 (It) seems that (he) is looking for keys (열쇠를 찾고 있다)
2 (It) seems that (she) works on Saturday (토요일에 일하다)
3 (It) seems that (they) sold the house (집을 팔다)
4 (It) seems that (he) will quit the job (직장을 그만두다)
5 (It) seems that the soup is spicy (국이 짜다)
6 (It) seems that the ring is too expensive (반지가 너무 비싸다)
7 (It) seems that the size will be too small (사이즈가 너무 작다)
8 (It) seems that the room will be too cold (방이 너무 춥다)

Exercise 17.5

Conjugate the predicate using ~는/(으)ㄴ 듯하다. Then translate the sentence.

Example: 오빠가 녹차를 시키고 있다
= 오빠가 녹차를 시키고 있는 듯해요.
"(It) seems that (my) older brother is ordering green tea."

1 친구를 돕고 있다
2 일본 노래를 부르고 있다
3 컴퓨터를 고치고 있다
4 눈이 오다
5 음식이 짜다

Exercise 17.6

Conjugate the predicate using ~나/(으)ㄴ가 보다. Then translate the sentence.

    Example: 케빈이 신문을 읽다
            = 케빈이 신문을 읽나 봐요. "(I) guess that Kevin reads newspapers."

1 낸시가 다음 달에 한국에 가다
2 져스틴이 병원에서 일하다
3 나오미가 이번 봄에 결혼하다
4 샘이 로라를 좋아하다
5 티모티가 아프다
6 김치가 싱겁다
7 오늘 날씨가 덥다
8 음식이 맛없다
9 첼시가 대학원생이다
10 브래드가 영국 사람이다

Exercise 17.7

Finish the following translation using ~어/아 보이다 and the adjective cue provided in parenthesis, as shown in the example.

    Example: "(He) looks anxious." (불안하다)
            = 불안해 보여요.

1 (She) looks joyful (기쁘다)
2 (He) looks scary (무섭다)
3 (You) look lonely (외롭다)
4 (You) look bored (심심하다)
5 (They) look happy (행복하다)
6 (He) looked excited (흥분되다)
7 (She) looked nervous (긴장되다)
8 (They) looked to be in high spirits (신나다)
9 (You) looked annoyed (짜증나다)
10 (He) looked angry (화나다)

17

Describing
the
appearance
of actions or
states of
affair

Exercise 17.8

Conjugate the predicate using ~어/아 보이다. Then translate the sentence.

Example: 브라이언이 친절하다
= 브라이언이 친절해 보여요. "Brian looks kind."

1 케이트가 젊다
2 윌리엄이 바쁘다
3 린다가 아프다
4 사이몬이 슬프다
5 제시가 예쁘다
6 애플파이가 맛있다
7 귀걸이가 비싸다
8 안경이 싸다
9 집안이 깨끗하다
10 노트북이 가볍다

UNIT 18
Post modifiers I

Korean has a number of idiomatic expressions that consist of one of three noun-modifying endings (e.g., ~는, ~은, and ~을) and a noun, such as 길, 적, 동안, and so forth. Since these nouns always appear after the noun-modifying endings (e.g., ~는 길 or ~은 적), they are called "post modifiers." This unit introduces seven special expressions that are made by combining one of three noun-modifying endings with one of the following post modifiers: 길, 적, 일, 동안, 도중, 중, and 편.

~는 길

~는 길 "on the way" is the combination of the noun-modifying ending ~는 and the noun 길 "way/road/street." ~는 길 is normally used with a verb of movement, such as 가다 "go" (e.g., 가는 길 "on the way to") and 오다 "come" (e.g., 오는 길 "on the way from").

> 보스톤으로 가는 길이에요. "(I) am on (my) way to Boston."
> 우리는 김 교수님을 만나러 가는 길이었어요. "As for us, (we) were on (our) way to meet Professor Kim."
> 우체국으로 가는 길에 어머니를 만났어요. "(I) met (my) mother on (my) way to the post office."
> 공항에서 오는 길에 선물을 살 거예요. "(I) will buy the present on (my) way from the airport."
> 학교에서 오는 길에 백화점에 들렀어요 "(I) stopped by the department store on (my) way from school."

~(으)ㄴ 적/일

~(으)ㄴ 적/일 is the combination of the noun-modifying ending ~(으)ㄴ and the noun 적 or 일 "experience." Typically, ~(으)ㄴ 적 or ~(으)ㄴ 일 is followed by 있다 "exist/have" or 없다 "not exist/not have," and they are used to indicate whether the subject "has an/no experience (of doing something)." Consider the following examples:

제니퍼의 집에 <u>간 적이 있어요</u>. "(I) have been to Jennifer's house."
골프를 <u>배운 적이 없어요</u>. "(I) have never learned golf."

The auxiliary verb ~어/아 보다 "try (doing) something" is often used with the form ~(으)ㄴ 적/일이 있다/없다, as shown below:

서울에 <u>가 본 적이 있어요</u>. "(I) have been to Seoul."
선생님을 <u>만나 본 적이 없어요</u>. "(I) have never met the teacher."
일본에서 <u>일해 본 적이 있어요</u>? "Have (you) ever worked in Japan?"
한국 음식을 <u>먹어 본 일이 있어요</u>? "Have (you) ever tried Korean food?"

Notice that ~어/아 본 적/일이 있다/없다 highlights whether the subject has an/no experience of doing something. In addition, when it is used in an interrogative sentence, the form expresses "Have you ever?"
Various time-related expressions, such as 한 달 전에 "a month ago" and 작년에 "last year," can be used with ~어/아 본 적/일이 있다/없다. However since ~어/아 본 일/적이 있다/없다 normally refers to a temporarily distant experience, the use of relatively recent time-related expressions, such as 지난 주에 "last week" and 어제 "yesterday," is inappropriate.

(O) <u>작년에</u> 한국어를 배워 본 적이 있어요. "(I) have an experience of learning Korean last year."
(X) <u>어제</u> 한국어를 배워 본 적이 있어요. "(I) have an experience of learning Korean yesterday."

~는 동안

The noun 동안 means "a while/an interval," as in 오랫 동안 "for a long time," 삼 년 동안 "for three years," and 겨울 방학 동안 "during winter vacation." The combination of 동안 and the noun-modifying ending ~는 as in ~는 동안, expresses two situations or activities that overlap in time. The form ~는 동안 is equivalent to "while" or "during," as shown below:

커피를 <u>마시는 동안</u> "while drinking coffee"
도서관에서 책을 <u>읽는 동안</u> "while reading the book in the library"
친구한테 <u>전화하는 동안</u> "while making a phone call to (my) friend"

Since ~는 동안 indicates this temporal relation, the particle 에 can be used optionally after the form, as in ~는 동안에.

수잔이 사무실에서 <u>일하는 동안에</u> 내가 로비에서 기다렸어요. "While Susan worked in the office, (I) waited in the lobby."

밖에서 조깅을 하는 동안에 제 컴퓨터를 쓰세요. "While (I) jog outside, use my computer."

누나가 점심을 먹고 있는 동안에 자고 있었어요. "While (my) older sister was eating lunch, (I) was sleeping."

아내가 자고 있는 동안에 저녁을 만들었어요. "While (my) wife was sleeping, (I) made dinner."

제가 없는 동안에 남동생을 돌봐 주세요. "While I am away, please take care of (my) younger brother."

~는 도중

The noun 도중 means "on the road." The combination of the noun-modifying ending ~는 and the noun 도중, as in ~는 도중, indicates "on the way to/from" or "in the middle of ."

시험을 치는 도중에 질문이 있으면 저한테 물으세요. "If (you) have questions in the middle of taking the test, ask me."

백화점에서 오는 도중에 차 사고가 있었어요. "(I) had a car accident on (my) way from the department store."

집에 가는 도중에 아버지를 만날 거예요. "(I) will meet (my) father on my way home."

이야기하는 도중에 화장실에 갔어요. "(He) went to the restroom in the midst of conversation."

공부하는 도중에 잠들었어요. "(I) fell asleep in the middle of studying."

아마 영화를 보는 도중에 잘 거예요. "Perhaps, (she) will fall asleep in the middle of (seeing the) movie."

~는 중이다

~는 중이다 means "be in the process/middle of (doing something)." This form is constructed from the noun-modifying ending ~는, the noun 중 "middle," and the copula 이다.

저희 모두 요리하는 중입니다. "We are all in the middle of cooking."

도서관에서 그 책을 찾는 중이에요. "(I) am in the middle of looking for that book in the library."

태권도를 배우는 중이었어요. "(We) were in the middle of learning Taekwondo."

운전하는 중일 거예요. "(I guess that he) is in the middle of driving."

The meaning of ~는 중이다 is similar to that of the progressive ~고 있다, since both involve progressive actions. Compare the following examples:

159

친구하고 이야기하고 있어요. "(I) am talking to (my) friend."
친구하고 이야기하는 중이에요. "(I) am in the middle (or process) of talking to (my) friend."

However, while ~고 있다 simply indicates the progressive meaning, ~는 중이다 tends to highlight the process.

~는/(으)ㄴ 편이다

~는/(으)ㄴ 편이다 is the combination of the noun-modifying ending ~는 (for a verb stem) or ~(으)ㄴ (for an adjective stem), the noun 편 "side/ way/party," and the copula 이다. ~는/(으)ㄴ 편이다 means "tends to" or "kind of" in English, as shown in the following examples:

유니스가 저보다 수영장에 더 자주 가는 편이에요. "Eunice tends to go to the swimming pool more often than I do."
남동생이 영어를 더 잘 하는 편이에요. "(My) younger brother kind of speaks English better (than I)."
주말에 골프를 치는 편이에요. "(I) tend to play golf on the weekend."
리사가 한국말을 잘 하는 편이에요. "Lisa kind of speaks Korean well."
제 차가 작은 편이에요. "My car is kind of small."
도서관이 제 집에서 먼 편이에요. "The library is kind of far from my house."
나보다 형이 키가 더 큰 편이에요. "(My) older brother is kind of taller than me."
이 가게 물건들이 비싼 편이에요. "The items in this store are kind of expensive."

Exercises

Key vocabulary for Unit 18 exercises

가다 to go
나가다 to go out
날씨 weather
내 I/my
다투다 to quarrel/to argue
돼지고기 pork
맥주 beer
모자 hat

받다 to receive
배우다 to learn

사다 to buy
슈퍼마켓 supermarket
스키 ski
시키다 to order/to ask (someone to do)
시험 test/exam
싸다 to pack
썰다 to cut up/to slice
쓰다 to use
아내 wife
양복 suit/dress
어렵다 to be difficult
어머니 mother
오늘 today
요리 cooking
음식 food
이야기하다 to talk
일요일 Sunday
일하다 to work
입다 to wear/to put on

자다 to sleep
자리 seat
잔소리 useless talk/scolding/preaching
잘 well/expertly
장학금 scholarship
조깅 jogging
좋아하다 to like/to be fond of/to rejoice
중국 China
짐 loads/packages
찾다 to look for/to seek for
치다 to play (tennis or piano)/to strike
친구 friend
타다 to ride
태권도 Taekwondo
한국 Korea
형 older brother
화장실 toilet
흐리다 to be cloudy

Exercise 18.1

Finish the following translation using ~는 길에 and the sentence cue provided in parenthesis, as shown in the example.

Example: "(I) stopped by the supermarket on (my) way from school."
(슈퍼마켓에 들르다 / 학교에서 오다)
= 학교에서 오는 길에 슈퍼마켓에 들렀어요.

1 (We) will send the package on (our) way to school (소포를 보내다 / 학교에 가다)
2 (They) ran into the teacher on (their) way to the hospital (선생님하고 마주치다 / 병원에 가다)
3 (She) lost (her) wallet on (her) way from the library (지갑을 잃어 버리다 / 도서관에서 오다)
4 (He) fell on (his) way from the church (쓰러지다 / 교회에서 오다)
5 (I) met John on (my) way from the store (존을 만나다 / 가게에서 오다)

Exercise 18.2

Finish the following translation using ~(으)ㄴ 적이 있다/없다 and the sentence cue provided in parenthesis, as shown in the example.

Example: "(I) have tried Philippine food." (필리핀 음식을 먹어 보다)
= 필리핀 음식을 먹어 본 적이 있어요.

1 (I) have never failed the test (시험에 떨어져 보다)
2 (I) have been to Manhattan (맨하턴에 가 보다)
3 (I) have tried kimchi (김치를 먹어 보다)
4 (I) have never been married (결혼을 해 보다)
5 (I) have an experience of shooting a gun (총을 쏴 보다)

Exercise 18.3

Conjugate the predicate using ~(으)ㄴ 적이 있다. Then translate the sentence.

Example: 토마스를 만나 보다
= 토마스를 만나 본 적이 있어요.
"(I) have an experience of meeting Thomas."

1 장학금을 받아 보다
2 태권도를 배워 보다
3 형과 다퉈 보다
4 한국에서 스키를 타 보다
5 일요일에 일해 보다

Exercise 18.4

Finish the following translation using ~는 동안에 and the sentence cues provided in parenthesis, as shown in the example.

> Example: "While (my) older brother was sleeping, (I) used (his) computer."
> (형이 자고 있다 / 컴퓨터를 썼어요)
> = 형이 자고 있는 동안에 컴퓨터를 썼어요.

1 While Harry does the laundry, Kate cooks (해리가 빨래를 하다 / 케이트가 요리해요)
2 While I look for keys, Gina will pack loads (내가 열쇠를 찾다 / 지나가 짐을 쌀 거예요)
3 While John drove (the car), Sally read the map (존이 운전을 하다 / 샐리가 지도를 봤어요)
4 While Charles worked, Cindy waited (for him) at the coffee shop (찰스가 일하다 / 씬디가 커피숍에서 기다렸어요)
5 While I negotiated with the salesman, (my) wife looked around the shop (내가 세일즈맨하고 흥정을 하다 / 아내가 가게를 구경했어요)

Exercise 18.5

Connect the following two sentences using ~는 동안에. Then translate the sentence.

> Example: 수잔이 전화를 하다 / 톰이 집에 들어왔어요
> = 수잔이 전화를 하는 동안에 톰이 집에 들어왔어요.
> "While Susan was on the phone, Tom entered (my) house."

1 에드워드가 모자를 사고 있다 / 피터가 화장실에 갔어요
2 내가 조깅을 하고 있다 / 아내가 슈퍼마켓에 갔어요
3 루이스가 친구하고 이야기하다 / 에리카가 음식을 시켰어요
4 메건이 자고 있다 / 조이스가 TV를 봤어요
5 우리가 자리를 찾고 있다 / 샘이 팝콘을 사러 나갔어요

Exercise 18.6

Finish the following translation using ~는 중이다 and the sentence cue
provided in parenthesis, as shown in the example.

>   Example: "(I) am in the middle of shaving." (면도를 하다)
>   = 면도를 하는 중이에요.

1 (She) is in the middle of driving (운전하다)
2 (We) are in the middle of planting a tree (나무를 심다)
3 (He) is in the middle of fixing the computer (컴퓨터를 고치다)
4 (I) am in the middle of writing a letter (편지를 쓰다)
5 (We) are in the middle of crossing the bridge (다리를 건너다)

Exercise 18.7

Conjugate the predicate using ~는 중이다. Then translate the sentence.

>   Example: 저녁을 만들다
>   = 저녁을 만드는 중이에요. "(I) am in the middle of making
>   dinner."

1 짐을 싸다
2 중국 음식을 시키다
3 에릭하고 테니스를 치다
4 돼지고기를 썰다
5 양복을 입다

Exercise 18.8

Finish the following translation using ~는/(으)ㄴ 편이다 and the sentence
cue provided in parenthesis, as shown in the example.

>   Example: "Kevin kind of eats a lot." (케빈이 많이 먹다)
>   = 케빈이 많이 먹는 편이에요.

1 The house is kind of noisy (집이 시끄럽다)
2 The room is kind of dark (방이 어둡다)
3 Nancy's food is kind of salty (낸시의 음식이 짜다)
4 Naomi tends to skip breakfast (나오미가 아침을 굶다)
5 (I) tend to exercise everyday (매일 운동하다)

Exercise 18.9

Conjugate the predicate using ~는/(으)ㄴ 편이다. Then translate the sentence.

Example: 알바니에 눈이 많이 오다
= 알바니에 눈이 많이 오는 편이에요.
"(It) kind of snows a lot in Albany."

1 스티브가 맥주를 좋아하다
2 헬렌이 요리를 잘 하다
3 어머니가 잔소리를 하시다
4 시험이 어렵다
5 오늘 날씨가 흐리다

UNIT 19
Post modifiers II

~는/(으)ㄴ 대로

~는/(으)ㄴ 대로 means "as soon as" or "in accordance with." It is the combination of the noun-modifying ending ~는 (for a verb stem) or ~(으)ㄴ (for an adjective stem) and the noun 대로 "according to/the same/just as."

집에 <u>도착하는 대로</u> 전화하세요. "Give (me) a call as soon as (you) arrive home."
<u>시키는 대로</u> 하겠어요? "Will (you) do according to (what I) ask (you to do)?"
날씨가 <u>좋아지는 대로</u> 시작합시다. "(Let us) begin as soon as the weather becomes better."
<u>주는 대로</u> 먹었어요. "(I) ate whatever (she) gave (me)."
날이 <u>밝는 대로</u> 떠날 거예요. "(I) will leave as soon as the dawn breaks."
<u>하고 싶은 대로</u> 하세요. "Do as (you) like to do."
<u>먹고 싶은 대로</u> 먹을 수 있어요. "(You) can eat as much as (you) like to eat."

~(으)ㄴ 후에

~(으)ㄴ 후에 means "afterward" or "later." It is the combination of the noun-modifying ending ~(으)ㄴ, the noun 후 "after," and the particle 에.

아침을 <u>먹은 후에</u> 보통 커피를 마셔요. "(I) usually drink coffee after having breakfast."
집에 <u>돌아온 후에</u> 샤워를 했어요. "(He) took a shower after coming back home."
아파트로 <u>이사를 한 후에</u> 새 소파를 샀어요. "(We) bought new sofas after moving in to the apartment."

손님이 <u>돌아간 후에</u> 설거지를 할 거예요. "(I) will do the dishes after guests return."
숙제를 다 <u>한 후에</u> 운동할 거예요. "(I) will exercise after doing all (my) homework."

The use of noun, such as 다음 "next" or 뒤 "behind" (instead of 후), indicates a similar meaning, as shown below:

3 과를 <u>읽은 다음에</u> 4 과를 공부하십시오. "After reading chapter 3, study chapter 4."
운동을 <u>한 다음에</u> 보통 샤워를 해요. "After exercising, (I) usually take a shower."
영화를 <u>본 뒤에</u> 감상문을 쓰세요. "After seeing the movie, write a reaction paper."

~는/(으)ㄴ 척/체하다

~는/(으)ㄴ 척/체하다 means "pretend." It is the combination of the noun-modifying ending ~는 (for verbs in the present meaning) or ~(으)ㄴ (for verbs in the past meaning; for adjectives/copulas in the present meaning), the noun 척(or 체) "pretence," and the verb 하다 "do."

~는 척/체하다

그녀가 나를 <u>모르는</u> 척합니다. "She pretends that (she) does not know me."
엄마가 돌아오면 열심히 <u>공부하는</u> 척할 거예요. "When (my) mom returns, (I) will pretend that (I) study hard."
고기만 <u>먹는</u> 척할 거예요? "Will (you) pretend that (you) eat only meat?"
저를 <u>아는</u> 체하지 마세요. "Do not pretend that (you) know me."
소파에서 <u>자는</u> 척하십시오. "Pretend that (you) are asleep on the sofa."
맥주를 못 <u>마시는</u> 척합시다. "(Let us) pretend that (we) cannot drink beer."

~(으)ㄴ 척/체하다

열심히 <u>공부한</u> 척해요. "(He) pretends that (he) studied hard."
커피를 <u>마신</u> 척합시다. "(Let us) pretend that (we) drank coffee."
영화를 안 <u>본</u> 척할 거예요. "(I) will pretend that (I) did not see the movie."

그 부부는 늘 <u>행복한 척해요</u>. "As for that couple, (they) always pretend to be happy."
친구들을 만나면 <u>슬픈 척하세요</u>. "When (you) meet (your) friends, pretend that (you) are sad."
목이 <u>아픈 척했어요</u>. "(I) pretended that (my) throat was sore."
<u>고마운 척할 거예요</u>. "(We) will pretend that (we) are grateful."
<u>부지런한 척할 거예요</u>? "Will (you) pretend that (you) are diligent?"
수잔이 캐나다 <u>사람인 척해요</u>. "Susan pretends that (she) is a Canadian."

~는 바람에

~는 바람에 is the combination of the noun-modifying ending ~는, the noun 바람 "wind," and the particle 에. It means "as a result of/because of," and the effects for which ~는 바람에 is used are generally negative and incidental. Consider the following example:

늦게 <u>일어나는 바람에</u> 학교에 못 갔어요. "(I) could not go to school because of getting up late."

Notice that ~는 바람에 indicates the cause (e.g., getting up late) for the negative or unpleasant consequence of the main clause (e.g., could not go to school). Here are more examples:

집을 <u>사는 바람에</u> 돈이 없어요. "(I) do not have money as a result of buying the house."
비가 많이 <u>오는 바람에</u> 병원에 못 갔어요. "(I) could not go to the hospital because (it) rained a lot."
<u>서두르는 바람에</u> 차 사고가 났어요. "(I) had a car accident because (I) hurried up."
열쇠를 잃어 <u>버리는 바람에</u> 약속을 못 지켰어요. "(I) could not keep the promise because (I) lost the key."

~는/(으)ㄴ 것이다

~는/(으)ㄴ 것이다 is used to give an account of events or states of affairs. It can be translated as "the fact is," or "what happened is that." This form is the combination of the noun-modifying ending ~는 (for verbs in the present meaning) or ~(으)ㄴ (for verbs in the past meaning or for adjectives/copulas in the present meaning), the dependent noun 것 (or 거 for colloquial usage) "fact/thing," and the copula 이다.

~는 것이다

앤드류가 베이스 기타를 <u>치는 거예요</u>. "The fact is that Andrew plays the base guitar."
이제부터 매일 <u>뛰는 거예요</u>. "The fact is that (we will) run everyday from now on."

~(으)ㄴ 것이다

엘리자베스가 피아노를 <u>친 거예요</u>. "The fact is that Elizabeth played the piano."
오늘 날씨가 <u>따뜻한 거예요</u>. "The fact is that today's weather is warm."
장미가 <u>아름다운 거예요</u>. "The fact is that roses are beautiful."
데니엘이 <u>한국 사람인 거예요</u>. "The fact is that Daniel is a Korean."

~(으)ㄹ 뻔했다

~(으)ㄹ 뻔했다 is the combination of the noun-modifying ending ~(으)ㄹ, the noun 뻔 "almost/about to," and the verb 했다 "did." ~(으)ㄹ 뻔했다 indicates that some events almost happened. It corresponds to "almost" or "to be nearly" in English.

날씨가 추워서 <u>감기에 걸릴 뻔했어요</u>. "(I) almost caught a cold, since the weather was cold."
공항에 늦게 도착해서 비행기를 <u>놓칠 뻔했어요</u>. "(I) almost missed the flight, since (I) arrived in the airport late."
어제 길에서 수잔하고 <u>마주칠 뻔했어요</u>. "(I) almost ran into Susan on the street yesterday."
피곤해서 아침에 <u>못 일어날 뻔했어요</u>. "(I) almost could not get up in the morning for (I) was tired."

~(으)ㄹ 때

~(으)ㄹ 때 means "when." It is the combination of the noun-modifying ending ~(으)ㄹ and the noun 때 "time/occasion."

시카고로 <u>떠날 때</u> 차로 갈 거예요. "(We) will go by car, when (we) leave for Chicago."
배가 <u>아플 때</u> 이 약을 먹어요? "Do (you) take this medicine, when (your) stomach aches?"
로션을 밖에 <u>나갈 때</u> 얼굴에 바르십시오. "Apply the lotion on (your) face, when (you) go outside."

시간 있을 때 연락합시다. "(Let us) contact (them) when (we) have time."

날씨가 좋을 때 공원에 가세요. "Go to the park, when the weather is good."

날씨가 따뜻할 때 바닷가에서 수영합시다. "When the weather is warm, (let us) swim at the beach."

싱글일 때 여행을 많이 하고 싶어요. "While (I) am a single, (I) want to travel a lot."

아직 학생일 때 많이 배우십시오. "Learn a lot when (you) are still a student."

There are two things to remember when using ~(으)ㄹ 때 with verbs in the past tense. When only the main clause is conjugated for the past tense, the action of the 때 clause co-occurred with that of the main clause. Consider the following example:

뉴욕시에 갈 때 버스를 탔어요. "Going to New York City, (I) took a bus."

Notice in the example above that the action of the first clause "going" co-occurred with the action of the main clause "taking the bus," and the tense is marked only in the main clause. However, when both clauses are conjugated for the past tense, the actions of both clauses do not co-occur: The action of the first clause happened prior to that of the main clause. Consider the following example:

뉴욕시에 갔을 때 수잔을 처음 만났어요. "When (I) went to New York City, (I) met Susan for the first time."

Notice that the first clause "going to New York City" happened prior to the action of the main clause "meeting Susan." Here are more examples:

일본인 친구하고 대화할 때 일본어를 했어요. "Conversing with (my) Japanese friend, (I) talked in Japanese."

도서관에 갈 때 지하철을 탔어요. "Going to the library, (I) took a subway."

일을 끝낼 때 전화했어요. "Finishing (my) work, (I) called (her)."

파리에 갔을 때 날씨가 추웠어요. "When (I) went to Paris, the weather was cold."

비행기가 공항에 도착했을 때 이미 새벽이었어요. "When the airplane arrived in the airport, (it) was already dawn."

하와이에 갔을 때 어느 호텔에 있었어요? "When (you) went to Hawaii, at which hotel did (you) stay?"

Exercises

Key vocabulary for Unit 19 exercises

가다 to go
감기 걸리다 to catch a cold/flu
갑자기 suddenly
건너다 to cross/to go over
결혼식 wedding ceremony
경기 game
경찰 police
고장이 나다 to get out of order/to break down
골다 to snore
공부 study/learning
관심이 없다 to be uninterested
기분 feeling/mood
길 road/street
끄다 to switch off/to extinguish
끓이다 to boil

나쁘다 to be bad/to be wrong
날씨 weather
남자 man
넣다 to put (something) into/to insert
노래 song
늦게 late
다치다 to hurt (oneself)/to be wounded
닫다 to close
대학 college
덥다 to be hot
도움 help
돈 money
돌려주다 to return (a thing)/to give (a thing) back
돌아가다 to return/to go back
되다 to become
듣다 to listen/to take (a class)

라면 ramyon/instant noodle
마시다 to drink
마치다 to finish/to accomplish
많다 to be many/to be much
많이 a lot
맥주 beer
먹다 to eat
모자 hat

171

문 door
물 water
미끄러지다 to slide
바지 pants
받다 to receive
보다 to see/to watch
부르다 to sing
비 rain
빠지다 to fall into/to be drowned
사고가 나다 to have an accident
사무실 office
새벽 dawn
생일 birthday
서류 documents
서점 bookstore
선물 gift/present
소금 salt
수업 class
숙제 homework
스트레스 stress
시간 hour/time
시작하다 to start
시키다 to order (something from a person)/to force (a person to do)
식사 meal
싫어하다 to dislike
심심하다 to be bored
싸우다 to quarrel/to fight

아이들 children
약속 promise/appointment
양복 suit/dress
어리다 to be juvenile/to be childish
연락 contact
열쇠 keys
영화 movie
오다 to come
옷 clothes
와인 wine
우산 umbrella
운동 exercises
월급 salary
음식 food
음악 music
의사 doctor
이기다 to win/to overcome

이메일 e-mail
일 work
일어나다 to get up
일하다 to work
잃다 to lose
입다 to wear/to put on
잊다 to forget

자다 to sleep
잠 sleeping
잠그다 to lock
전등 electric lamp
전화 telephone
젖다 to get wet
좋다 to be good/to be nice
준비 preparation
졸업하다 to graduate
지각하다 to be late/to be tardy
지다 to lose/to get defeated
집 house
짜다 to be salty
짧다 to be short

차 car/tea
창문 window
찾다 to look for/to seek for
취직 employment
친구들 friends
코 nose
필요하다 to be in need of
행복하다 to be happy
화내다 to get angry
허리 waist
회사 company
흐리다 to be cloudy

Exercise 19.1

Finish the following translation using ~는/(으)ㄴ 대로 and the sentence
cues provided in parenthesis, as shown in the example.

> Example: "Comply with whatever (they) request." (요구하다 / 들어주
> 세요)
> = 요구하는 대로 들어주세요.

1 (We) will do as Simon orders (us to do) (사이몬이 지시하다 / 할 거 예요)
2 The mail arrived (here) yesterday as (we) expected (기대하다 / 편지가 어제 도착했어요)
3 Will (you) drink as much as (you) want? (마시고 싶다 / 마실 거예요?)
4 Sleep as long as (you) want (자고 싶다 / 자세요)
5 (Let us) eat as much as (we) want (먹고 싶다 / 먹읍시다)

Exercise 19.2

Connect the following two sentences using ~는/(으)ㄴ 대로. Then translate the sentence.

> Example: 공항에 도착하다 / 전화해 주세요
> = 공항에 도착하는 대로 전화해 주세요.
> "Call (me) as soon as (you) arrive at the airport."

1 일어나다 / 샤워를 할 거예요
2 식사를 마치다 / 사무실로 돌아갈 거예요?
3 열쇠를 찾다 / 떠나세요
4 서류를 받다 / 일을 시작하십시오
5 책을 받다 / 돌려줍시다

Exercise 19.3

Finish the following translation using ~(으)ㄴ 후에 and the sentence cues provided in parenthesis, as shown in the example.

> Example: "(I) will buy (it) after (I) look around the store."
> (가게를 구경하다 / 살래요)
> = 가게를 구경한 후에 살래요.

1 Usually, (I) shave after brushing (my) teeth (보통 이를 닦다 / 면도를 해요)
2 (He) leaves home for work after having breakfast (아침 식사를 하다 / 출근해요)
3 (She) returned to school after sending the package (소포를 보내다 / 학교로 돌아왔어요)
4 (We) will go to the party after buying a gift (선물을 사다 / 파티에 갈 거예요)
5 (I) want to rest after finishing (my) work (일을 끝내다 / 쉬고 싶어요)

Exercise 19.4

Connect the following two sentences using ~(으)ㄴ 후에. Then translate the sentence.

> Example: 컴퓨터를 켜다 / 전화를 걸었어요
> = 컴퓨터를 켠 후에 전화를 걸었어요.
> "(I) made a phone call after turning (my) computer on."

1 샤워를 하다 / 잘 거예요
2 물을 끓이다 / 라면을 넣으세요
3 대학을 졸업하다 / 취직 준비를 하겠어요
4 창문을 닫다 / 전등을 끄십시오
5 일을 마치다 / 집에 갔습니다

Exercise 19.5

Finish the following translation using ~는/(으)ㄴ 척하다 and the sentence cue provided in parenthesis, as shown in the example.

> Example: "Do not pretend that (you) are drunk." (술에 취하다)
> = 술에 취한 척하지 마세요.

1 Do not pretend that (you) are sleeping (자고 있다)
2 Do not pretend that (you) are working hard (열심히 일하고 있다)
3 (She) pretends that (she) likes the present (선물을 좋아하다)
4 (He) pretended that (he) could swim (수영할 수 있다)
5 Will (you) pretend that (you) are an American? (미국 사람이다)

Exercise 19.6

Conjugate the predicate using ~는/(으)ㄴ 척하다. Then translate the sentence.

> Example: 킴벌리가 아프다
> = 킴벌리가 아픈 척해요.
> "Kimberly pretends that (she) is sick."

1 제임스가 비밀 번호를 알다
2 지나하고 로날드가 행복하다
3 패트릭이 항상 돈이 없다
4 제임스가 제시카를 싫어하다
5 앤서니가 공부에 관심이 없다

Exercise 19.7

Finish the following translation using ~는/(으)ㄴ 거예요 and the sentence cue provided in parenthesis, as shown in the example.

> Example: "The fact is that (we) leave for London tomorrow."
> (내일 런던으로 출발하다)
> = 내일 런던으로 출발하는 거예요.

1 The fact is that (we) meet the professor together (교수님을 함께 만나다)
2 The fact is that (we) all wear contact lenses (우리 모두 콘텍트 렌즈를 끼다)
3 The fact is that (we) live together from now on (이제부터 같이 살다)
4 The fact is that prices are high (물가가 높다)
5 The fact is that George is honest (조지가 솔직하다)
6 The fact is that James is smart (제임스가 똑똑하다)
7 The fact is that (they) bought a new car (새 차를 사다)
8 The fact is that (he) lost the wallet (지갑을 잃어버리다)
9 The fact is that (she) invited Gina to the party as well (지나도 파티에 초청하다)
10 The fact is that (he) majored in the Korean language (한국어를 전공하다)

Exercise 19.8

Connect the following two sentences using ~는 바람에. Then translate the sentence.

> Example: 길이 막히다 / 약속 시간에 늦었어요
> = 길이 막히는 바람에 약속 시간에 늦었어요.
> "(I) was late for the appointment, because the road was congested."

1 늦게 일어나다 / 수업에 지각했어요
2 갑자기 비가 오다 / 옷이 젖었어요
3 차가 고장이 나다 / 회사에 못 갔어요
4 감기에 걸리다 / 공부를 못 했어요
5 바람이 불다 / 모자를 잃어 버렸어요
6 소금을 많이 넣다 / 음식이 너무 짰어요
7 코를 골다 / 잠을 못 잤어요
8 길에서 미끄러지다 / 허리를 다쳤어요
9 차 사고가 나다 / 전화를 못 했어요
10 새벽에 일하다 / 감기에 걸렸어요

Exercise 19.9

Connect the following two sentences using ~(으)ㄹ 때. Then translate the sentence.

> Example: 길이 막히다 / 지름길을 이용합니다
> = 길이 막힐때 지름길을 이용합니다.
> "When the roads are congested, (I) use a short cut."

1 월급을 받다 / 기분이 좋습니다
2 영화가 시작하다 / 팝콘을 먹읍시다
3 숙제를 하다 / 음악을 듣습니까?
4 맥주를 마시다 / 노래를 부르십시오
5 스테이크를 먹다 / 와인을 마십니다
6 스트레스가 많다 / 운동을 하십시오
7 도움이 필요하다 / 친구들한테 연락할 겁니다
8 결혼식에 가다 / 양복을 입었습니다
9 비가 오다 / 우산이 필요합니다
10 시간이 있다 / 코미디 영화를 보십시오
11 날씨가 흐리다 / 기분이 나쁩니다
12 여자친구 생일이다 / 무슨 생일 선물을 준비합니까?
13 심심하다 / 서점에 갑니다
14 어렸다 / 의사가 되고 싶었습니까?
15 날씨가 덥다 / 짧은 바지를 입읍시다

Exercise 19.10

Conjugate the predicate using ~(으)ㄹ 뻔하다. Then translate the sentence.

> Example: 차 사고가 나다
> = 차 사고가 날 뻔했어요. "(I) almost had a car accident."

1 친구하고 싸우다
2 물에 빠지다
3 약속을 잊다
4 문을 잠그다
5 게임을 지다
6 우리 팀이 경기를 이기다
7 길에서 미끄러지다
8 아이들한테 화내다
9 와인을 마시다
10 길을 건너다

UNIT 20
Ability and possibility

~(으)ㄹ 수 있다/없다

~(으)ㄹ 수 있다/없다 is used to indicate an ability or possibility of doing something. This form is constructed from the noun-modifying ending ~(으)ㄹ, the noun 수 "means/way," and the verb 있다 "have/exist." For negation, 없다 "not have/not exist" is used instead of 있다.

~(으)ㄹ 수 있다 is equivalent to English translation "one can do/be" or "it is possible to," as shown in the examples below:

피아노를 칠 수 있어요. "(I) can play a piano" or "(It) is possible to play a piano."
서울에 갈 수 있어요. "(I) can go to Seoul" or "(It) is possible to go to Seoul."
그 책을 읽을 수 있어요. "(I) can read that book" or "(It) is possible to read that book."

On the other hand, ~(으)ㄹ 수 없다 is used to express "cannot do/be" or "it is not possible to."

집에서 공부할 수 없어요. "(I) cannot study at home" or "(It) is not possible to study at home."
파티에 갈 수 없어요. "(I) cannot go to the party" or "(It) is not possible to go to the party."
매일 수영할 수 없어요. "(I) cannot swim everyday" or "(It) is not possible to swim everyday."

The meaning of ~(으)ㄹ 수 없어요 is similar to that of the negative expression with 못 "cannot/unable." For instance, compare the following two sentences:

빵을 못 먹어요 (or 빵을 먹지 못해요). "(I) cannot eat bread."
빵을 먹을 수 없어요. "(I) cannot eat bread" or "(It) is not possible to eat bread."

Notice that while the first sentence with the negative 못 simply emphasizes one's inability (e.g., whether one can eat bread or not), the second sentence with ~(으)ㄹ 수 없어요 indicates one's ability as well as the possibility of the action (e.g., whether eating bread is possible or not).

When ~(으)ㄹ 수 있다/없다 is used with adjectives, it indicates the possibility of the state or quality, as shown below:

월요일 시험이 <u>어려울 수 있어요</u>. "(It) is possible that the test on Monday can be difficult."
내일의 날씨가 <u>추울 수 있습니다</u>. "(It) is possible that the tomorrow's weather can be cold."

Meanwhile, some particles, such as 도 "also," 만 "only," and 밖에 "except/but," can appear after the noun 수 to indicate additional meanings. Consider the following examples:

내일의 날씨가 <u>더울 수도 있어요</u>. "(It) is possible that the tomorrow's weather can be <u>also</u> hot."
서울에서 <u>살 수만 있다면</u> 좋겠어요. "(It) would be wonderful, <u>only</u> if (I) can live in Seoul."

Notice that the particle 도 adds a special meaning of "also" to the first sentence, and the particle 만 adds a meaning of "only" to the second sentence.

When the noun 수 is followed by the particle 밖에, which means "except/but," as in ~(으)ㄹ 수밖에 없어요, it creates an expression of "have no other way to/can't help (doing)," as shown below:

커피를 <u>마실 수밖에 없어요</u>. "(I) cannot help drinking coffee."
매일 조깅을 <u>할 수밖에 없어요</u>. "(I) cannot help jogging everyday."
제 집을 <u>팔 수밖에 없었어요</u>. "(I) couldn't help selling my house."

~(으)ㄹ 줄 알다/모르다

~(으)ㄹ 줄 알다/모르다 is used to express a specific ability of the subject, equivalent to "know how to" in English. This form is constructed from the noun-modifying ending ~(으)ㄹ, the noun 줄 "the way (how to)," and the verb 알다 "know" or 모르다 "do not know."

와인을 <u>마실 줄 알아요</u>. "(I) know how to drink wine."
넥타이를 <u>맬 줄 알았어요</u>. "(I) knew how to wear a tie."
영어를 <u>할 줄 알아요</u>? "(Do you) know how to speak English?"
한국어를 <u>할 줄 몰라요</u>. "(I) do not know how to speak Korean."

179

한국 음식을 <u>만들 줄 몰랐어요</u>. "(I) did not know how to make Korean food."

돈을 <u>쓸 줄 몰라요</u>? "Don't (you) know how to spend money?"

When the subject of ~(으)ㄹ 줄 알았다/몰랐다 is a third person, it indicates the speaker's presumed thought, as shown below:

톰이 와인을 <u>마실 줄 알았어요</u>. "(I) thought that Tom would drink wine."

날씨가 <u>더울 줄 알았어요</u>. "(I) thought that the weather would be hot."

니콜라스가 일을 일찍 <u>끝낼 줄 알았어요</u>. "(I) thought that Nicolas would finish (his) work early."

수잔이 한국어를 <u>할 줄 몰랐어요</u>. "(I) did not think that Susan would speak Korean."

톰이 여기에 쓰레기를 <u>버릴 줄 몰랐어요</u>. "(I) did not expect that Tom would throw the garbage away here."

아내가 그 집을 <u>좋아할 줄 몰랐어요</u>. "(I) did not think that (my) wife would like that house."

~(으)ㄹ 리가 없다

~(으)ㄹ 리가 없다 is constructed from the noun-modifying ending ~(으)ㄹ, the dependent noun 리 "possibility," the subject particle 가, and the verb 없다 "not have/not exist." ~(으)ㄹ 리가 없다 indicates that content of the ~(으)ㄹ 리 ending clause is not true or far from the reality. It can be translated as "it is not possible that..." or "there is no possibility that..." in English.

앤지가 한국에 <u>갈 리가 없어요</u>. "There is no possibility that Angie goes to Korea."

그 친구들이 나를 <u>싫어할 리가 없어요</u>. "(It) is not possible that those friends dislike me."

여름에 코트를 <u>입을 리가 없어요</u>. "(It) is not possible that (she) wears a coat in summer."

시험이 <u>쉬울 리가 없어요</u>. "(It) is not possible that the test is easy."

날씨가 <u>추울 리가 없어요</u>. "(It) is not possible that the weather is cold."

빌이 <u>가난할 리가 없어요</u>. "(It) is not possible that Bill is poor."

룸메이트가 <u>여자일 리가 없어요</u>. "(It) is not possible that (his) roommate is a woman."

Exercises

Key vocabulary for Unit 20 exercises

가게 store
가다 to go
갈아타다 to change (cars/trains)
같이 together
골프 golf
김치 kimchi
노래 song
느끼다 to feel
닫다 to close
대학 college
더위 the heat/sun stroke
디자인 design
떠나다 to depart/to take leave of
마시다 to drink
만들다 to make
미국 U.S.A.
부르다 to sing/to call out

사귀다 to make friends
생활 living/life
수영하다 to swim
쉽다 to be easy
싸다 to be cheap
어떻게 how
예쁘다 to be pretty
오늘 today
와인 wine
요금 fee
운동 exercise/sports
운전하다 to drive
월요일 Monday
일본 Japan
일찍 early

잘 well/expertly
재미있다 to be interesting
지하철 subway
치다 to play (tennis/golf/piano)
친구 friend
토요일 Saturday
트럭 truck

편하다 to be convenient/to be comfortable
한국 Korea
형 older brother
회사 company

Exercise 20.1

Finish the following translation using ~(으)ㄹ 수 있다/ 없다 and the sentence cue provided in parenthesis, as shown in the example.

Example: "(They) can repair the car." (차를 고치다)
= 차를 고칠 수 있어요.

1 (I) can open the store alone (혼자 가게를 열다)
2 (We) can give a hope to them (그들에게 희망을 주다)
3 (They) can dance on the stage (무대 위에서 춤을 추다)
4 (She) cannot sell the house (집을 팔다)
5 (I) cannot solve this math problem (이 수학 문제를 풀다)

Exercise 20.2

Conjugate the predicate using ~(으)ㄹ 수 있다. Then translate the sentence.

Example: 그 아이한테 영어를 가르치다
= 그 아이한테 영어를 가르칠 수 있어요.
"(I) can teach English to that child."

1 트럭을 운전하다
2 더위를 느끼다
3 와인을 마시다
4 한국 노래를 부르다
5 미국 친구를 사귀다

Exercise 20.3

Finish the following translation using ~(으)ㄹ 줄 알다/~(으)ㄹ 줄 알았다 and the sentence cue provided in parenthesis, as shown in the example.

Example: "(I) know how to speak Spanish." (스페인어를 하다)
= 스페인어를 할 줄 알아요.

1 (I) know how to sing a Japanese song (일본 노래를 부르다)
2 (I) know how to make Chinese food (중국 음식을 만들다)
3 (I) thought that Scarlet would have a key (스칼릿이 열쇠를 가지고 있다)
4 (I) thought (they) would open the store even on Sunday (일요일에도 가게를 열다)
5 (I) thought that (he) would be in church today (오늘 교회에 있다)

Exercise 20.4

Conjugate the predicate using ~(으)ㄹ 줄 알다. Then translate the sentence.

Example: 일본어 신문을 읽다
= 일본어 신문을 읽을 줄 알아요.
"(I) know how to read Japanese newspapers."

1 김치를 만들다
2 골프를 치다
3 자전거를 타다
4 여기서 회사까지 가다
5 수영하다

Exercise 20.5

Finish the following translation using ~(으)ㄹ 줄 몰랐다 and the sentence cue provided in parenthesis, as shown in the example.

Example: "(I) did not think that Lisa would order Chinese food."
(리사가 중국 음식을 시키다)
= 리사가 중국 음식을 시킬 줄 몰랐어요.

1 (I) did not think that Jerry would be popular (제리가 유명하다)
2 (I) did not think that Professor Chang would be a Korean (장 교수님이 한국 사람이다)
3 (We) did not think that Kate would study well (케이트가 공부를 잘 하다)
4 (I) did not think that (she) would have a boyfriend (남자 친구가 있다)
5 (I) did not think that George would be a policeman (조지가 경찰관이다)

Exercise 20.6

Conjugate the predicate using ~(으)ㄹ 줄 몰랐다. Then translate the sentence.

> Example: 리사가 독일 사람이다
> = 리사가 독일 사람일 줄 몰랐어요.
> "(I) did not think that Lisa would be a German."

1 형이 월요일에 일본으로 가다
2 매튜가 토요일에 가게를 일찍 닫다
3 수잔이 한국에 가다
4 사이먼이 운동을 잘 하다
5 찰스가 오늘 런던으로 떠나다

Exercise 20.7

Finish the following translation using ~(으)ㄹ 리가 없다 and the sentence cue provided in parenthesis, as shown in the example.

> Example: "There is no possibility that Paul is a college student."
> (폴이 대학생이다)
> = 폴이 대학생일 리가 없어요.

1 There is no possibility that the dress size fits (옷 사이즈가 맞다)
2 There is no possibility that the weather is nice (날씨가 좋다)
3 There is no possibility that the movie is interesting (그 영화가 재미 있다)
4 There is no possibility that Andrew is lazy (앤드류가 게으르다)
5 There is no possibility that William majors in Korean history (윌리엄 이 한국 역사를 전공하다)

Exercise 20.8

Conjugate the predicate using ~(으)ㄹ 리가 없다. Then translate the sentence.

> Example: 제이슨이 돈이 많다
> = 제이슨이 돈이 많을 리가 없어요.
> "There is no possibility that Jason has a lot of money."

1 대학 생활이 재미있다
2 지하철이 편하다
3 테니스가 쉽다
4 택시 요금이 싸다
5 디자인이 예쁘다

UNIT 21
Indirect question form

Questions can be either direct or indirect.

> Direct question: "What does Peter drink?"
> Indirect question: "Do you know what Peter drinks?"

In English the indirect question is often marked by the relative clause, introduced by question words such as "whether," "what," "where," and "which." Notice in the second example above that the actual question is a relative clause (e.g., what Peter drinks), which is marked by the question word "what."

This unit introduces the form ~는/(으)ㄴ/(으)ㄹ지, which is used to construct indirect questions in Korean as well as to indicate the speaker's uncertain or wondering mindset.

Indirect question

The form ~는/(으)ㄴ/(으)ㄹ지 consists of one of three noun-modifying endings and the special noun 지 "whether/given the state of being/since then/until."

~는지 is used after a verb stem for the present meaning (e.g., 먹다 => 먹는지); ~(으)ㄴ지 is used after an adjective/copula stem for the present meaning (e.g., 작다 => 작은지); ~(으)ㄹ지 is used after a verb or adjective/copula stem for the unrealized or prospective meaning (e.g., 가르치다 => 가르칠지; 바쁘다 => 바쁠지). For a verb as well as adjective/copula in the past meaning, ~었/았는지 is used (e.g., 먹다 => 먹었는지; 작다 => 작았는지).

~는/(으)ㄴ/(으)ㄹ지 is often used with certain verbs or adjectives, such as 알다 "know," 모르다 "do not know," and 궁금하다 "curious." Consider the following two sentences:

> 이사벨이 몇 시에 돌아와요? "What time does Isabel return?"
> 이사벨이 몇 시에 돌아오는지 알아요? "Do (you) know what time Isabel returns?"

The first sentence is a direct question, and the second sentence is an indirect question. Notice in the second sentence that ~는지 is used after the verb stem (e.g., 돌아오 + 는지), and followed by the verb 알다.

The use of the adverb 얼마나 "how much/many" with the form ~는/(으)ㄴ/(으)ㄹ 지 may add an exclamatory sense to the content, as shown below:

데이빗이 요즘 얼마나 열심히 시험 공부를 하는지 아세요? "Do (you) know how hard David studies for tests nowadays?"
그 차가 얼마나 비싼지 아세요? "Do (you) know how expensive that car is?"

Here are more examples.

After the verb stem in the present meaning

폴이 어디에 가고 있는지 아세요? "Do (you) know where Paul is going to?"
에리카가 어디에 사는지 아세요? "Do (you) know where Erica lives?"

After the adjective or copula stem in the present meaning

호놀룰루의 날씨가 얼마나 좋은지 아세요? "Do (you) know how nice Honolulu's weather is?"
그들이 행복한지 궁금해요? "Are (you) curious whether they are happy?"
브래드가 누구인지 아세요? "Do (you) know who Brad is?"

After the verb, adjective and/or copula stem in the past meaning

앤지가 어제 무엇을 했는지 아세요? "Do (you) know what Angie did yesterday?"
어제 밤 몇 시까지 공부했는지 아세요? "Do (you) know what time (he) studied until last night?"
지난 주에 얼마나 바빴는지 아세요? "Do (you) know how busy (I) was last week?"
시험이 얼마나 어려웠는지 아세요? "Do (you) know how hard the test was?"

After the verb, adjective and/or copula stem in the prospective meaning

크리스틴이 몇 시에 출근할지 아세요? "Do (you) know at what time Christine will go to work?"
그 차가 얼마나 비쌀지 아세요? "Do (you) know how expensive that car will be?"

Indicating a speculative mindset

When ~는/(으)ㄴ/(으)ㄹ지 is used in a non-interrogative sentence, it indicates the speaker's speculative or uncertain mindset. Consider the following sentence:

캐티가 몇 시에 학교에 가는지 몰라요. "(I) do not know what time Cathy goes to school."

Notice that 몇 시에 학교에 가는지 "what time Cathy goes to school" implies the speaker's wondering mindset. Here are more examples:

애플을 쓰는지 PC 를 쓰는지 기억이 안 나요. "(I) do not remember whether (he) uses an Apple or a PC."
오빠가 어디서 사는지 모르겠어요. "(I) do not know where (my) older brother lives."

존한테 그 책이 비싼지 물어보세요. "Ask John whether that book is expensive."
시험이 얼마나 어려운지 몰라요. "(They) do not know how difficult the test is."
지미 스미스가 누구인지 몰라요. "(I) do not know who Jimmy Smith is."
오늘 어느 팀이 이길지 궁금해요. "(I) am curious which team will win today."
다음 학기에 어떤 수업을 들을지 모르겠어요. "(I) am not sure what kind of courses (I) will take next semester."
음식이 맛있을지 모르겠습니다. "(I) am not sure whether the food will be tasty."
열쇠를 어디에 감추었는지 모르겠어요. "(I) do not know where (she) hid the key."
그 영화가 재미있었는지 이야기해 주세요. "Please tell (us) whether that movie was interesting."
작년 겨울이 얼마나 추웠는지 모를 거예요. "(They probably) do not know how cold the last winter was."

~어/아야 할지 모르다

The form ~어/아야 할지 모르다 is used when the speaker is uncertain about what he/she must do. This form is constructed from ~어/아야 하다 "must/should," the form ~(으)ㄹ지, and the verb 모르다 "do not know/be unaware of."

제니퍼의 이야기를 믿어야 할지 모르겠어요. "(I) do not know whether (I) should believe Jennifer's story."

그 남자를 계속 <u>만나야 할지 모르겠어요</u>. "(I) do not know whether (I) should continue to meet with that man."

~어/아야 할지 모르다 is often used with a question word, such as 무엇 "what," 언제 "when," and 어디 "where," as shown below:

먼저 <u>무엇을</u> 사야 할지 모르겠어요. "(I) do not know what (I) have to buy first."
<u>언제</u> 부탁을 해야 할지 모르겠어요. "(I) do not know when (I) should ask for a favor."
비가 오는데 우산을 사러 <u>어디로</u> 가야 할지 모르겠어요. "(It) rains, but (I) do not know where (I) should go to buy an umbrella."

~(으)ㄴ지…되다/지나다

The form ~(으)ㄴ지…되다/지나다 is constructed from ~(으)ㄴ지, and the verb 되다 "become" (or the verb 지나다 "pass/elapse"). The ~(으)ㄴ 지…되다/지나다 is used to express the amount of time that has elapsed since a certain temporal point, and it can be translated as "since" in English.

브라이언한테 <u>전화를 한지</u> 삼 주가 됐어요. "(It) has been three weeks since (I) called Brian."
가을 학기가 <u>시작한지</u> 삼 일이 지났어요. "(It) has been three days since the fall semester began."
서울에 한국어를 공부하러 <u>온지</u> 일 년이 지났어요. "(It) has been a year since (I) came to Seoul to study Korean."
골프를 <u>배운지</u> 얼마나 됐어요? "How long has (it) been, since (you) learned golf?"

Exercises

Key vocabulary for Unit 21 exercises

가게 store
가다 to go
감기 cold/flu
공부 study
기다리다 to wait
길 road
날씨 weather
눈 snow
늦다 to be late
닫다 to close

덥다 to be hot
도착하다 to arrive
떠나다 to leave/to depart
마시다 to drink
막히다 to be blocked/to be held up
많이 a lot
먹다 to eat
문제 problem

방 room
번호 number
보다 to see/to watch/to read
비행기 airplane
살 age/one's years
시끄럽다 to be noisy
시작하다 to begin
시험 test/examination
싸다 to be cheap/to be inexpensive
어렵다 to be difficult
여자 친구 girlfriend
영화 movie
오다 to come
요즈음 nowadays
운동 exercise/sports
음식 food
이틀 two days
일하다 to work

재미있게 interestingly
저녁 dinner
전화 telephone
점심 lunch
집 house
짜다 to be salty
차 car
취직하다 to get employed
층 floor
타다 to ride
팔다 to sell
편지 letter
풀다 to solve
학교 school
헤어지다 to break up
화장실 toilet

회사 company

Exercise 21.1

Connect the following two sentences using ~는/(으)ㄴ지. Then translate the sentence.

> Example: 몇 시에 사무실로 돌아가요? / 아세요?
> = 몇 시에 사무실로 돌아가는지 아세요?
> "Do (you) know what time (they) return to the office?"

1 제리가 몇 살이에요? / 아세요?
2 영화가 몇 시에 시작해요? / 아세요?
3 어디에서 일해요? / 아세요?
4 어디에서 버스를 타요? / 아세요?
5 제임스의 방이 몇 층에 있어요? / 아세요?
6 줄리가 왜 파리로 떠나요? / 아세요?
7 집이 왜 시끄러워요? / 아세요?
8 방이 왜 더워요? / 아세요?
9 이 국이 왜 짜요? / 아세요?
0 이 컴퓨터가 왜 싸요? / 아세요?

Exercise 21.2

Connect the following two sentences using ~(으)ㄹ지. Then translate the sentence.

> Example: 몇 시에 일을 마쳐요? / 아세요?
> 몇 시에 일을 마칠지 아세요?
> "Do (you) know what time (they) will finish (their) work?"

1 마이클이 무슨 일을 해요? / 아세요?
2 어디서 저녁을 먹어요? / 아세요?
3 요즈음 로마의 날씨가 어때요? / 아세요?
4 비행기가 공항에 몇 시에 도착해요? / 아세요?
5 내일 몇 시에 가게를 닫아요? / 아세요?

Exercise 21.3

Finish the following translation using ~는/(으)ㄴ/(으)ㄹ지 모르겠어요 and the sentence cue provided in parenthesis, as shown in the example.

Example: "(I) do not know why Edward went to Korea."
(에드워드가 왜 한국에 가다)
= 에드워드가 왜 한국에 갔는지 모르겠어요.

1 (I) do not know whether Paul passed the test (폴이 시험에 합격하다)
다)
2 (I) do not know where (they) have a wedding ceremony (어디서 결혼식을 하다)
3 (I) do not know what (I) should buy (뭘 사야 하다)
4 (I) do not know what (her) name is (이름이 무엇이다)
5 (I) do not know when (I) should marry (언제 결혼을 해야 하다)
6 (I) do not know when the package will arrive (언제 소포가 도착하다)
다)
7 (I) do not know whether Peter has a car (폴이 차가 있다)
8 (I) do not know whether the test was easy (시험이 쉽다)
9 (I) do not know whether the price is expensive (가격이 비싸다)
10 (I) do not know how heavy the bag will be (가방이 얼마나 무겁다)

Exercise 21.4

Translate the following into English.

Example: 얼마나 짐이 무거운지 못 가져왔어요.
= "How heavy the load was, (I) could not bring (it)."

1 얼마나 집이 시끄러운지 공부를 못 하겠어요
2 얼마나 길이 막혔는지 파티에 1 시간이나 늦었어요
3 얼마나 시험이 어려웠는지 한 문제도 못 풀었어요
4 얼마나 영화를 재미있게 보는지 화장실도 안 가요
5 얼마나 눈이 많이 오는지 학교에 못 갈 것 같아요

Exercise 21.5

Conjugate the predicate using ~어/아야 할지 모르다. Then translate the sentence.

Example: 언제 집으로 돌아가다
= 언제 집으로 돌아가야 할지 모르겠어요.
"(I) am not sure when (I) should return home."

1 몇 시까지 기다리다
2 어느 차를 사다

3 얼마에 집을 팔다

왜 여자 친구와 헤어지다
무엇을 마시다

Exercise 21.6

Finish the following translation using ~(으)ㄴ지...되다 and the cues provided in parenthesis, as shown in the example.

> Example: "(It) has been three days since my back hurts." (허리가 아프다 / 3 일)
> = 허리가 아픈지 3 일이 됐어요.

1 (It) has been 4 days since snow started falling (눈이 오기 시작하다 / 4 일)
2 (It) has been a year since (we) moved to Canada (캐나다로 이사오다 / 1 년)
3 (It) has been 3 weeks since (I) learned Korean (한국어를 배우다 / 3 주)
4 (It) has been 6 months since (I) quitted smoking (담배를 끊다 / 6 개월)
5 (It) has been 10 minutes since (I) began cooking (요리를 시작하다 / 10 분)
6 (It) has been 2 days since (I) bought the car (차를 사다 / 이틀)
7 (It) has been a week since Jennifer left for London (제니퍼가 런던으로 떠나다 / 일 주일)
8 How long has (it) been since (you) had a hair cut? (머리를 자르다 / 얼마나 됐어요?)
9 How long has (it) been since (you) returned home? (집에 돌아오다 / 얼마나 됐어요?)
10 How long has (it) been since (you) last saw him? (그를 마지막으로 보다 / 얼마나 됐어요?)

Exercise 21.7

Write a sentence using the cues provided and ~(으)ㄴ지...되다, as shown in the example. Then translate the sentence.

> Example: 데니엘이 한국으로 떠나다 / 3 일
> = 데니엘이 한국으로 떠난지 3 일이 됐어요.
> "(It) has been three days since Daniel left for Korea."

21

Indirect
question
form

1 점심을 먹다 / 2 시간
2 감기 걸리다 / 이틀
3 편지를 받다 / 1 주일
4 운동을 시작하다 / 4 일
5 취직하다 / 1 년

UNIT 22
The retrospective suffix

~더

The retrospective suffix 더 indicates a speaker's past observation and/or experience. This unit introduces several grammatical forms that incorporate the suffix 더. These patterns include a sentence-ending, a noun-modifying ending, and clausal conjunctives.

~더라구요

The sentence ending ~더라구요 is primarily used in spoken communication. The ending is constructed from the retrospective suffix 더, the statement suffix 라, the quotation particle 구 (the informal counterpart of 고), and the politeness marker 요.

~더라구요 is used to report what a speaker has experienced or observed. It also stresses the authenticity of the speaker's experience and adds meanings such as "I am telling you" and "you know." Consider the following examples:

경치가 아주 <u>아름답더라구요</u>. "(I am telling you that) the scenery was really beautiful."
존이 한국어를 잘 <u>하더라구요</u>. "John spoke Korean well (you know)."

Notice in the examples above that the ending ~더라구요 emphasizes the validity of the speaker's experiences or observation. Here are more examples:

집이 정말 <u>크더라구요</u>. "The house was really huge (you know)."
나는 한국 음식이 제일 <u>맛있더라구요</u>. "As for me, the Korean food was the most delicious (you know)."
건강을 위해서 매일 야채만 <u>먹더라구요</u>. "For the sake of health, (they) ate only vegetables (you know)."

~던

In Unit 16, three Korean noun-modifying endings, ~는, ~(으)ㄴ, and ~(으)ㄹ were introduced. It was noted that any phrase (whether it be an adjective or a verb) can be made into a modifier by attaching a noun-modifying ending to the stem of the predicate. Korean has one more noun-modifying ending, ~던. It is the retrospective noun-modifying ending that indicates a speaker's past experience and/or observation of the action or state. When it is used with a verb stem, the ending ~던 indicates an habitual action in the past. When it is used with an adjective stem, it implies that the past state that no longer exists.

Verb	Verb stem + 던
만나다 "meet"	만나던 여자 "the woman that (I) used to meet"
먹다 "eat"	먹던 음식 "the food that (I) used to eat"
찾다 "find"	찾던 사람 "the person that (I) used to look for"
읽다 "read"	읽던 책 "the book that (I) used to read"

Adjective	Adjective stem + 던
예쁘다 "pretty"	예쁘던 꽃 "the flower that used to be pretty"
조용하다 "quiet"	조용하던 방 "the room that used to be quiet"
유명하다 "famous"	유명하던 노래 "the song that used to be popular"
어렵다 "difficult"	어렵던 시험 "the test that used to be difficult"

One can make the past action or state even more temporarily remote by using it with the past tense marker 었/았 as in 었/았던. Compare the following two sentences:

한국어를 <u>공부하던</u> 학생 "the student who used to study the Korean language."

한국어를 <u>공부했던</u> 학생 "the student who used to study the Korean language (a long time ago)."

Here are more examples:

신문을 <u>읽던</u> 사람 "the person who used to read the newspaper."
신문을 <u>읽었던</u> 사람 "the person who used to read the newspaper (a long time ago)."

어둡던 방 "the room that used to be dark."
어두웠던 방 "the room that used to be dark (a long time ago)."

~더니

The clausal conjunctive ~더니, consisting of the retrospective suffix 더 and the suffix 니, means "but (now)/as/since/and as a result." The conjunctive ~더니 is used when the speaker recollects what he/she has directly observed or experienced. Consider the following examples:

어제는 날씨가 <u>덥더니</u> 오늘은 춥네요. "As for yesterday, the weather was hot, but as for today, (it) is cold."
아침에 눈이 <u>오더니</u> 이제 비가 와요. "(It) snowed in the morning, but (it) rains now."

Notice in the first example that the ~더니 ending clause (e.g., the weather was hot) is based on the speaker's direct experience. In the second example, the first clause with 더니 (e.g., snow in the morning) is based on the speaker's direct observation.

Since ~더니 involves the speaker's past observation/experience, it implies the past connotation. Consequently, the use of the past tense marker 었/았 would be optional for the past action or state. Consider the following examples:

편지를 <u>읽더니</u> 웃기 시작했어요. "As (she) read the letter, (she) began to laugh."
매일 <u>조깅을 하더니</u> 건강해졌네요. "Since (you) have jogged everyday, (now I see that you) became healthy."
어머니와 <u>전화하더니</u>, 울기 시작했어요. "As (he) talked to (his) mother over the phone, (he) began to cry."

Notice in the examples above that only the main clauses are conjugated for the past tense.

When ~더니 is used with the past tense marker 었/았, as in ~었/았 더니, the speaker's past observation/experience sounds even more temporarily distant.

아침을 많이 <u>먹었더니</u> 배가 아파요. "Since (I) ate a lot of breakfast, (my) stomach aches."
집에 <u>갔더니</u> 아무도 없었어요. "(I) went home, but nobody was there."
밤 늦게까지 텔레비전을 <u>봤더니</u> 피곤해요. "Since (I) watched TV until late at night, (I) feel tired."

~었/았더라면

The clausal conjunctive ~었/았더라면 means "if (something had/had not been the case)." This conjunctive is constructed from the past tense marker 었/았, the retrospective suffix 더, the statement suffix 라, and the conjunctive ~(으)면 "if." The conjunctive ~었/았더라면 is used when the speaker wishes to express a sense of regret or supposition. Consider the following examples:

담배를 안 피웠더라면 더 건강했을 거예요. "If (it was the case that he) did not smoke, (he) would have been healthier."
그 때 대학을 졸업했더라면 더 좋은 직장을 가질 수 있었을 거예요. "If (it was the case that I) graduated from college at that time, (I) could have had a better job."

Notice that the main clauses of both examples indicate the sense of disappointment or assumption. Here are more examples:

그 날 학교에 안 갔더라면 차 사고가 안 났을 거예요. "If (it was the case that I) didn't go to school on that day, the car accident might not have occurred."
제인을 더 일찍 만났더라면 리사하고 결혼 안 했을 거예요. "If (it was the case that he) met Jane earlier, (he) might not have married Lisa."
교수님의 조언이 없었더라면 화가가 안 됐을 거예요. "If (it was the case that) there was not the professor's advice, (he) might not have become a painter."

~더라도

The clausal conjunctive ~더라도 means "even though (it may be the case)." It is constructed from the retrospective suffix 더, and the clausal conjunctive ~어/아도 "although." This conjunctive is used when the speaker acknowledges the content of the ~더라도 ending clause but stresses that the following clause must be the case. Consider the following example:

비가 오더라도 꼭 가게에 들르세요. "Even though (it) may rain, stop by the store for sure."

Notice that the content of the first clause is acknowledged but the content of the main clause is highlighted (e.g., stopping by the store). Here are more examples:

길이 막히더라도 걱정하지 마세요. "Even though the road may get congested, do not worry (about it)."

시험에 떨어지더라도 좌절하지 마세요. "Even though (you) may fail the test, do not be discouraged."

친구를 못 만나더라도 여기서 기다릴 거예요. "Even though (I) may not be able to meet (my) friend, (I) will wait (for her) here."

Exercises

Key vocabulary for Unit 22 exercises

가다 to go
가져오다 to bring
같이 together
고기 meat
교복 school uniform
기다리다 to wait
기분 feeling/mood
꼭 surely
나쁘다 to be bad/to be wrong
나오다 to come out
대학교 college
돈 money
동료 colleague
드라마 drama
떠나다 to depart/to take leave of/to leave
마시다 to drink
만나다 to meet
맥주 beer
머리 head
먹다 to eat
무겁다 to be heavy

반지 (a finger) ring
배우다 to learn
병원 hospital
보다 to see/to watch/to read
부지런하다 to be diligent
사귀다 to make friends/to go out with
사다 to buy
사람 person/people
사장 president (of company)/CEO
살다 to live

소설책 novel
슬프다 to be sad
시끄럽다 to be noisy

아침 morning/breakfast
아파트 apartment
아프다 to be sore
약 medicine
어제 yesterday
여자 woman
영화 movie
오빠 older brother
오후 afternoon
요리하다 to cook
울다 to cry
웃다 to smile
음식 food
이번 주 this week

재미없다 to be uninteresting
전에 before
조용하다 to be quiet
졸다 to doze off
중학교 middle school
즐겨 willingly/frequently
지난 주 last week
집 house
차 car
책 book
친구 friend
토요일 Saturday
피곤하다 to be tired
한국어 the Korean language
회사 company/firm

Exercise 22.1

Finish the following translation using ~더라구요 and the sentence cue
provided in parenthesis, as shown in the example.

> Example: "(They) served various side dishes (you know)"
> (여러가지 반찬을 주다)
> = 여러가지 반찬을 <u>주더라구요</u>.

1 There were many customers (you know) (손님이 많다)
2 The service was great (you know) (서비스가 좋다)
3 The apartment rent was expensive (you know) (아파트세가 비싸다)
4 (It) took five hours (you know) (다섯 시간 걸리다)
5 The house was huge (you know) (집이 크다)

Exercise 22.2

Conjugate the predicate using ~더라구요. Then translate the sentence.

Example: 모두 바쁘다
= 모두 바쁘더라구요. "Everyone was busy (you know)."

1 윌리엄이 부지런하다
2 수잔의 오빠가 회사 사장이다
3 톰이 택시를 기다리다
4 제인의 생일이 어제이다
5 캐서린이 반지를 사고 있다

Exercise 22.3

Finish the following translation using ~던 and the cues provided in parenthesis, as shown in the example.

Example: "The friend that (I) used to study with."
(같이 공부하다 / 친구)
= 같이 공부하던 친구

1 The song that (I) used to listen to (듣다 / 노래)
2 The bicycle that (I) used to ride (타다 / 자전거)
3 The company that (we) used to work for (일하다 / 회사)
4 The food that (we) used to like (좋아하다 / 음식)
5 The toothbrush that (you) used to use (쓰다 / 칫솔)
6 The man who used to be brave (씩씩하다 / 남자)
7 The skin that used to be soft (부드럽다 / 피부)
8 The room that used to be dark (어둡다 / 방)
9 The weather that used to be warm (따뜻하다 / 날씨)
10 The store that used to be crowded with customers (손님으로 붐비다 /
가게)

Exercise 22.4

Respond to each question using ~던 and the cues provided in parenthesis, as shown in the example. Then translate the response.

> Example: 여기가 어디예요? (내가 다니다 / 고등학교)
> = 내가 다니던 고등학교예요.
> "(It) is the high school that I used to attend."

1 이 책은 뭐예요? (대학교 때 읽다 / 소설책)
2 저 사람은 누구예요? (사귀다 / 여자 친구)
3 이 드라마는 무슨 드라마예요? (한국에서 즐겨 보다 / TV 드라마)
4 여기가 어디예요? (10 년전에 살다/ 아파트)
5 그 것은 뭐예요? (중학교 때 입다 / 교복)
6 저 사람은 누구예요? (같이 일하다 / 동료)

Exercise 22.5

Connect the following two sentences using ~더니. Then translate the sentence.

> Example: 남자 친구를 사귀다 / 성격이 많이 변했어요
> = 남자 친구를 사귀더니 성격이 많이 변했어요.
> "As (she) made a boyfriend, (her) personality changed a lot."

1 아침에는 집이 조용하다 / 오후에는 시끄러워요
2 지난 주까지 일본 드라마를 보다 / 이번 주는 한국 드라마를 봐요
3 한국어를 배우다 / 한국 영화만 봐요
4 십 분 기다렸다 / 음식이 나왔어요
5 어제 맥주를 많이 마셨다 / 머리가 아파요

Exercise 22.6

Finish the following translation using ~었/았더라면 and the sentence cues provided in parenthesis, as shown in the example.

> Example: "If (it was the case that I) studied harder, (I) might have entered medical school."
> (더 열심히 공부하다 / 의과 대학에 들어갔을 거예요)
> = 더 열심히 공부했더라면 의과 대학에 들어갔을 거예요.

1 If (it was the case that I) had time, (I) might have met (her) (시간이 있다 / 만났을 거예요)
2 If (it was the case that I) was not busy, (I) might have stopped by home (바쁘지 않다 / 집에 들렀을 거예요)
3 If (it was the case that they) were happy, (they) might not have divorced (행복하다 / 이혼하지 않았을 거예요)
4 If (it was the case that he) knew the secret, (he) might have succeeded (비밀을 알다 / 성공했을 거예요)
5 If (it was the case that they) practiced harder, (they) might have won the game (연습을 더 열심히 하다 / 경기를 이겼을 거예요)

Exercise 22.7

Connect the following two sentences using ~었/았더라면. Then translate the sentence.

> Example: 집에 있다 / 드라마를 봤을 거예요.
> = 집에 있었더라면 드라마를 봤을 거예요.
> "If (it was the case that I) stayed home, (I) might have watched the drama."

1 병원에 가다 / 살았을 거예요
2 약을 먹다 / 안 아팠을 거예요
3 돈이 있다 / 떠났을 거예요
4 고기가 있다 / 샀을 거예요
5 차가 있다 / 만났을 거예요

Exercise 22.8

Finish the following translation using ~더라도 and the sentence cues provided in parenthesis, as shown in the example.

> Example: "Even if (it) may be cold, do not put on a coat."
> (춥다 / 코트를 입지 마세요)
> = 춥더라도 코트를 입지 마세요.

1 Even if (you) may be curious, do not ask (궁금하다 / 묻지 마세요)
2 Even if (you) may be itchy, do not scratch (가렵다 / 긁지 마세요)
3 Even if (you) may be angry, control (yourself) (화나다 / 참으세요)
4 Even if (you) may feel bored, stay home (심심하다 / 집에 있으세요)
5 Even if (he) may come late, do not nag at (him) (늦게 오다 / 잔소리 하지 마세요)

Exercise 22.9

Connect the following two clauses using ~더라도. Then translate the sentence.

Example: 덥다 / 밖에 나가지 마세요
= 덥더라도 밖에 나가지 마세요.
"Even if (it) may be hot, do not go outside."

1 피곤하다 / 졸지 마세요
2 영화가 재미없다 / 꼭 보세요
3 기분이 나쁘다 / 웃으세요
4 무겁다 / 가져오세요
5 슬프다 / 울지 마세요

UNIT 23
Nominalizing endings

Nominalizing endings change a verb or an adjective into a noun form. Examples of English nominalzing endings include the gerund "~ing" (e.g., studying), "~ment" (e.g., accomplishment), and "~ation" (e.g., legalization). This unit introduces two Korean nominalizing endings, ~기 and ~(으)ㅁ, as well as some useful expressions that incorporate one of these two nominalizing endings.

The nominalizing ending ~기

When the nominalizing ending ~기 is attached to a verb stem, it modifies the meaning of the verb as "the act of ~ing" (e.g., 듣다 "listen" => 듣기 "listening"). When it appears after an adjective stem, it changes the meaning of the adjective to "state of being~" (e.g., 반갑다 "glad" => 반갑기 "state of being glad"). Consider the following examples:

혼자서 영화 보기를 좋아해요. "(I) like seeing a movie alone."
주로 말하기를 배워요. "(We) mainly learn speaking."
외국에 나가기가 쉬워졌어요. "Going abroad became easier."
날씨가 덥기때문에 집에 있어요. "(I) stay home because the weather is hot."
이 카페가 커피가 맛있기로 유명해요. "This cafe is famous for (its) delicious coffee."

What follows are some major expressions that contain the nominalizing ending ~기.

~기는 커녕

~기는 커녕 means "far from ~ing." It is constructed from the nominalizing ending ~기, the topic particle 는, and the particle 커녕 "not at all." ~기는 커녕 is used to negate the content of the ~기 ending predicate emphatically, as shown below:

즐겁기는 커녕 아주 불쾌해요. "Far from being joyful, (I) feel very unpleasant."

주말에 쉬기는 커녕 바쁘게 일했어요. "Far from resting over the week-end, (I) worked busily."

칭찬을 듣기는 커녕 꾸지람만 들을 거예요. "In place of hearing praise, (he) will (probably) hear only reproach."

~기 전에

~기 전에 means "before *verb*~ing." It is constructed from the nominalizing ending ~기, the noun 전 "before," and the particle ~에.

빨래를 하기 전에 방 청소를 합니다. "(I) clean the room before doing the laundry."

런던으로 떠나기 전에 호텔에 전화 할 거예요. "(I) will make a phone call to the hotel before (I) leave for London."

자기 전에 샤워해요? "Do (you) take a shower before going to bed?"

점심을 먹기 전에 손을 씻으십시오. "Wash (your) hands before having a lunch."

강의를 듣기 전에 책을 읽으십시오. "Read the book before listening to (his) lecture."

학교에 가기 전에 빵집에 들릅시다. "(Let us) stop by the bakery, before going to school."

~기는요

~기는요 is constructed from the nominalizing ending ~기, the topic particle 는, and the politeness marker 요. This form is used to mildly contend another speaker's comment. It is corresponding to English expressions, like "What do you mean…?" or "No way!" Consider the following dialogue:

A: 서울의 날씨가 추웠지요? "The weather of Seoul was cold, right?"
B: 춥기는요, 생각보다 따뜻했어요. "No way, (it) was much warmer than (my) thought."

Frequently, ~기는요 is used to express humility, when receiving a complimentary remark or praise.

A: 차가 참 좋아요. "(Your) car is really nice."
B: 좋기는요. 싸게 샀어요. "Good? (no way). (I) bought (it) at a bargain price."

~기에는

~기에는 is constructed from the nominalizing ending ~기, the particle 에, and the topic particle 는. It means "as for (doing something)," as shown below:

이 집은 혼자 살기에는 작아요. "As for this house, (it) is small for living alone."
이 방이 조용히 공부하기에는 시끄러워요. "This room is noisy for studying quietly."
집에 하루종일 있기에는 날씨가 너무 좋았어요. "As for staying home whole day, the weather was too nice."

~기 때문에

~기 때문에 means "because of ~ing." It is constructed from the nominalizing ending ~기, the dependent noun 때문 "cause," and the particle 에.

매일 아침 조깅을 하기 때문에 일찍 일어나야 해요. "(I) must get up early since (I) jog every morning."
고기를 많이 안 먹기 때문에 건강해요. "(I) am healthy since (I) don't eat meat much."
날씨가 덥기 때문에 선풍기를 살 거예요. "Since the weather is hot, (we) will buy a fan."
머리가 아프기 때문에 공부하고 싶지 않아요. "Because (my) head aches, (I) don't want to study."

~기 때문에 can take the past tense marker, when it refers to the past activity or state, as shown below:

그 때 여권이 없었기 때문에 캐나다에 못 갔어요. "(I) could not go to Canada because (I) did not have the passport at that time."
와인을 많이 마셨기 때문에 골치가 심했어요. "(My) headache was terrible because of excessive wine drinking."
이가 아팠기 때문에 치과에 갔어요. "(I) went to the dentist office because of the toothache."
너무 비쌌기 때문에 못 샀어요. "(We) could not buy (it) because (it) was too expensive."

~기 위해서

~기 위해서 means "in order to." This form is constructed from the nominalizing ending ~기 and 위해서 "for the sake of."

존을 <u>만나기 위해서</u> 20 분이나 기다렸어요. "(I) waited as long as 20 minutes in order to meet John."
호텔에 <u>돌아가기 위해서</u> 택시를 불렀어요. "(I) called a taxi in order to return to the hotel."
유학을 <u>가기 위해서</u> 영어를 배우고 있어요. "(I) am learning English in order to study abroad."
변호사가 <u>되기 위해서</u> 더 열심히 공부할 거예요. "(I) will study harder in order to become a lawyer."

~기로 하다

~기로 하다 means "plans to" or "decides to." This form is constructed from the nominalizing ending ~기, the particle 로, and the verb 하다 "do." It is used when one wishes to express a decision or determination.

내일 집으로 <u>돌아가기로 했어요</u>. "(We) decided to return home tomorrow."
중국 식당에서 저녁을 <u>먹기로 할 거예요</u>. "(We) will decide to eat dinner at Chinese restaurant."
어디에서 <u>만나기로 했습니까</u>? "Where did (you) decide to meet?"
오후 10 시에 <u>떠나기로 하십시오</u>. "Plan to leave at 10 p.m."
신혼여행은 하와이로 <u>가기로 합시다</u>. "As for (our) honeymoon, (let us) decide to go to Hawaii."

Instead of 하다, other verbs such as 결정하다 "make a decision," 결심하다 "make up one's mind," and 정하다 "fix up" can be used as well.

초청 연사로 최 박사님을 <u>모시기로 결정했습니다</u>. "(We) made a decision to invite Dr. Choi as a guest speaker."
언제 담배를 <u>끊기로 결심했어요</u>? "When did (you) make up (your) mind to quit smoking?"
추우니까 가게 안에서 <u>만나기로 정합시다</u>. "Since it is cold, (let us) decide on meeting inside the store."

~기 시작하다

~기 시작하다 means "begins to." It is constructed from the nominalizing ending ~기 and the verb 시작하다 "begin."

어제부터 <u>읽기 시작했어요</u>. "(I) started reading (it) since yesterday."
지금 <u>쓰기 시작하십시오</u>. "Start writing now."
오후 9 시부터 영화를 <u>보기 시작할 거예요</u>. "(We) will start seeing the movie from 9 p.m."

~기가 어렵다

~기가 어렵다 is used to express how difficult a certain action is. It can be translated as "(it) is difficult to" in English. This form is constructed from the nominalizing ending ~기, the subject particle 가, and the adjective 어렵다 "difficult."

글자가 너무 작아서 읽기가 어려워요. "Since the letters are too small, (it) is difficult to read (them)."
목이 부어서 침도 삼키기가 어려웠어요. "Since (my) throat was swollen, even swallowing (my) saliva was difficult."

Instead of 어렵다, other adjectives, as shown below, can be used to convey different messages:

~기가 쉽다 *"(it) is easy to"*

그 수업은 A 를 받기가 쉬워요. "As for that class, receiving an A is easy."
이 접시가 깨지기가 쉬우니까 조심하세요. "Since this dish is easy to be broken, be careful."

~기가 힘들다 *"(it) is laborious to"*

사무실 안이 너무 더워서 일하기가 힘들어요. "Since the inside of the office is too hot, working is toilsome."

~기가 좋다 *"(it) is good to"*

오늘 날씨는 자전거 타기가 좋아요. "As for today's weather, (it) is good to ride a bicycle."

~기가 편하다 *"(it) is convenient to"*

도서관이 가까워서 책을 빌리기가 편해요. "Since the library is close, borrowing books is convenient."

~기가 싫다 *"(it) is unwilling/unpleasant to"*

피터를 도와주기가 싫어요. "(I) am unwilling to help Peter / Helping Peter is unpleasant."

~기가 재미있다 *"(it) is fun to"*

한국어로 말하기가 재미있어요. "(It) is fun to talk in Korean / Talking in Korean is fun."

~기가 귀찮다 *"(it) is bothersome to"*

숙제를 하기가 귀찮아요. "Doing homework is bothersome."

~기도 하다

~기도 하다 is used to indicate that a nominalized activity is a less common activity. It is translated as "also does (something)." This form is constructed from the nominalizing ending ~기, the particle 도 "also," and the verb 하다 "do." Consider the following example:

커피를 주로 마시지만 녹차를 마시기도 해요. "(I) normally drink coffee, but (I) also drink green tea."

Notice in the example above that ~기도 해요 adds a less common activity (e.g., drinking green tea) to the main activity (e.g., drinking coffee). Here are more examples:

가끔 친구들하고 농구를 하기도 해요. "(I) also play basketball with (my) friends once in a while."
주로 지하철을 이용했지만 비가 올 때는 가끔 택시를 타기도 했어요. "Normally, (we) used the subway, but when (it) rained, (we) sometimes took a taxi."
전공은 일본학이지만 한국어 수업도 가끔 듣기도 할 거예요. "Although (my) major is Japanese Studies, (I) will also take the Korean language class occasionally."

The nominalizing ending ~(으)ㅁ

The use of the nominalizing ending ~(으)ㅁ is much more restricted and less frequent than that of ~기. For instance, the ending ~(으)ㅁ is used only when the activity or state of the predicate has already occurred, and has been actualized and/or confirmed. Consider the following examples:

존이 서울에 갔음을 몰랐어요. "(We) did not know that John went to Seoul."
하와이 물은 깨끗함과 맑음으로 유명합니다. "As for Hawaii's water, (it) is well known for its purity and clarity."

Notice that the ~(으)ㅁ ending phrases imply that the activity or state has already been ensured, or determined. Here are more examples:

톰은 자신이 죄인임을 깨닫지 못했습니다. "As for Tom, (he) could not realize that he was a sinner."

우리 모두 이별의 <u>아픔</u>을 경험했어요. "We all experienced the pain of separation."

Meanwhile, a number of Korean nouns are made of ~(으)ㅁ. The ~(으)ㅁ ending nouns include:

살다 "to live"	삶 "life"
죽다 "to die"	죽음 "death"
웃다 "to smile"	웃음 "smile/laughter"
울다 "to cry"	울음 "weeping"
자다 "to sleep"	잠 "sleep"
아프다 "to be sore"	아픔 "pain"
기쁘다 "to be joyous"	기쁨 "joy"
즐겁다 "to be glad"	즐거움 "gladness"
어렵다 "to be hard"	어려움 "hardship/distress"

In limited contexts, such as when one wishes to state, inform, and/or record a certain fact in a concise manner, the nominalizing ending ~(으)ㅁ can be used as a sentence ending. Consider the following examples:

저녁 <u>안 먹었음</u> "Did not eat dinner."
오늘 수업 <u>없음</u> "No class today."
집에 오면 <u>연락</u> 바람 "Let us know when you come home."
친구 <u>찾았음</u> "Found a friend."

Exercises

Key vocabulary for Unit 23 exercises

가끔 sometimes
가다 to go
감기 걸리다 to catch a cold
같이 together
개 dog
결혼하다 to marry
경기 game/competitive sport
고치다 to fix/to repair
교수님 professor
구경 sightseeing/looking around
구하다 to seek
기간 period
기숙사 dormitory
기차 train

까맣다 to be black/dark
끊다 to quit

나가다 to go out
날씨 weather
내년 next year
내일 tomorrow
너무 too (much)/ever so much
노래 song
농구 basketball
느리다 to be slow
늦게 late
늦다 to be late
다운로드 download
다음 next
달 month
담배 cigarette
도서관 library
돈 money
돌아오다 to return/to come back
듣다 to take (a class)/to listen
들르다 to stop by
등산 mountaineering

마시다 to drink
만나다 to meet
만들다 to make
많다 to be many/to be much
많이 a lot
매다 to wear (a tie)
매일 everyday
머리 hair (from a head)/head
먹다 to eat
멀다 to be far
모자라다 to be short of
받다 to receive
배우다 to learn
보관하다 to keep/to take custody of
보다 to see/to read/to watch
봄 spring
부르다 to sing/to call out
불편하다 to be inconvenient/to be uncomfortable
비 rain
비싸다 to be expensive
빨래 laundry/washing (clothes)

사다 to buy
사람 person/people
살을 빼다 to lose weight
살다 to live
상담하다 to consult
새 new
생일 birthday
선물 gift/present
선생님 teacher
손 hand
수업 class/course
수영 swimming
시간 time/hour
시험에 떨어지다 to fail a test
시험을 보다 to take a test
신문 newspaper
심심하다 to be bored
씻다 to wash

아버지 father
아침 morning/breakfast
어리다 to be juvenile/to be childish
연습하다 to practice
열심히 earnestly
영화 movie
예약하다 to reserve
오전 a.m.
옷 clothes
요가 yoga
요리하다 to cook
운동하다 to exercise
운전하다 to drive
음식 food
의과 대학 medical college
의논하다 to consult
이기다 to win
이사하다 to move into/to change one's residence
이용하다 to use
일하다 to work
잃다 to lose

자르다 to cut off
자다 to sleep
작다 to be small
잠 sleeping

재미없다 to be uninteresting
저녁 dinner/evening
전공 major
전화하다 to make a phone call
점심 lunch
정비소 repair shop
정하다 to decide
조금 little
주다 to give
주말 weekend
준비하다 to prepare
지갑 wallet
지하철 subway
진학하다 to go on to next stage of education
집 house

차 car
찾다 to look for/to seek for
출근하다 to leave home for work
춥다 to be cold
충분히 sufficiently
취소되다 to be canceled
치다 to play (tennis/golf/piano)/to hit
친구 friend
침대 bed
키 height
타다 to ride
토요일 Saturday
팔다 to sell
표 ticket
한국어 the Korean language
학기 semester
학교 school
혼자 alone
화장 makeup

Exercise 23.1

Construct a sentence using the sentence cues provided and ~기 전에. Then
translate the sentence, as shown in the example.

> Example: 자다 / 샤워를 했어요.
> = 자기 전에 샤워를 했어요.
> "(I) took a shower before going to bed."

23.2

1 아침을 먹다 / 손을 씻으세요
2 시험을 보다 / 잠을 충분히 자세요
3 기차를 타다 / 기차 표를 예약해야 돼요
4 레스토랑에 가다 / 집에 들릅시다
5 출근하다 / 신문을 보세요?
6 화장을 하다 / 샤워를 해요
7 새 집으로 이사하다 / 아파트에서 살았어요?
8 전공을 정하다 / 교수님하고 상담해야 합니다
9 피터를 만나러 나가다 / 전화합시다
10 차를 팔다 / 아버지하고 의논하세요

Exercise 23.2

Construct a sentence using the sentence cues provided and ~기는 커녕, as shown below. Then translate the sentence.

> Example: 샤워를 하다 / 얼굴도 못 씻었어요
> = 샤워를 하기는 커녕 얼굴도 못 씻었어요.
> "Far from taking a shower, (I) could not even wash (my) face."

1 점심을 먹다 / 아침도 안 먹었어요
2 등산을 하다 / 집 밖에도 안 나갔어요
3 저녁을 먹다 / 커피도 못 마셨어요
4 새 차를 사다 / 구경도 못 했어요
5 생일 파티를 하다 / 선물도 못 받았어요

Exercise 23.3

Construct a sentence using the sentence cues provided and ~기에는. Then translate the sentence.

> Example: 혼자 밤에 걸어다니다 / 위험해요.
> = 혼자 밤에 걸어다니기에는 위험해요.
> "(It) is dangerous for walking around alone at night."

1 두 사람이 자다 / 침대가 너무 작아요
2 영화를 다운로드 받다 / 제 컴퓨터가 너무 느려요
3 수영을 하다 / 날씨가 너무 추워요
4 영화를 보다 / 시간이 없어요
5 전화를 하다 / 너무 늦었어요
6 농구를 하다 / 키가 작았어요

7 커피를 마시다 / 너무 어렸어요
8 혼자 운전하다 / 너무 멀었어요
9 노트북을 사다 / 돈이 모자랐어요
10 선물로 주다 / 너무 비쌌어요

Exercise 23.4

Construct a sentence using the sentence cues provided and ~기 때문에.
Then translate the sentence, as shown in the example.

> Example: 차 사고가 났다 / 늦었어요
> = 차 사고가 났기 때문에 늦었어요.
> "Because there was a car accident, (I) was late."

1 감기 걸렸다 / 학교에 못 가요
2 아침을 늦게 먹었다 / 점심을 먹고 싶지 않아요
3 비가 오다 / 경기가 취소될 거예요
4 버스가 불편하다 / 지하철을 이용해요
5 시험 기간이다 / 도서관에 사람이 많아요

Exercise 23.5

Construct a sentence using the sentence cues provided and ~기 위해서.
Then translate the sentence, as shown in the example.

> Example: 용돈을 벌다 / 주말마다 일했어요
> = 용돈을 벌기 위해서 주말마다 일했어요.
> "(I) worked every weekend to earn extra money."

1 살을 빼다 / 저녁을 조금 먹을 거예요
2 의과 대학에 진학하다 / 준비하고 있어요
3 차를 고치다 / 정비소에 가고 있어요
4 다음 경기를 이기다 / 매일 열심히 연습해요
5 한국에 있는 친구한테 전화하다 / 전화 카드를 샀어요

Exercise 23.6

Conjugate the predicate using ~기로 하다. Then translate the sentence.

> Example: 매일 운동하다
> = 매일 운동하기로 했어요. "(I) decided to exercise everyday."

1 내년 봄에 결혼하다
2 학교 기숙사에서 살다
3 다음 학기에 한국어 수업을 듣다
4 내일부터 담배를 끊다
5 다음 달부터 태권도를 배우다

Exercise 23.7

Conjugate the predicate using ~기도 하다. Then translate the sentence.

> Example: 주말에 영화를 보다
> = 주말에 영화를 보기도 해요.
> "(We) also see a movie on the weekend."

1 토요일마다 테니스를 치다
2 가끔 까만 넥타이를 매다
3 주말에 친구들하고 농구를 하다
4 심심하면 영화를 보다
5 토요일 아침에 조깅을 하다

Exercise 23.8

Construct a sentence using the cues provided, as shown in the example.
Then translate the sentence.

> Example: 대학에 들어가다 / ~기가 어렵다
> = 대학에 들어가기가 어려워요. "Entering a college is
> difficult."

1 매일 요가를 하다 / ~기가 어렵다
2 프랑스 음식을 만들다 / ~기가 어렵다
3 시험에 떨어지다 / ~기가 쉽다
4 이사하다 / ~기가 힘들다
5 노래를 부르다 / ~기가 좋다
6 차를 타다 / ~기가 편하다
7 일하다 / ~기가 싫다
8 요리하다 / ~기가 재미있다
9 빨래를 하다 / ~기가 귀찮다
10 매일 운동하다 / ~기가 힘들다

Exercise 23.9

Complete the dialogue using ~기는요, as shown in the example.

Example:　A: 매일 테니스를 치세요?
　　　　　B: <u>매일 치기는요</u>, 1 주일에 2 번정도 쳐요.

1　A: 차가 좋네요.
　　B: ＿＿＿＿＿＿＿＿＿. 자주 고장이 나요.

2　A: 오늘 영화 봐요?
　　B: ＿＿＿＿＿＿＿＿＿ 월요일에 시험이 있어서 공부해야 해요.

3　A: 남자 친구랑 자주 만나세요?
　　B: ＿＿＿＿＿＿＿＿ 요즈음 바빠서 자주 못 봐요.

4　A: 방이 따뜻하네요.
　　B: ＿＿＿＿＿＿＿＿ 매일 히터를 켜고 자요.

5　A: 부지런하시네요.
　　B: ＿＿＿＿＿＿＿＿ 오늘만 일찍 일어났어요.

Exercise 23.10

Conjugate the predicate using ~(으)ㅁ, as shown in the example. Then translate the sentence.

Example:　저녁 안 먹었어요
　　　　　= 저녁 안 먹었음. "Did not eat dinner."

1　내일 오전 10 시에 돌아와요
2　오늘 저녁은 스테이크예요
3　차 고쳤어요
4　집에 안 갔어요
5　옷 샀어요
6　어제 머리 잘랐어요
7　우리가 지갑을 보관하고 있어요
8　잃어버린 개를 찾았습니다
9　룸메이트를 구합니다
10　영화가 재미없어요

UNIT 24
Direct and indirect quotation

A direct quotation conveys the exact spoken or written message. Consider the following sentence:

"Jane said that 'I will come to the party no matter what happens!'"

This sentence is a direct quotation. It reports what has been said or written verbatim, using quotation marks. On the other hand, an indirect quotation delivers only the main message. In an indirect quotation, the speaker delivers what somebody said or wrote without using the original speaker's exact words. Consequently, an indirect quotation involves the modification of the original utterance. Consider the following example:

"Jane said that she would come to the party no matter what happens."

Notice that the personal pronoun and the tense are modified so that they represent the speaker's voice and perspective. This unit introduces direct and indirect quotations in Korean.

Direct quotation

Direct quotation in Korean is constructed from the original utterance, a quotation particle (이)라고, and a quoting verb, such as 말하다 "speak," 대답하다 "answer," 묻다 "ask," 부탁하다 "request," and 제언하다 "suggest." Consider the following examples:

수잔이 "우리 이제 점심 먹읍시다" 라고 했어요. "Susan said 'Let us have lunch now.'"
피터가 선생님한테 "곧 갈게요" 라고 대답했어요. "Peter replied to the teacher, '(I) promise to go (there) soon.'"
사이몬이 "이번 주말 내 생일 파티에 올 거예요?" 라고 물었어요. "Simon asked (me) 'Will (you) come to my birthday party this weekend?'"

문 앞에 "금연!" 이라고 써 있었어요. "(It) was written 'No Smoking!'
in front of the door."
윌리엄이 "제 고향은 서울입니다" 라고 대답했어요. "William answered
'As for my hometown, (it) is Seoul.'"

When quoting mimetic expressions and/or when quoting the exact forms
involved along with the tone and intonation of the quoted utterance, the
particle 하고 is used instead of (이)라고. Consider the following examples:

학교 종이 "땡땡" 하고 울렸습니다. "The school bell rang 'ttang
ttang.'"
찰스는 "똑똑" 하고 문을 두드렸어요. "Charles knocked on the door
'knock knock.'"
사람들이 "불이야!" 하고 소리를 질렀어요. "People shouted 'It's
fire!'"
앤드류가 "와, 가을이다!" 하고 소리쳤습니다. "Andrew shouted 'Wow,
it's Autumn!'"
존이 제니퍼에게 차분한 목소리로 "이번 주말에 영화 보러 가자" 하고
물었어요. "John asked Jennifer in a calm tone of voice, saying 'Let us
go see a movie this weekend.'"
제시카가 "선생님!" 하고 불렀습니다. "Jessica called out, 'Professor!'"

Indirect quotation

Generally speaking in Korean, the use of indirect quotation is more frequent than that of direct quotation. The function of indirect quotation
in Korean is twofold: (1) to convey what somebody has said or written
without using the original speaker's or writer's exact words, and (2) to
report one's own thoughts or feelings (e.g., internal speech).

Reporting without using the speaker's or writer's exact words

Indirect quotation in Korean is constructed from the following: the quoted
utterance, the indirect quotation particle 고, and a verb, such as 말하다
(or 하다) "say," 묻다 "ask," 대답하다 "answer," and the adjective 그렇다
"be that way."
When a direct quoted utterance is converted to an indirect reported
utterance, part of the original utterance (e.g., tense, personal pronouns,
and honorifics) is modified to fit the perspective of the speaker. Compare
the following two sentences:

리사가 "제가 이번 주말에 일하겠어요" 라고 말했어요. "Lisa said 'I will
work this weekend.'"

리사가 자기가 이번 주말에 일하겠다고 말했어요. "Lisa said that (her-self/she) would work this weekend."

The first sentence is a direct quotation, whereas the second is an indirect quotation. Notice that the first person pronoun 저 in the first sentence was replaced by the noun 자기 "herself" in the second sentence. In addition, the polite speech level ending in the first sentence is replaced by the plain speech level ending in the second (e.g., 일하겠어요 vs. 일하겠다).

Note that the plain speech level has different endings depending on the sentence type:

Declarative	Interrogative	Imperative	Propositive
~(느)ㄴ다	~(으)니/냐	~어라/아라	~자

Consequently, depending on the sentence type of the quoted utterance, one of the four plain speech level endings is used accordingly before the quotation particle 고.

Declarative

~(느)ㄴ다고 하다 *(for verbs)*

매일 한국 음식을 먹는다고 했어요. "(They) said that (they) would eat Korean food everyday."
오늘 밤 중국으로 떠난다고 말했어요. "(He) said that (he) would leave for China tonight."
일본 문학을 전공한다고 해요. "(She) says that (she) majors in Japanese literature."

~다고 하다 *(for adjectives)*

시험이 쉽다고 해요. "(He) said that the test is easy."
어제 음식이 매웠다고 말했어요. "(She) said that yesterday's food was spicy."

~라고 하다 *(for copulas)*

내일부터 봄 방학이라고 해요. "(They) say that (it) is the spring break from tomorrow."
룸메이트가 오늘 밤 늦게 잘 거라고 했어요. "(My) roommate said that (he) would go to bed late tonight."
아버지가 의사라고 해요. "(She) says the (her) father is a doctor."

221

Interrogative

~느냐고 하다/묻다 *(for verbs)*

이사벨이 에릭에게 어느 은행에 <u>가냐고 물었어요</u>. "Isabel asked Eric which bank (he) goes to."
다음 금요일에 어디에 <u>갈 거냐고 물었습니다</u>. "(I) asked (her) where (she) would go next Friday."
오늘 저녁 메뉴가 <u>뭐냐고 해요</u>. "(He) asks (her) what the dinner menu for today is."

~냐고 하다/묻다 *(for adjectives and copulas)*

서울의 날씨가 <u>춥냐고 물었어요</u>. "(I) asked (them) whether Seoul's weather is cold."
수잔이 누가 한국 사람<u>이냐고 물었습니다</u>. "Susan asked (me) who is a Korean."

Imperative

~(으)라고 하다 *(for verbs only)*

자기 전에 약을 <u>먹으라고 했어요</u>. "(I) told (him) to take the medicine before going to bed."
여동생한테 조심해서 <u>운전하라고 했어요</u>. "(I) told (my) younger sister to drive safely."
Note that ~(으)라 is used instead of the plain speech level ending ~어라/아라.

Propositive

~자고 하다 *(for verbs only)*

데니엘이 이번 주말에 <u>만나자고 했어요</u>. "Daniel suggested that (we) meet this weekend."
내일부터 같이 <u>테니스 치자고 해요</u>. "(They) suggest that (we) play tennis together from tomorrow (onward)."
마리오가 같이 저녁 <u>먹자고 합니다</u>. "Mario suggests that (we) eat dinner together."

Abbreviation of the indirect quotation endings in colloquial usages

In conversational settings, some of the aforementioned indirect quotation endings can be abbreviated, as shown below:

~(느)ㄴ다고 하다 is shortened to ~(느)ㄴ대요.
매튜가 한국 음식을 <u>좋아한대요</u>. "(They) say that Matthew likes Korean food."

~라고 하다 is shortened to ~래요.
형이 변호사<u>래요</u>. "(He) says that (his) older brother is a lawyer."

~(으)라고 하다 is shortened to ~(으)래요.
학교에 가기전에 아침을 <u>먹으래요</u>. "(She) tells (us) to eat breakfast before going to school."

~자고 하다 is shortened to ~재요.
내일 같이 골프 <u>치재요</u>. "(They) suggest that (we) play golf tomorrow together."

Reporting one's thoughts or feelings

Beside reporting the speech or writing of a third person, indirect quotation is also used to report one's own thoughts or feelings. It is constructed from the following: the quoted utterance, the indirect quotation particle 고, and a verb, such as 생각하다 "think" or 느끼다 "feel." Consider the following example:

어제 시험이 <u>어려웠다고 생각했다</u>. "(I) thought that yesterday's test was difficult."

Notice that the form reports one's thought rather than quotes someone else's idea. Here are more examples:

제인의 성격이 참 <u>좋다고 생각한다</u>. "(I) think that Jane's personality is really nice."
존의 행동이 <u>옳았다고 생각했다</u>. "(I) thought that John's action was right."
직원들의 태도가 안 <u>좋았다고 느꼈다</u>. "(I) felt that the employees' attitudes were not good."

Exercises

Key vocabulary for Unit 24 exercises

가다 to go
같이 together
계절 season
공부하다 to study

그만두다 to quit/to stop (doing)
금요일 Friday
끝 an end/the tip
나중 next time
내려오다 to come down
내리다 to get off/to come down
내일 tomorrow
놀다 to play
다시 again
돌아가다 to go back
돕다 to help
들르다 to stop by
따라오다 to follow
마시다 to drink
만나다 to meet
만들다 to make
맵다 to be spicy
먹다 to eat
밤 night
보다 to see/to watch/to read
빨래 laundry
빨리 fast/immediately
소나기 a passing rain/shower
수업 class
시간 time/hour
시작하다 to begin
열쇠 keys
열심히 earnestly/enthusiastically/hard
영화 movie
오늘 today
오르다 to climb/to go up
오후 p.m.
우유 milk
이따 after a while
일어나다 to get up
일찍 early

잘 well/expertly
저녁 dinner/evening
전화하다 to make a phone call
정말 really
제발 please/for heaven's sake
주말 weekend

지내다 to spend (time)/to get along

직장 one's place of work
집 house
집세 house rent
찌개 pot stew
찾다 to look for/to seek for
친구 friends
타다 to ride (a train/car/bus/airplane)
한국어 the Korean language
화내다 to get angry

Exercise 24.1

Quote the following directly, as shown in the example. Then translate the sentence.

Example: The speaker: 제인 / The original utterance: "집에 갑시다"
= 제인이 "집에 갑시다"라고 했어요. "Jane said 'Let us go home.'"

1 The speaker: 누나 / The original utterance: "제발 일찍 일어나라"
2 The speaker: 앤드류 / The original utterance: "빨리 따라오세요"
3 The speaker: 이사벨 / The original utterance: "정말 우유를 잘 마시네요"
4 The speaker: 리사 / The original utterance: "저녁에 저희 집에 들르세요"
5 The speaker: 선생님 / The original utterance: "오늘 수업 끝"
6 The speaker: 폴 / The original utterance: "피자 먹자"
7 The speaker: 마리아 / The original utterance: "찌개가 맵다"
8 The speaker: 브래드 / The original utterance: "우리 금요일에 만나자"
9 The speaker: 니콜 / The original utterance: "이따 시간 있으면 전화해"
0 The speaker: 지나 / The original utterance: "집에 안 가세요?"

Exercise 24.2

Quote the following indirectly as shown in the example. Then translate the sentence.

Example: The speaker: 폴 / The original utterance: 오후에 집에 갑니다
= 폴이 오후에 집에 간다고 했어요.
"Paul said that (he) would go home in the afternoon."

1 The speaker: 모니카 / The original utterance: 뉴욕에 4 계절이 있습니다

2 The speaker: 앤서니 / The original utterance: 내일 소나기가 내리겠습니다

3 The speaker: 사브리나 / The original utterance: 집세가 올랐습니다

4 The speaker: 제이슨 / The original utterance: 오늘 스파게티를 만들어요

5 The speaker: 조디 / The original utterance: 내일 다시 전화하겠습니다

6 The speaker: 스티브 / The original utterance: 언제 직장을 그만뒀어요?

7 The speaker: 쥴리아 / The original utterance: 언제 집에 와요?

8 The speaker: 에스더 / The original utterance: 이 차가 누구 거예요?

9 The speaker: 제리 / The original utterance: 잘 지내고 있어요?

10 The speaker: 데이지 / The original utterance: 몇 시예요?

Exercise 24.3

Quote the following indirectly as shown in the example. Then translate the sentence.

> Example: The speaker: 테렌스 / The original utterance: 열심히 공부합시다.
> = 테렌스가 열심히 공부하자고 했어요.
> "Terrence suggested that (we) study hard."

1 The speaker: 에릭 / The original utterance: 버스를 탑시다

2 The speaker: 나오미 / The original utterance: 오후 2 시에 만납시다

3 The speaker: 클라라 / The original utterance: 같이 요가를 시작합시다

4 The speaker: 조지 / The original utterance: 이번 주말에 같이 영화를 봅시다

5 The speaker: 나탈리 / The original utterance: 그 친구를 도와 줍시다

6 The speaker: 아비가일 / The original utterance: 빨래를 하십시오

7 The speaker: 케빈 / The original utterance: 열심히 공부하십시오

8 The speaker: 다이에나 / The original utterance: 20 분안에 내려오십시오

9 The speaker: 져스틴 / The original utterance: 화내지 마십시오

10 The speaker: 일레인 / The original utterance: 열쇠를 찾으십시오

Exercise 24.4

Finish the following translation using the cues provided in parenthesis, as shown in the example.

Example: "Luis suggested that (we) buy a wine." (루이스 / 와인을 삽시다)
= 루이스가 와인을 사자고 했어요.

1 Sam said that (he) leaves tonight (샘 / 오늘 밤 떠나요)
2 Lisa asked (me) what time (I) go to bed (리사 / 몇 시에 자요?)
3 Paul suggested that (we) eat Korean food (폴 / 한국 음식을 먹읍시다)
4 Teacher told (us) to be quiet (선생님 / 조용히 하십시오)
5 Susan said that (she) would call (me) tonight (수잔 / 오늘 밤 전화할 거
예요)

Exercise 24.5

Finish the following translation using the sentence cue provided in parenthesis, as shown in the example.

Example: "(I) think that the room was too noisy." (방이 너무 시끄러
웠다)
= 방이 너무 시끄러웠다고 생각한다.

1 (I) think that (their) food is delicious (음식이 맛있다)
2 (I) think that (their) service is great (서비스가 좋다)
3 (I) think that the coffee was too strong (커피가 너무 진했다)
4 (I) thought that (I) would start exercising from tomorrow (내일부터
운동을 시작해야겠어요)
5 (I) thought that (I) would write an e-mail to John (존한테 이메일을
써야겠다)

KEY TO EXERCISES

Unit 1

Exercise 1.1

1 다리를 건너. "Cross a bridge."
2 문을 열어. "Open the door."
3 차를 팔아. "(Let us) sell the car."
4 쓰레기를 버려. "(I) throw away the trash."
5 창문을 닫아. "Close the window."
6 공연을 일찍 마쳐. "End the concert early."
7 접시를 빌려. "(Let us) borrow dishes."
8 발을 씻어. "(I) wash (my) feet."
9 일찍 자. "(Let us) go to bed early."
10 자전거를 타? "Do (you) ride a bicycle?"
11 느낌이 좋아. "The feeling is good."
12 강의가 재미있어. "The lecture is interesting."
13 프랑스 사람이야? "Is (she) a Frenchman?"
14 일을 해 "Work."
15 경찰관이 아니야? "Isn't (he) a policeman?"
16 집이 멀어. "The house is far."
17 사과가 달아. "The apple is sweet."
18 머리가 아파? "Does (your) head ache?"
19 하늘이 흐려. "The sky is cloudy."
20 과일이 싱싱해? "Is the fruit fresh?"

Exercise 1.2

1 아침을 먹는다. "(I) eat breakfast."
2 중국어를 가르친다. "(I) teach Chinese."
3 누나를 기다린다. "(I) wait for (my) older sister."
4 물을 마신다. "(I) drink water."
5 소포를 받는다. "(I) receive a package."
6 일본어를 배운다. "(I) learn Japanese."

7 사무실이 깨끗하다 "The office is clean."
8 버스가 느리다. "The bus is slow."
9 커피가 뜨겁다. "The coffee is hot."
10 이번 주말에 바쁘다. "(I) am busy this weekend."

Exercise 1.3

1 언제 가게 문을 닫니? "When do (you) shut the store door?"
2 어디서 친구를 만나니? "Where do (you) meet (your) friend?"
3 언제 떠나니? "When do (you) depart?"
4 어디서 공부하니? "Where do (you) study?"
5 담배를 피우니? "Do (you) smoke?"
6 열쇠를 찾니? "Do (you) look for keys?"
7 날씨가 따뜻하니? "Is the weather warm?"
8 시험이 어렵니? "Is the test difficult?"
9 기분이 나쁘니? "Is (your) mood bad?"
10 집이 조용하니? "Is the house quiet?"

Exercise 1.4

1 다리를 건너라. "Cross the bridge."
2 아래로 내려가라. "Go down to the bottom."
3 가방을 던져라. "Throw the bag."
4 창문을 열어라. "Open the window."
5 아버지를 따라라. "Follow (your) father."
6 앤드류를 믿어라. "Trust Andrew."
7 양말을 신어라. "Put on (your) socks."
8 셔츠를 입어라. "Wear the shirt."
9 손을 잡아라. "Take (my) hand."
10 크게 외쳐라. "Shout aloud."

Exercise 1.5

1 사진을 보내자. "(Let us) send (him) the picture."
2 그림을 그리자. "(Let us) draw a picture."
3 범인을 잡자. "(Let us) catch the criminal."
4 신문을 읽자. "(Let us) read the newspaper."
5 일을 마치자. "(Let us) finish the work."
6 택시를 타자. "(Let us) take a taxi."
7 커피숍에서 헤어지자. "(Let us) get scattered at the coffee shop."
8 로맨스 영화를 보자. "(Let us) see a romance movie."
9 책을 주자. "(Let us) give (them) a book."
10 쓰레기를 버리자. "(Let us) throw garbage away."

Exercise 1.6

1 Read page 19.
2 (Let us) wash (our) hands.
3 Close the door.
4 (Let us) borrow (his) money.
5 Go out from the room.
6 Drink green tea.
7 (Let us) give (them) homework.
8 (Let us) wear jeans.
9 Learn English.
10 (Let us) leave for London.

Exercise 1.7

1 오후 2 시에 영화가 시작해.
2 조용히 해.
3 집을 청소해.
4 톰을 어디서 만나?
5 어디에 갔어?
6 담배를 끊었어.
7 날씨가 맑았어.
8 와인을 사.
9 얼마나 기다렸어?
10 한국에서 영어를 가르쳤어.

Exercise 1.8

1 경제학을 전공한다.
2 작년에 서울을 여행했다.
3 커피가 뜨겁다.
4 캐나다 사람이니?
5 지하철이 편했니?
6 행복하니?
7 창문을 열어라.
8 쓰레기를 버려라.
9 자신감을 가지자.
10 노래를 부르자.

Unit 2

Exercise 2.1

1 웬디가 중국 사람이지요?
2 에드워드를 만나지요?

3 나를 믿지요?
4 가격이 비싸지요?
5 저기서 버스를 타지요?

Exercise 2.2

1 오늘 날씨가 덥지요? "Today's weather is hot, right?"
2 경치가 아름답지요? "The scenery is beautiful, right?"
3 방이 조용하지요? "The room is quiet, right?"
4 집이 시끄럽지요? "The house is noisy, right?"
5 커피가 맛있지요? "The coffee is delicious, right?"

Exercise 2.3

1 집으로 돌아가지요.
2 커피를 시키지요.
3 에어컨을 켜지요.
4 린다한테 전화를 걸지요.
5 현금으로 지불하지요.
6 생일 카드를 사지요.
7 한국 영화를 빌리지요.
8 지하철을 이용하지요.
9 조디의 친구들도 초대하지요.
10 담배를 끊지요.

Exercise 2.4

1 크리스가 코고네요.
2 아비게일이 노래를 잘 하네요.
3 로날드가 부지런하네요.
4 다이에나가 퇴근했네요.
5 리디아가 돈을 벌었네요.
6 반지가 비쌌네요.

Exercise 2.5

1 조셉이 집에 없네요. "(Oh, I see that) Joseph is not home."
2 레이첼이 김치를 먹네요. "(Oh, I see that) Rachel eats kimchi."
3 니콜라스가 나탈리하고 이야기하네요. "(Oh, I see that) Nicolas talks to Natalie."
4 데이빗이 알렉스의 형이네요. "(Oh, I see that) David is Alex's older brother."
5 씬디가 아직 안 자네요. "(Oh, I see that) Cindy does not sleep yet."
6 방이 깨끗하네요. "(Oh, I see that) the room is clean."

Exercise 2.6

1 날씨가 싸늘하군요.
2 어제 바람이 많이 불었군요.
3 보스톤이 바닷가재로 유명하군요.
4 쥴리아가 간호사이군요.
5 이제부터 여름이군요.
6 짐이 보너스를 받았군요.

Exercise 2.7

1 나오미가 패션 모델이군요. "(Oh, I see that) Naomi is a fashion
   model."
2 유럽으로 신혼 여행을 가는군요. "(Oh, I see that they) go to Europe
   for (their) honeymoon."
3 오후 9 시에 가게를 닫았군요. "(Oh, I see that they) closed (their) store
   at 9 p.m."
4 해리가 변호사로 일했군요. "(Oh, I see that) Harry worked as a
   lawyer."
5 물가가 비싸군요. "(Oh, I see that) prices are expensive."
6 어제 방이 더웠군요. "(Oh, I see that) the room was hot yesterday."

Unit 3

Exercise 3.1

1 리사보다 찰스가 인기가 더 많아요.
2 한국보다 필리핀이 더 더워요.
3 봄보다 가을을 더 좋아했어요.
4 과학보다 문학을 더 전공하고 싶어했어요.
5 디지탈 카메라보다 노트북을 더 사고 싶었어요?
6 차보다 비행기가 더 빠릅니다.
7 호놀룰루보다 뉴욕시가 더 큽니다.
8 어제보다 오늘이 덜 춥습니다.
9 해리보다 샘이 테니스를 더 잘 칩니까?
10 데이브보다 제인이 고기를 더 좋아합니까?

Exercise 3.2

1 주스가 얼음처럼 차가워요.
2 리디아가 형사처럼 행동해요.
3 크리스가 물개처럼 수영을 잘 해요?
4 제리가 양처럼 순했어요.
5 야채가 금처럼 비쌀 거예요.

6 존이 농구 선수처럼 키가 커요.
7 샌디가 모델처럼 날씬해요.
8 앤서니가 아인슈타인처럼 똑똑해요.
9 사라가 오페라 가수처럼 노래를 잘 했어요.
10 토마스가 마라톤 선수처럼 잘 뛸 거예요.

Exercise 3.3

1 캐서린이 닐만큼 한국어를 잘 합니다.
2 부엌이 거실만큼 큽니다.
3 데니엘이 필립만큼 부지런합니다.
4 패트릭이 에리카만큼 와인을 좋아했습니까?
5 레베카가 제니퍼만큼 얌전했습니다.
6 서울이 뉴욕만큼 비싸요.
7 이 차가 저 차만큼 좋아요.
8 필립이 아담만큼 돈을 벌어요?
9 지하철이 택시만큼 편했어요.
10 에드워드가 토마스만큼 마셨어요.

Exercise 3.4

1 저녁마다 산책합니다.
2 겨울마다 스키를 탑니까?
3 여름마다 바닷가에 갔습니다.
4 가게마다 바쁠 거예요.
5 밤마다 만납시다.
6 슈퍼마켓마다 주스를 팔아요.
7 학교마다 교가가 있어요.
8 방마다 창문이 있었어요.
9 학생마다 시험 공부를 하고 있어요.
10 친구들이 토요일마다 골프를 쳤어요?

Exercise 3.5

1 사브리나마저 거짓말을 했어요.
2 누나마저 사실을 감췄어요.
3 날씨마저 추웠어요.
4 제 방마저 어두웠어요.
5 에어컨마저 고장났어요.
6 매튜마저 학교에 안 갔어요.
7 부인마저 미국으로 돌아갈 거예요.
8 모니카마저 시험에 떨어졌어요.
9 편의점마저 문을 닫았어요?
10 폴마저 차를 팔 거예요.

Exercise 3.6

1 사과 주스밖에 안 마셔요. "(I) drink only apple juice."
2 샐러드밖에 안 먹어요. "(I) eat only salad."
3 엄마는 아빠밖에 안 좋아해요. "As for Mom, (she) likes only Dad."
4 손님이 7 명밖에 없어요. "There are only seven customers."
5 낮잠을 1 시간밖에 안 잘 거예요. "(I) will take a nap only one hour."
6 어머니밖에 생각 안 했어요. "(I) thought of only (my) mother."
7 재즈밖에 안 좋아했어요. "(I) liked only jazz."
8 어제 5 시간밖에 안 잤어요. "(I) slept only 5 hours yesterday."
9 10 분밖에 안 기다릴 거예요. "(I) will wait only 10 minutes."
10 언니밖에 안 만날 거예요. "(I) will meet only (my) older sister."

Unit 4

Exercise 4.1

1 인도 음식을 먹어 봤습니다. "(I) tried Indian food."
2 도자기를 만들어 봤습니다. "(I) tried making ceramics."
3 한복을 입어 봤습니다. "(I) tried wearing Hanbok."
4 베이징에 가 봤습니다. "(I) have been to Beijing."
5 병원에 전화해 봤습니다. "(I) tried calling the hospital."

Exercise 4.2

1 무역 회사에서 일해 봤습니까? "Have (you) tried working for a trading company?"
2 낚시를 해 봤습니까? "Have (you) tried fishing?"
3 타이 음식을 먹어 봤습니까? "Have (you) tried (eating) Thai food?"
4 한국어를 배워 봤습니까? "Have (you) tried learning the Korean language?"
5 교회에 가 봤습니까? "Have (you) been to church?"

Exercise 4.3

1 영어를 가르쳐 보십시오. "Try teaching English."
2 산을 올라가 보십시오. "Try climbing the mountain."
3 아파트에서 살아 보십시오. "Try living in an apartment."
4 여자친구랑 헤어져 보십시오. "Try breaking up with (your) girlfriend."
5 컴퓨터를 고쳐 보십시오. "Try fixing the computer."

Exercise 4.4

1 기도해 봅시다. "(Let us) try praying."
2 선생님한테 부탁해 봅시다. "(Let us) try asking a favor to the teacher."
3 차를 고쳐 봅시다. "(Let us) try fixing the car."
4 구멍을 막아 봅시다. "(Let us) try filling up a hole."
5 에어컨을 켜 봅시다. "(Let us) try turning on the air conditioner."

Exercise 4.5

1 아프리카에 가 봤습니다.
2 한국어를 공부해 볼 겁니다.
3 한국 맥주를 마셔 봤습니다.
4 스웨덴에 가 봤습니까?
5 기타를 쳐 봤습니까?
6 집 전화 번호를 외워 보십시오.
7 마사지 기계를 사용해 보십시오.
8 한국 사람하고 사귀어 보십시오.
9 요리를 배워 봅시다.
10 컴퓨터를 고쳐 봅시다.

Exercise 4.6

1 형이 좋은 소식을 전해 왔어요.
2 개가 이쪽으로 달려 와요.
3 윌리엄이 감기로 고생해 왔어요.
4 로버트로부터 도움을 받아 오고 있어요.
5 물이 얼어 가고 있어요.

Exercise 4.7

1 우리 할머니는 해마다 늙어 가십니다. "As for my grandmother, (she) continues to get old."
2 이제부터 혼자 살아갑니까? "Do (you) go on living alone from now on?"
3 행복한 가정을 만들어 가십시오. "Continue to make a happy family."
4 물을 절약해 갑시다. "(Let us) continue to save water."
5 조금씩 스케줄을 바꿔 갑시다. "(Let us) continue to change the schedule gradually."

Unit 5

Exercise 5.1

1 큰 물고기를 낚아 냈어요.
2 강물을 막아 냈어요.
3 프로젝트를 따 냈어요.
4 돈을 받아 냈어요.
5 논문을 써 냈어요.

Exercise 5.2

1 비밀을 캐 냈어요. "(I) ferreted out a secret."
2 전화기를 만들어 냈어요. "(He) made a telephone."
3 고기를 구워 냈어요. "(I) roasted meat."
4 금하고 은을 구별해 냈어요. "(I) made a distinction between gold and silver."
5 그림을 그려 냈어요. "(I) drew a picture."

Exercise 5.3

1 앤드류가 사진을 찍어 버렸어요.
2 사라가 노트북을 빌려 버렸어요.
3 돈을 다 써 버렸어요.
4 케빈이 드라마를 끝까지 봐 버렸어요.
5 앤지가 직장을 옮겨 버렸어요.

Exercise 5.4

1 차가 또 고장이 나 버렸어요. "The car broke down again."
2 가게 문을 닫아 버렸어요. "(I) shut the store door."
3 파일을 지워 버렸어요. "(I) erased the file."
4 친구가 뉴욕으로 떠나 버렸어요. "(My) friend left for New York."
5 학교에서 나와 버렸어요. "(I) came out from school."

Exercise 5.5

1 늦게 일어나고 말았어요.
2 위스키를 마시고 말았어요.
3 여자 친구한테 사랑을 고백하고 말았어요.
4 결국 일을 그만두고 말았어요.
5 차가 고장이 나고 말았아요.

Exercise 5.6

1 로날드가 형하고 싸우고 말았어요. "Ronald ended up disputing with (his) older brother."
2 샐리가 남자 친구하고 헤어지고 말았어요. "Sally ended up breaking up with (her) boyfriend."
3 테렌스가 노트북을 팔고 말았어요. "Terrence ended up selling (his) notebook."
4 씬디가 길에서 미끄러지고 말았어요. "Cindy ended up sliding down on the road."
5 조앤이 언니한테 화내고 말았어요. "Joan ended up getting mad at (her) older sister."

Exercise 5.7

1 티나가 프로젝트를 도와 줬어요.
2 오빠가 가방을 사 줬어요.
3 존이 차를 팔아 줬어요.
4 메건이 사진을 찍어 줄 거예요.
5 언니가 설거지를 해 줄 거예요.
6 책을 빌려 주세요.
7 컴퓨터를 고쳐 주세요.
8 옷을 환불해 주세요.
9 피아노를 쳐 주세요.
10 라디오를 틀어 주세요.

Exercise 5.8

1 책을 읽어 드렸어요. "(I) read a book (for her)."
2 편지를 써 드렸어요. "(I) wrote a letter (for her)."
3 전화를 받아 드렸어요. "(I) received the phone call (for her)."
4 창문을 닫아 드렸어요. "(I) shut the window (for him)."
5 전등을 켜 드렸어요. "(I) switched on the electric lamp (for her)."
6 문을 열어 드렸어요. "(I) opened the door (for him)."
7 옷을 바꿔 드렸어요. "(I) changed the dress (for him)."
8 노래를 불러 드렸어요. "(I) sang the song (for her)."
9 점심을 만들어 드렸어요. "(I) made lunch (for him)."
10 커피를 시켜 드렸어요. "(I) ordered coffee (for him)."

Unit 6

Exercise 6.1

1 숙제를 끝내 놓으세요.
2 지도를 그려 놓으세요.
3 소스를 만들어 놓으세요.
4 물을 끓여 놓으세요.
5 돈을 받아 놓으세요.

Exercise 6.2

1 전화 번호를 기억해 두세요. "Remember the telephone number for later."
2 신문을 읽어 두세요. "Read newspapers for later."
3 좌석을 예약해 두세요. "Reserve a seat for later."
4 지리를 익혀 두세요. "Make (yourself) familiar with the geographical features for later."
5 야채를 씻어 두세요. "Wash vegetables for later."

Exercise 6.3

1 문이 닫혀 있어요.
2 사진이 벽에 걸려 있어요.
3 가게가 열려 있어요.
4 손님이 소파에 앉아 있어요.
5 제임스가 문 앞에 서 있어요.

Exercise 6.4

1 버스가 와 있어요. "Bus is here."
2 정원에 꽃이 피어 있어요. "Flowers are in bloom in the garden."
3 친구가 집에 와 있어요. "The friends are (here) home."
4 환자가 침대에 누워 있어요. "The patient is lying on the bed."
5 전등이 꺼져 있어요. "The electric lamp is off."

Exercise 6.5

1 행복해해요.
2 기뻐해요.
3 지루해할 거예요.
4 우울해했어요.
5 괴로워했어요.

Exercise 6.6

1 더워해요. "(He) feels hot."
2 아파해요. "(He) feels sore."
3 고마워해요. "(He) feels thankful."
4 궁금해해요. "(He) feels curious."
5 부러워해요. "(He) envies."

Exercise 6.7

1 머리가 어지러워졌어요.
2 성격이 차분해졌어요.
3 목소리가 부드러워졌어요.
4 몸이 튼튼해졌어요.
5 차가 더러워질 거예요.

Exercise 6.8

1 아이의 키가 커졌어요. "The child's height has become tall."
2 제시카가 예뻐졌어요. "Jessica has become pretty."
3 음식 값이 비싸졌어요. "Food price has become expensive."
4 날씨가 맑아졌어요. "The weather has become clear."
5 얼굴이 까매졌어요. "(My) face has become dark."

Unit 7

Exercise 7.1

1 소포를 받으러 우체국에 오세요.
2 차를 고치러 정비소에 가고 있어요.
3 낚시질 하러 바닷가로 갑시다.
4 비행기를 타러 공항에 갈 거예요.
5 컴퓨터 게임을 하러 친구 집에 자주 가세요?

Exercise 7.2

1 커피를 마시러 스타벅스에 갔어요. "(I) went to Starbucks to drink coffee."
2 시험 공부하러 도서관에 가십시오. "Go to the library to study for the test."
3 얼굴을 씻으러 화장실에 가고 있어요. "(I) am going to toilet to wash (my) face."
4 점심을 먹으러 중국 식당에 갑시다. "(Let us) go to the Chinese restaurant to have lunch."

5 케이트를 만나러 공항에 갑니까? "Do (you) go to the airport to meet Kate?"

Exercise 7.3

1 살을 빼려고 운동해요.
2 선생님을 만나려고 사무실에서 기다리고 있었어요.
3 의과 대학에 들어가려고 열심히 공부하고 있어요.
4 이번 여름에 한국에 가려고 비행기표를 예약했어요.
5 취직하려고 노력하고 있었어요.

Exercise 7.4

1 남편한테 생일 선물로 주려고 선물을 고르고 있어요. "(I) am choosing a gift intending to give (it) to (my) husband for (his) birthday present."
2 파리로 떠나려고 기차 역에 갔어요. "(I) went to the train station intending to leave for Paris."
3 같이 점심을 먹으려고 로비에서 친구를 기다려요. "(I) wait for (my) friend at lobby intending to have lunch together."
4 싸게 차를 사려고 흥정을 하고 있어요. "(I) am negotiating intending to buy the car at a cheap price."
5 돈을 벌려고 아르바이트를 했어요. "(I) had a side job intending to earn (some) money."

Exercise 7.5

1 책을 빌리려고
2 야채를 사려고
3 여자 친구한테 주려고
4 학교에 빨리 가려고
5 남자 친구의 가족을 만나려고

Exercise 7.6

1 뉴스를 들을 수 있도록 라디오를 켜 주세요.
2 차를 쓸 수 있도록 허락해 주세요.
3 건강을 회복할 수 있도록 도와 주세요.
4 취직할 수 있도록 추천서를 써 주세요.
5 잘 수 있도록 전등을 꺼 주세요.

Exercise 7.7

1 앰블란스가 지나갈 수 있도록 길을 비켜 주세요. "Please get out of the way so that the ambulance can pass by."

2 좋은 인상을 줄 수 있도록 웃어 주세요. "Please smile so that (you) can give (them) a good impression."

3 시험에 붙을 수 있도록 열심히 공부하십시오. "Study hard so that (you) can pass the test."

4 아침에 일찍 일어날 수 있도록 알람을 맞추어 주세요. "Please set the alarm, so that (he) can get up early in the morning."

5 열심히 공부할 수 있도록 혼내 주세요. "Please teach (him) a lesson, so that (he) can study hard."

Unit 8

Exercise 8.1

1 여행사에 전화해서 항공 요금에 대해서 물어 볼 거예요.
2 학교에 가서 교수님을 만났어요.
3 딸기를 씻어서 먹었어요?
4 그 반지를 사서 여자 친구한테 주세요.
5 한국어를 배워서 서울에서 취직합시다.

Exercise 8.2

1 아침에 일찍 일어나서 운동할래요. "(I) will get up early in the morning and then exercise."

2 친구 집에 가서 요리하십시오. "Go to (your) friend's house and then cook."

3 언제 뉴욕에 가서 뮤지컬을 볼 거예요? "When will (you) go to New York and then see a musical?"

4 선물을 포장해서 생일 파티 때 줬어요. "(I) wrapped up the gift and then gave (it to her) at (her) birthday party."

5 파티에 가서 흥겹게 놉시다. "(Let us) go to the party and then play merrily."

Exercise 8.3

1 교통이 막혀서 수업에 늦었어요.
2 아침을 늦게 먹어서 아직 점심을 안 먹었어요.
3 배가 아파서 집에 일찍 가고 싶어요.
4 방이 너무 더러워서 오늘 청소할 거예요.
5 생일이어서 일찍 집에 갔어요.

Exercise 8.4

1 어제가 친구 생일이어서 생일 파티에 갔습니다. "Since yesterday was
(my) friend's birthday, (I) went to (his) birthday party."
2 이 식당 음식이 맛있어서 자주 와요. "Since this restaurant's food is
delicious, (we) come (here) often."
3 눈이 많이 와서 학교에 못 갈 것 같아요. "Since (it) snows much, (I)
guess that (I) will not be able to go to school."
4 감기 걸려서 약을 먹고 있어요. "Since (I) caught a cold, (I) am taking
medicines."
5 약속 시간에 늦어서 미안합니다. "(I) am sorry in that (I) am late for
the appointment."

Exercise 8.5

1 커피를 못 마시니까 대신 녹차를 삽시다.
2 퇴근 시간이니까 교통이 막힙니다.
3 시간이 없으니까 용건만 말하십시오.
4 허리가 아프니까 누구도 만나고 싶지 않습니다.
5 추우니까 창문을 닫으십시오.

Exercise 8.6

1 내일 바쁘니까 모래 전화할게요. "Since (I) am busy tomorrow, (I) will
call (you) the day after tomorrow."
2 도서관이니까 크게 이야기하지 마십시오. "Since (here) is the library,
do not talk aloud."
3 머리가 아프니까 약을 사 주세요. "Since (my) head aches, please buy
medicines (for me)."
4 내일 아침에 이사하니까 오전 8 시까지 오세요. "Since (we) move (into
the new residence) tomorrow morning, come by 8 a.m."
5 음식이 싱거우니까 소금을 넣으십시오. "Since the food is watery, put
(some) salt in (it)."
6 더우니까 에어콘을 틀어 주세요. "Since (it) is hot, please turn on the
air conditioner."
7 이제 곧 피자가 도착하니까 조금 더 기다립시다. "Since the pizza will
arrive (here) soon, (let us) wait a little more."

Exercise 8.7

1 맥주를 사느라고 돈을 다 썼어요.
2 컴퓨터를 고치느라고 아직 퇴근을 못 했어요.
3 오래 통화하느라고 저녁을 같이 못 먹었어요.
4 동전을 넣느라고 지갑을 떨어뜨렸어요.
5 열쇠를 찾느라고 늦었어요.

Exercise 8.8

1 숙제를 하느라고 밤을 새웠어요. "(I) stayed up all night because of doing (my) homework."
2 라디오를 듣느라고 초인종 소리를 못 들었어요. "(I) could not hear the doorbell sound because of listening to the radio."
3 사라를 기다리느라고 늦었어요? "Were (you) late waiting for Sarah?"
4 다이어트를 하느라고 저녁을 많이 안 먹습니다. "(I) do not eat dinner much because (I) am on diet."
5 은행을 찾느라고 사람들한테 물어보고 있었어요. "(I) was asking people because (I) was looking for a bank."

Unit 9

Exercise 9.1

1 시간이 있으면 빌한테 전화할 거예요.
2 길이 막히면 지하철을 탑시다.
3 비싸면 사겠어요?
4 내일 아침 일찍 일어나면 깨워 주세요.
5 이야기했으면 화냈을 거예요.

Exercise 9.2

1 배가 아프면 병원에 가세요. "If (your) stomach hurts, go to hospital."
2 날씨가 너무 추우면 히터를 켜겠어요. "If the weather is too cold, (I) will turn on the heater."
3 모르면 물어 보세요. "If (you) do not know, try asking (someone)."
4 더우면 창문을 엽시다. "If (it) is hot, (let us) open the window."
5 도움이 필요하면 누구한테 전화하세요? "When (you) need help, who do (you) call?"

Exercise 9.3

1 공항에서 만나면 좋겠어요.
2 생일 선물로 시계를 받으면 좋겠어요.
3 레드 와인을 시키면 좋겠어요.
4 저녁으로 한국 음식을 먹으면 좋겠어요.
5 돈을 많이 벌면 좋겠어요.

Exercise 9.4

1 룸메이트가 한국 사람이면 좋겠어요. "(I) wish that (my) roommate is a Korean."
2 캐나다로 유학가면 좋겠어요. "(I) wish that (I) go abroad for study to Canada."
3 직장이 집에서 가까우면 좋겠어요. "(I) wish that (my) place of work is near from home."
4 내일 날씨가 따뜻하면 좋겠어요. "(I) wish that tomorrow's weather is warm."
5 남편이 일찍 자면 좋겠어요. "(I) wish that (my) husband goes to bed early."
6 다음 학기에 김교수님이 가르치시면 좋겠어요. "(I) wish that Professor Kim teaches next semester."
7 남자 친구가 담배를 끊으면 좋겠어요. "(I) wish that (my) boyfriend quits smoking."
8 노트북을 생일 선물로 받으면 좋겠어요. "(I) wish that (I) receive a notebook for (my) birthday present."

Exercise 9.5

1 물을 끓이려면 냄비가 필요해요. "If (you) intend to boil water, (you) need a pot."
2 이 식당에서 저녁을 먹으려면 예약하십시오. "If (you) intend to have dinner in this restaurant, make a reservation."
3 병원에 가려면 지하철을 타세요. "If (you) intend to go to hospital, take a subway."
4 미국에 입국하려면 비자를 받아야 해요. "If (you) intend to enter the States, (you) have to receive a visa."
5 이 회사에 취직하려면 대학 졸업장을 제출하세요. "If (you) intend to get employed in this company, submit (your) college diploma."
6 브로드웨이 쇼를 보려면 뉴욕에 가야 돼요. "If (you) intend to see a Broadway show, (you) must go to New York."
7 테니스를 치려면 공하고 라켓이 필요해요. "If (you) intend to play tennis, (you) need a ball and a racket."
8 화장실을 사용하려면 요금을 내세요. "If (you) intend to use a toilet, pay the fee."

Exercise 9.6

1 편지를 읽으면 읽을수록 화가 나요.
2 날씨가 흐리면 흐릴수록 추워요.
3 시간이 지나면 지날수록 옛날이 그리워요.
4 크면 클수록 비쌌어요.
5 그 책을 읽으면 읽을수록 재미있었어요.

Exercise 9.7

1 한국에 살면 살수록 좋아요. "The more (I) live in Korea, the better (it) is."
2 사람들을 만나면 만날수록 피곤합니다. "The more (I) meet people, the more tired (I) am."
3 돈을 쓰면 쓸수록 필요합니다. "The more (I) spend money, the more (I) need (it)."
4 여행을 하면 할수록 많이 배울 거예요. "The more (you) travel, the more (you) will learn."
5 바쁘면 바쁠수록 건강 조심하세요. "The busier (you) are, take more care of (your) health."

Exercise 9.8

1 아기가 울거든 아기를 안아 주세요.
2 맛있거든 더 시킵시다.
3 크리스마스 트리를 만들거든 사진을 찍으세요.
4 이번 주말에 일하거든 파티에 오지 마세요.
5 나중에 메리를 만나거든 메세지를 전해 줍시다.

Exercise 9.9

1 추천서가 필요하거든 저한테 연락하세요. "If (you) need a recommendation letter, contact me."
2 또 머리가 아프거든 약을 드세요. "If (your) head aches again, take medicines."
3 걱정거리가 있거든 말하세요. "If (you) have a source of anxiety, talk (to me)."
4 심심하거든 TV 보세요. "If (you) feel bored, watch TV."
5 병원에 가거든 박선생님을 만나세요. "If (you) go to the hospital, meet Dr. Park."

Exercise 9.10

1 점심을 늦게 먹었거든요. "(I) ate lunch late, you know."
2 목이 아프거든요. "(My) throat hurts, you know."
3 다이어트를 하고 있거든요. "(I) am on diet, you know."
4 돈이 없거든요. "(I) do not have money, you know."
5 술을 못 마시거든요. "(I) cannot drink alcohol, you know."
6 사이즈가 작았거든요. "The size was small, you know."

Exercise 9.11

1 여자 친구가 행복해야 저도 행복해요.
2 세일을 해야 살 수 있어요.
3 열심히 공부해야 의사가 될 수 있어요.
4 일을 그만둬야 여행을 할 수 있어요.
5 담배를 끊어야 병이 나을 수 있어요.

Exercise 9.12

1 시험을 잘 봐야 법대에 들어갈 수 있어요. "Only if (you) do well on the test, (you) can enter law school."
2 아르바이트를 해야 학비를 낼 수 있어요. "Only if (I) do a side job, (I) can pay (my) tuition."
3 저금을 해야 새 소파를 살 수 있어요. "Only if (we) save money, (we) can buy a new sofa."
4 파리에 가야 에펠타워를 볼 수 있어요. "Only if (you) go to Paris, (you) can see Eiffel Tower."
5 크리스틴을 만나야 책을 받을 수 있어요. "Only if (you) meet Christine, (you) can receive the book."

Unit 10

Exercise 10.1

1 아침을 먹고 운동합니다.
2 이를 닦고 자요.
3 선생님한테 먼저 물어 보고 화장실에 갑니까?
4 예약을 하고 떠납시다.
5 대학교를 졸업하고 취직하고 싶어요.
6 수잔은 눈이 크고 조용해요.
7 팀은 목소리가 좋고 유머가 있어요.
8 앤드류는 겸손하고 부지런해요.

Exercise 10.2

1 세수를 하고 옷을 갈아 입으세요. "Wash (your) face and then change (your) clothes."
2 숙제를 하고 인터넷을 쓰겠어요. "(I) will do (my) homework and then use the internet."
3 샤워를 하고 저녁을 먹읍시다. "(Let us) take a shower and then eat dinner."
4 키가 크고 얼굴이 작았어요 "(His) height was tall and (his) face was small."
5 존이 31 살이고 의사입니다. "John is 31 years old and (he) is a doctor."

Exercise 10.3

1 폴의 목소리가 크며 부드럽습니다.
2 제임스가 과학자이며 발명가입니다.
3 웬디가 배우이며 가수입니다.
4 오늘 날씨가 맑으며 선선합니다.
5 그 학교가 좋으며 유명합니다.
6 기차가 안전하며 편합니다.

Exercise 10.4

1 테렌스가 커피를 마시며 신문을 읽고 있어요. "Terrence is reading newspapers, drinking coffee."
2 그레이스가 텔레비전을 보며 저녁을 먹었어요. "Grace ate dinner, watching TV."
3 리처드가 팝콘을 먹으며 영화를 봐요. "Richard sees a movie, eating popcorn."
4 에스더가 땀을 흘리며 테니스를 치고 있어요. "Esther is playing tennis, sweating."
5 로버트가 울며 소리 질렀어요. "Robert shouted crying."
6 니콜이 날씬하며 착해요. "Nicole is slender and tenderhearted."
7 클라라가 예쁘며 성격이 좋아요. "Clara is pretty and (her) personality is good."
8 로라는 머리가 길며 친절했어요. "As for Laura, (her) hair was long, and (she) was nice."
9 서울은 날씨가 흐리며 비가 오겠어요. "As for Seoul, the weather will be cloudy and rain may fall."
10 이 방이 크며 시원해요. "This room is big and cool."

Exercise 10.5

1 부자이거나 거지이거나 제 형이에요.
2 어렵거나 쉽거나 한국어를 공부하고 싶어요.
3 오거나 안 오거나 기다릴 거예요.
4 빌려주거나 안 빌려주거나 물어 볼 거예요.
5 재미있거나 재미없거나 그 드라마를 다시 보십시오.

Exercise 10.6

1 보통 언제 영화를 보거나 외식을 합니까? "When (do) you usually see movies or dine out?"
2 꽃을 사거나 케이크를 만드십시오. "Buy flowers or make cakes."
3 아침에 조깅을 하거나 요가를 해요. "In the morning, (I) jog or do yoga."

4 현금으로 내거나 카드로 지불할 거예요. "(I) will pay by cash or defray by a card."
5 산으로 가거나 바닷가로 갑시다. "(Let us) go to mountains or beach."

Exercise 10.7

1 점심을 먹든지 커피를 마실 거예요.
2 집에 가든지 커피숍에 갑시다.
3 사과 주스를 마시든지 토마토 주스를 마시세요.
4 액션 영화를 보든지 공포 영화를 봅시다.
5 춥든지 덥든지 테니스를 칠 거예요.

Exercise 10.8

1 콜라를 사든지 주스를 사겠어요. "(I) will buy cola or juice."
2 소고기를 먹든지 돼지고기를 먹읍시다. "(Let us) eat beef or pork."
3 커피를 마시든지 케이크를 먹어요. "Drink coffee or eat cake."
4 날씨가 흐리든지 추울 거예요. "The weather will be cloudy or cold."
5 신문을 읽든지 TV 를 볼 거예요. "(I) will read newspapers or watch TV."

Unit 11

Exercise 11.1

1 울면서 전화를 하고 있어요.
2 여행을 하면서 친구를 사귈 거예요?
3 일어나면서 침대에서 떨어지지 마십시오.
4 요리하면서 접시를 깨뜨리지 맙시다.
5 자전거를 타면서 넘어졌습니까?

Exercise 11.2

1 톰하고 제리가 웃으면서 이야기하고 있어요. "Tom and Jerry are talking, smiling."
2 스티브가 책을 읽으면서 혼자 중얼거려요. "Steve murmurs alone, while reading a book."
3 루이스가 자면서 코를 골았어요. "Lewis snored, while sleeping."
4 해리가 노래를 하면서 샤워를 해요. "Harry takes a shower, singing."
5 조디가 길을 걸으면서 무언가 찾고 있었어요. "Jodie was looking for something, while walking on the road."

Exercise 11.3

1 취직하자마자 결혼하고 싶습니다.
2 남자 친구를 만나자마자 울었어요.
3 침대에 눕자마자 코를 골 거예요.
4 대학을 졸업하자마자 무엇을 하고 싶어요?
5 런던에 도착하자마자 누나한테 전화하십시오.
6 영화관에 들어가자마자 팝콘을 삽시다.

Exercise 11.4

1 일어나자마자 세수를 합니다. "(I) wash (my) face as soon as (I) get up."
2 새 집으로 이사를 하자마자 주소를 바꿨어요. "(I) changed (my) address as soon as (I) moved to the new house."
3 대학을 졸업하자마자 차를 살 거예요? "Will (you) buy a car as soon as (you) graduate from college?"
4 점심을 먹자마자 커피를 시킵시다. "(Let us) order coffee as soon as (we) eat lunch."
5 세수를 하자마자 양치질을 하십시오. "Brush (your) teeth as soon as (you) wash (your) face."

Exercise 11.5

1 텔레비전을 보다가 잤어요.
2 슈퍼마켓에서 야채를 사다가 친구와 마주쳤어요.
3 문을 열다가 손목을 다쳤어요.
4 농구를 하다가 발목을 삐었어요.
5 편지를 쓰다가 화장실에 갔어요.

Exercise 11.6

1 신문을 읽다가 졸았어요. "As (I) read newspapers, (I) dozed off."
2 영화를 보다가 울었어요. "As (I) saw the movie, (I) cried."
3 오른쪽으로 가다가 멈추세요. "Go to the right side and then stop."
4 계단을 올라가다가 넘어졌어요? "Did (you) fall as (you) went up the stairs?"
5 누가 요리를 하다가 접시를 깼어요? "Who broke dishes while cooking?"

Exercise 11.7

1 열심히 공부를 안 하다가는 대학에 못 들어가요.
2 담배를 계속 피우다가는 암에 걸릴 수 있어요.
3 과속을 하다가는 사고가 날 거예요.
4 연락을 안 하다가는 서로 잊어 버릴 수 있어요.
5 계속 거절하다가는 기회를 놓칠 수 있어요.
6 매일 위스키를 마시다가는 알콜 중독자가 될 거예요.

Exercise 11.8

1 자기 전에 많이 먹다가는 살찔 거예요. "If (she) eats a lot before going to bed, (she) may gain weight."
2 계속 놀다가는 시험에 떨어질 수 있어요. "If (you) continue to play, (you) can fail the test."
3 돈만 쓰다가는 거지가 될 거예요. "If (he) only spends money, (he may) become a beggar."
4 열심히 일을 안 하다가는 회사에서 쫓겨날 수 있어요. "If (you) do not work hard, (you) can be expelled out from the company."
5 많이 먹다가는 배탈날 거예요. "If (he) eats a lot, (he) may have a stomachache."

Unit 12

Exercise 12.1

1 껌을 씹고 있는데 이가 아파요.
2 길을 청소하고 있는데 도와 줄래요?
3 선물을 사야 하는데 백화점에 같이 갑시다.
4 어제 에릭을 만났는데 전하고 똑같았어요.
5 공부를 열심히 했는데 시험에 떨어졌어요.

Exercise 12.2

1 부엌을 수리하고 있는데 비싸요. "(They) are repairing the kitchen, but (it) is expensive."
2 지금 학교에 가는데 같이 갑시다. "(I) am going to school now, and (let us) go together."
3 물을 끓이고 있는데 마실래요? "(I) am boiling water, and will (you) drink (it)?"
4 백화점에 갔는데 사람들이 너무 많았어요. "(I) went to the department store, and there were too many people."
5 지난 주에 소포를 부쳤는데 도착했어요? "(I) mailed the package last week, and did (it) arrive (there)?"

Exercise 12.3

1 작년에 학생이었는데 이제 선생님이에요.
2 전에 사람들이 많았는데 이제 별로 없어요.
3 어제는 더웠는데 오늘은 선선해요.
4 값은 쌌는데 양이 적었어요.
5 날씨가 나빴는데 손님이 많았어요.

Exercise 12.4

1 기타를 배우고 싶은데 같이 배웁시다. "(I) want to learn (how to play) a guitar, and (let us) learn (it) together."
2 머리가 아픈데 약 있어요? "(My) head aches, and do (you) have medicines?"
3 가방이 무거운데 도와 주실래요? "The bag is heavy, and will (you) help (me)?"
4 앤드류는 미국 사람인데 스페인어도 잘 해요. "As for Andrew, (he) is an American, but (he) also speaks Spanish well."
5 요즈음 무척 바쁜데 다음 주에 연락주세요. "(I) am very busy nowadays, so contact (me) next week."

Exercise 12.5

1 내일은 좀 바쁜데요.
2 한국 음식이 먹고 싶은데요.
3 5 달라밖에 없는데요.
4 아직 음식이 안 나왔는데요.
5 시끄러운데요.

Exercise 12.6

1 영어 선생님인데도 영어를 잘 못해요.
2 양이 적은데도 맛있어요.
3 월급이 많은데도 그만둘 거예요.
4 시험이 어려웠는데도 합격했어요.
5 가난했는데도 행복했어요.

Exercise 12.7

1 약을 먹었는데도 머리가 아파요. "Although (I) took medicines, (my) head aches."
2 물을 두 컵이나 마셨는데도 목말라요? "(You) drank as many as two cups of water, but are (you) thirsty?"
3 그 차가 비싼데도 살 거예요. "Although that car is expensive, (I) will buy (it)."

4 히터를 켰는데도 방이 추웠어요. "Although (I) turned on the heater, the room was cold."
5 돈이 없었는데도 서울에 가고 싶었어요. "Although (I) did not have money, (I) wanted to go to Seoul."

Unit 13

Exercise 13.1

1 데이브가 서울에 있지만 바바라한테 매일 전화해요.
2 가방이 크지만 가벼워요.
3 같이 가고 싶지만 약속이 있어요.
4 내일 시험을 볼 거지만 공부를 안 했어요.
5 여름에 덥웠지만 겨울에 추웠어요.

Exercise 13.2

1 한국어는 어렵지만 재미있어요. "Although Korean is difficult, (it) is interesting."
2 미국으로 유학을 가고 싶지만 등록금때문에 걱정돼요. "Although (I) want to study abroad in America, (I) feel uneasy because of tuition."
3 고기를 좋아하지만 자주 먹지 못 해요. "Although (I) like meat, (I) cannot eat (it) often."
4 영문학을 전공했지만 영어를 잘 못해요. "Although (I) majored in English literature, (I) cannot speak English well."
5 초대장을 보냈지만 안 올 것 같아요. "Although (I) sent an invitation, (it) seems that (he) will not come."

Exercise 13.3

1 한국어를 일년 배웠으나 아직 어려워요.
2 한 시간 기다렸으나 안 왔어요.
3 오빠하고 다퉜으나 금방 화해 했어요.
4 거실이 넓으나 부엌이 좁아요.
5 방이 깨끗하나 시끄러워요.

Exercise 13.4

1 레이먼드는 키가 크나 뚱뚱해요. "As for Raymond, (his) height is tall, but (he) is chubby."
2 조지는 활발하나 데이빗은 내성적이에요. "As for George, (he) is active, but as for David, (he) is introverted."

3 백화점이 가까우나 지하철 역이 멀어요. "The department store is near,
but the subway station is far."
4 택시가 편하나 비싸요. "Taxi is convenient, but (it) is expensive."
5 음식은 쌌으나 서비스가 나빴어요. "As for food, (it) was cheap, but the
service was bad."

Exercise 13.5

1 음식이 맛있으나 맛없으나 다 먹읍시다.
2 시험이 쉬우나 어려우나 봐야 해요.
3 조깅을 하나 요가를 하나 매일 하십시오.
4 한국으로 가나 일본으로 가나 비자가 필요해요.
5 돼지고기나 소고기나 다 비싸요.

Exercise 13.6

1 히터를 켜도 여전히 추워요.
2 담배를 피웠어도 건강했어요.
3 많이 먹어도 살이 안 쪄요.
4 두 시간을 기다렸어도 연락이 없었어요.
5 아파도 학교에 갈 거예요.

Exercise 13.7

1 에밀리가 어려도 키가 커요. "Even if Emily is young, (she) is tall."
2 한국 음식이 매워도 맛있어요. "Even if Korean food is spicy, (it) is
delicious."
3 로버트가 게을러도 똑똑해요. "Even if Robert is lazy, (he) is smart."
4 옷이 비싸도 사고 싶었어요. "Even if the dress was expensive, (I) wanted
to buy (it)."
5 사이즈가 작아도 귀여웠어요. "Even if the size was small, (it) was
cute."

Unit 14

Exercise 14.1

1 피터의 이야기를 믿어도 돼요.
2 내 컴퓨터를 써도 돼요.
3 에어콘을 틀어도 돼요.
4 전등을 꺼도 돼요.
5 문을 닫아도 돼요.

Exercise 14.2

1 이제 퇴근해도 돼요. "(You) may go home now."
2 눈을 떠도 돼요. "(You) may open (your) eyes."
3 얼굴을 씻어도 돼요. "(You) may wash (your) face."
4 손을 잡아도 돼요. "(You) may hold (her) hand."
5 샤워를 해도 돼요. "(You) may take a shower."

Exercise 14.3

1 열쇠를 잃어 버리면 안 돼요.
2 다리를 건너면 안 돼요.
3 맥주를 마시면 안 돼요.
4 쓰레기를 버리면 안 돼요.
5 여기서 담배를 피우면 안 돼요.

Exercise 14.4

1 국이 싱거우면 안 돼요. "It would not be all right if the soup is watery."
2 반찬이 짜면 안 돼요. "It would not be all right if side dishes are salty."
3 영화가 재미없으면 안 돼요. "It would not be all right if the movie is uninteresting."
4 방이 작으면 안 돼요. "It would not be all right if the room is small."
5 길이 좁으면 안 돼요. "It would not be all right if the road is narrow."

Exercise 14.5

1 열심히 공부하지 않으면 안 돼요.
2 사무실을 청소하지 않으면 안 돼요.
3 설거지를 하지 않으면 안 돼요.
4 밖에 나가지 않으면 안 돼요.
5 집에 있지 않으면 안 돼요.

Exercise 14.6

1 시험 공부를 하지 않으면 안 돼요. "(I) must study for the test."
2 일을 시작하지 않으면 안 돼요. "(I) must begin (my) work."
3 손을 씻지 않으면 안 돼요. "(You) must wash (your) hands."
4 내일 아침 일찍 일어나지 않으면 안 돼요. "(You) must get up early tomorrow morning."
5 운전면허를 따지 않으면 안 돼요. "(I) must obtain a driver's license."

Exercise 14.7

1 의사이어야 돼요.
2 유니폼을 입어야 돼요.
3 돈을 벌어야 돼요.
4 얼굴을 씻어야 돼요.
5 병원에 가야 돼요.

Exercise 14.8

1 여행 가방을 싸야 됩니다. "(I) must pack a travel bag."
2 전기세를 내야 됩니다. "(I) must pay for electricity bill."
3 날씨가 좋아야 됩니다. "The weather has to be good."
4 가격이 싸야 됩니다. "The price has to be cheap."
5 고등학생이라야 됩니다. "(He) has to be a high-school student."

Exercise 14.9

1 쓰면 안 돼요.
2 퇴근해도 돼요.
3 닫아도 돼요.
4 타면 안 돼요.

Exercise 14.10

1 저기서 담배를 피워도 돼요.
2 방에서 사진을 찍어도 돼요.
3 한국어 수업을 안 들으면 안 돼요.
4 코트를 안 사면 안 돼요.
5 큰소리로 말하지 않으면 안 돼요.
6 안전 벨트를 매지 않으면 안 돼요.
7 여기에 주차해야 돼요.
8 파리를 떠나야 돼요.
9 냉장고를 열면 안 돼요.
10 그림을 만지면 안 돼요.

Unit 15

Exercise 15.1

1 a 팔아요.   b 팔려요.
2 a 들었어요.   b 들려요.
3 a 놓을까요?   b 놓여 있어요.

Exercise 15.2

1 올리브 기름만 씁니다.
2 이 풍선이 생일 파티에 쓰여요.
3 몇 시에 가게를 닫아요?
4 문이 바람에 닫혔어요.
5 쥐를 잡았어요.
6 도둑이 경찰한테 잡혔어요.
7 모기가 물어요.
8 존이 모기한테 많이 물렸어요.
9 아기가 울면 안으세요 (or 안아 주세요).
10 아기가 아빠한테 안겼어요.

Exercise 15.3

1 (I) heap a desk with books.
2 Because of the stress, stress is piled up.
3 (I) removed the laundry from a clothes-line.
4 Fortunately, fog was lifted up.
5 The bear bit a fish.
6 (I) was bitten by mosquitoes.
7 Please sell (it) at a cheap price.
8 Sweaters are sold well.
9 Please hang up the phone first.
10 The electricity is disconnected due to rain.

Exercise 15.4

1 깨웁니다.
2 입힙니다.
3 신깁니다.
4 앉힙니다.
5 재웁니다.

Exercise 15.5

1 아이를 울리지 마세요.
2 유니폼을 입혔어요?
3 학생들을 웃겨 주세요
4 저를 6 시에 깨워 주세요.
5 물을 끓여 주세요.
6 아기를 침대에 눕히세요.
7 고기를 태우지 마세요.

Exercise 15.6

1 What shall (we) eat today?
2 Susan feeds a cat.
3 Peter sleeps about 7 hours everyday.
4 Usually (my) older sister put the child to sleep around 8 o'clock.
5 Chris often wears jeans.
6 Please dress (him) a T-shirt.
7 Please sit in the back.
8 Please make Andrew sit in the front row.
9 Don't take off (your) sweater.
10 Please undress (his) jacket.

Exercise 15.7

1 국을 맵게 해 주세요.
2 방을 따뜻하게 해 주세요.
3 주위를 어둡게 해 주세요.
4 리사를 행복하게 해 주세요.
5 부인을 기쁘게 해 주세요.

Exercise 15.8

1 Please make (your) presentation longer.
2 Please make (it) delicious (for me).
3 Please make (it) cheap (for me).
4 Please make (him/her) drink coffee.
5 Please make (him/her) chew a gum.

Unit 16

Exercise 16.1

1 예쁜 디자인
2 한국에서 제일 유명한 관광지
3 한국에서 제일 인기있는 배우
4 제일 비싼 시계
5 긴 머리

Exercise 16.2

1 이 집에서 제일 조용한 방 "the quietest room in this house"
2 데니엘이 가고 싶은 학교 "the school Daniel wants to go to"
3 제일 아름다운 섬 "the most beautiful island"

4 미국에서 제일 높은 산 "the highest mountain in the U.S.A."
5 제일 싼 옷 "the cheapest clothes"

Exercise 16.3

1 피터가 요즈음 읽는 책
2 겨울에 즐기는 스포츠
3 한국 사람이 매일 먹는 음식
4 제시카가 일하는 가게
5 언니가 사귀는 남자

Exercise 16.4

1 친구가 사는 과일 "the fruit which (my) friend buys"
2 시카고에서 갈아타는 기차 "the train that (I) change at Chicago"
3 형이 사는 아파트 "the apartment where (my) older brother lives"
4 누나가 쓰는 컴퓨터 "the computer which (my) older sister uses"
5 내가 같이 일하는 사람 "the person that I work with"

Exercise 16.5

1 같이 찍은 사진
2 지난 달에 본 영화
3 어제 바꾼 옷
4 아침에 마신 우유
5 오후에 판 물건

Exercise 16.6

1 어제 부른 노래 "the song that (I) sang yesterday"
2 작년에 만난 사람 "the person that (I) met last year"
3 지난 주에 받은 선물 "the present that (I) received last week"
4 아침에 버린 쓰레기 "the garbage that (I) threw away in the morning"
5 내가 만든 음식 "the food that (I) made"

Exercise 16.7

1 내가 내일 요리할 음식
2 우유를 담을 병
3 환자가 마실 물
4 도서관에서 빌릴 책
5 우체국에서 부칠 소포

Exercise 16.8

1 제이슨이 입을 양복 "the suit which Jason will wear"
2 누나가 결혼할 사람 "the person whom (my) older sister will marry"
3 우리가 다음 주에 이사갈 집 "the house where we will move into next week"
4 네가 내일 빌릴 책 "the book which you will borrow tomorrow"
5 제임스가 앉을 자리 "the seat where James will sit"

Exercise 16.9

1 기타를 치는 마리아
2 내일 일본으로 떠날 사람
3 케이크를 만든 여자
4 내가 좋아하는 계절
5 공을 던진 아이
6 애플 컴퓨터가 있는 학생
7 화요일에 로라를 만날 남자
8 비싼 차가 있는 톰
9 경찰관인 데이브
10 어제 편지를 보낸 손님

Unit 17

Exercise 17.1

1 와싱턴에서 출발하는 것 같아요. "(It) seems that (they) depart from Washington."
2 오후에 도착하는 것 같아요. "(It) seems that (they) arrive (here) in the afternoon."
3 친구를 기다리는 것 같아요. "(It) seems that (he) waits for (his) friend."
4 돈이 별로 없는 것 같아요. "(It) seems that (he) does not have much money."
5 서울에 친구가 많은 것 같아요. "(It) seems that (she) has many friends in Seoul."
6 찌개가 짠 것 같아요. "(It) seems that the stew is salty."
7 앤드류가 성실하고 똑똑한 것 같아요. "(It) seems that Andrew is earnest and smart."
8 날씨가 춥고 흐린 것 같아요. "(It) seems that the weather is cold and cloudy."
9 친구가 부지런한 것 같아요. "(It) seems that (your) friend is diligent."
10 가격이 싼 것 같아요. "(It) seems that the price is cheap."

Exercise 17.2

1 신혼 여행은 라스베가스로 갈 것 같아요. "As for (their) honeymoon, (it) seems that (they) will go to Las Vegas."
2 폴이 담배를 끊을 것 같아요. "(It) seems that Paul will quit smoking."
3 다음 수요일에 집에 돌아갈 것 같아요. "(It) seems that (they) will return home next Wednesday."
4 형이 돈을 빌려 줄 것 같아요. "(It) seems that (my) older brother will lend (me) money."
5 다음 학기부터 기숙사에서 살 것 같아요. "(It) seems that (they) will live in the dormitory from next semester."
6 제인이 노래를 잘 할 것 같아요. "(It) seems that Jane will sing well."
7 음식이 맛없을 것 같아요. "(It) seems that the food will be tasteless."
8 매일 바쁠 것 같아요. "(It) looks like (I) will be busy everyday."
9 날씨가 더울 것 같아요. "(It) looks like the weather will be hot."
10 존이 겸손할 것 같아요. "(It) seems that John will be humble."

Exercise 17.3

1 제임스가 한국에서 영어를 가르치는 모양이에요. "(It) appears that James teaches English in Korea."
2 토마스가 부엌에서 요리하는 모양이에요. "(It) appears that Thomas cooks in the kitchen."
3 존이 다리를 건너는 모양이에요. "(It) appears that John crosses the bridge."
4 샌디가 친구를 기다리는 모양이에요. "(It) appears that Sandy waits for (her) friends."
5 앤서니가 차를 고치는 모양이에요. "(It) appears that Anthony repairs (his) car."
6 사라가 편지를 부치는 모양이에요. "(It) appears that Sarah sends the letter."
7 찰스가 커피를 시키는 모양이에요. "(It) appears that Charles orders coffee."
8 웬디가 가난한 모양이에요. "(It) appears that Wendy is poor."
9 케이트가 부지런한 모양이에요. "(It) appears that Kate is diligent."
10 샐리가 인기가 많은 모양이에요. "(It) appears that Sally is popular."

Exercise 17.4

1 열쇠를 찾고 있는 듯합니다.
2 토요일에 일하는 듯합니다.
3 집을 판 듯합니다.
4 직장을 그만둘 듯합니다.
5 국이 짠 듯합니다.

6 반지가 너무 비싼 듯합니다.
7 사이즈가 너무 작을 듯합니다.
8 방이 너무 추울 듯합니다.

Exercise 17.5

1 친구를 돕고 있는 듯해요. "(It) seems that (he) is helping (his) friends."
2 일본 노래를 부르고 있는 듯해요. "(It) seems that (they) are singing a Japanese song."
3 컴퓨터를 고치고 있는 듯해요. "(It) seems that (he) is repairing (his) computer."
4 눈이 오는 듯해요. "(It) seems that (it) snows."
5 음식이 짠 듯해요. "(It) seems that the food is salty."

Exercise 17.6

1 낸시가 다음 달에 한국에 가나 봐요. "(I) guess that Nancy goes to Korea next month."
2 져스틴이 병원에서 일하나 봐요. "(I) guess that Justin works at the hospital."
3 나오미가 이번 봄에 결혼하나 봐요. "(I) guess that Naomi marries this spring."
4 샘이 로라를 좋아하나 봐요. "(I) guess that Sam likes Laura."
5 티모티가 아픈가 봐요. "(I) guess that Timothy is sick."
6 김치가 싱거운가 봐요. "(I) guess that kimchi is watery."
7 오늘 날씨가 더운가 봐요. "(I) guess that today's weather is hot."
8 음식이 맛없나 봐요. "(I) guess that the food is tasteless."
9 첼시가 대학원생인가 봐요. "(I) guess that Chelsea is a graduate student."
10 브래드가 캐나다 사람인가 봐요. "(I) guess that Brad is a Canadian."

Exercise 17.7

1 기뻐 보여요.
2 무서워 보여요.
3 외로워 보여요.
4 심심해 보여요.
5 행복해 보여요.
6 흥분돼 보였어요.
7 긴장돼 보였어요.
8 신나 보였어요.
9 짜증나 보였어요.
10 화나 보였어요.

Exercise 17.8

1 케이트가 젊어 보여요. "Kate looks young."
2 윌리엄이 바빠 보여요. "William looks busy."
3 린다가 아파 보여요. "Linda looks sick."
4 사이몬이 슬퍼 보여요. "Simon looks sad."
5 제시가 예뻐 보여요. "Jessie looks pretty."
6 애플파이가 맛있어 보여요. "The apple pie looks delicious."
7 귀걸이가 비싸 보여요. "The earring looks expensive."
8 안경이 싸 보여요. "(His) glasses look inexpensive."
9 집안이 깨끗해 보여요. "The inside of the house looks clean."
10 노트북이 가벼워 보여요. "The notebook looks light."

Unit 18

Exercise 18.1

1 학교에 가는 길에 소포를 보낼 거예요.
2 병원에 가는 길에 선생님하고 마주쳤어요.
3 도서관에서 오는 길에 지갑을 잃어 버렸어요.
4 교회에서 오는 길에 쓰러졌어요.
5 가게에서 오는 길에 존을 만났어요.

Exercise 18.2

1 시험에 떨어져 본 적이 없어요.
2 맨하턴에 가 본 적이 있어요.
3 김치를 먹어 본 적이 있어요.
4 결혼을 해 본 적이 없어요.
5 총을 쏴 본 적이 있어요.

Exercise 18.3

1 장학금을 받아 본 적이 있어요. "(I) have an experience of receiving a scholarship."
2 태권도를 배워 본 적이 있어요. "(I) have an experience of learning Taekwondo."
3 형과 다퉈 본 적이 있어요. "(I) have an experience of quarrelling with (my) older brother."
4 한국에서 스키를 타 본 적이 있어요. "(I) have an experience of skiing in Korea."
5 일요일에 일해 본 적이 있어요. "(I) have an experience of working on Sunday."

Exercise 18.4

1 해리가 빨래를 하는 동안에 케이트가 요리해요.
2 내가 열쇠를 찾는 동안에 지나가 짐을 쌀 거예요.
3 존이 운전을 하는 동안에 샐리가 지도를 봤어요.
4 찰스가 일하는 동안에 씬디가 커피숍에서 기다렸어요.
5 내가 세일즈맨하고 흥정을 하는 동안에 아내가 가게를 구경했어요.

Exercise 18.5

1 에드워드가 모자를 사고 있는 동안에 피터가 화장실에 갔어요. "While Edward was buying a hat, Peter went to the restroom."
2 내가 조깅을 하고 있는 동안에 아내가 슈퍼마켓에 갔어요. "While I was jogging, (my) wife went to the supermarket."
3 루이스가 친구하고 이야기하고 있는 동안에 에리카가 음식을 시켰어요. "While Luis was talking to (his) friend, Erica ordered food."
4 메건이 자고 있는 동안에 조이스가 TV 를 봤어요. "While Megan was sleeping, Joyce watched TV."
5 우리가 자리를 찾고 있는 동안에 샘이 팝콘을 사러 나갔어요. "While we were looking for seats, Sam went out to buy popcorn."

Exercise 18.6

1 운전하는 중이에요.
2 나무를 심는 중이에요.
3 컴퓨터를 고치는 중이에요.
4 편지를 쓰는 중이에요.
5 다리를 건너는 중이에요.

Exercise 18.7

1 짐을 싸는 중이에요. "(I) am in the middle of packing loads."
2 중국 음식을 시키는 중이에요. "(I) am in the middle of ordering Chinese food."
3 에릭하고 테니스를 치는 중이에요. "(I) am in the middle of playing tennis with Eric."
4 돼지고기를 써는 중이에요. "(I) am in the middle of cutting pork (into piecies)."
5 양복을 입는 중이에요. "(I) am in the middle of wearing a suit."

Exercise 18.8

1 집이 시끄러운 편이에요.
2 방이 어두운 편이에요.

3 낸시의 음식이 짠 편이에요.
4 나오미가 아침을 굶는 편이에요.
5 매일 운동하는 편이에요.

Exercise 18.9

1 스티브가 맥주를 좋아하는 편이에요. "Steve kind of likes beer."
2 헬렌이 요리를 잘 하는 편이에요. "Helen kind of cooks well."
3 어머니가 잔소리를 하시는 편이에요. "(My) mother tends to do useless talk."
4 시험이 어려운 편이에요. "The test is kind of hard."
5 오늘 날씨가 흐린 편이에요. "Today's weather is kind of cloudy."

Unit 19

Exercise 19.1

1 사이몬이 지시하는 대로 할 거예요.
2 기대한 대로 편지가 어제 도착했어요.
3 마시고 싶은 대로 마실 거예요?
4 자고 싶은 대로 자세요.
5 먹고 싶은 대로 먹읍시다.

Exercise 19.2

1 일어나는 대로 샤워할 거예요. "(I) will take a shower as soon as (I) get up."
2 식사를 마치는 대로 사무실로 돌아갈 거예요? "Will (you) return to the office as soon as (you) finish (your) meal?"
3 열쇠를 찾는 대로 떠나세요. "Leave as soon as (you) find the key."
4 서류를 받는 대로 일을 시작하십시오. "Start working as soon as (you) receive the document."
5 책을 받는 대로 돌려줍시다. "(Let us) return the book (to them) as soon as (we) receive (it)."

Exercise 19.3

1 보통 이를 닦은 후에 면도를 해요.
2 아침 식사를 한 후에 출근해요.
3 소포를 보낸 후에 학교로 돌아왔어요.
4 선물을 산 후에 파티에 갈 거예요.
5 일을 끝낸 후에 쉬고 싶어요.

Exercise 19.4

1 샤워를 한 후에 잘 거예요. "(I) will go to bed after taking a shower."
2 물을 끓인 후에 라면을 넣으세요. "Put ramyon after boiling water."
3 대학을 졸업한 후에 취직 준비를 하겠어요. "(I) will prepare for employment after graduating from college."
4 창문을 닫은 후에 전등을 끄십시오. "Turn off the electric lamp after closing the window."
5 일을 마친 후에 집에 갔습니다. "(They) went home after finishing (their) work."

Exercise 19.5

1 자고 있는 척하지 마세요.
2 열심히 일하고 있는 척하지 마세요.
3 선물을 좋아하는 척해요.
4 수영할 수 있는 척했어요.
5 미국 사람인 척할 거예요?

Exercise 19.6

1 제임스가 비밀 번호를 아는 척해요. "James pretends that (he) knows the secret code."
2 지나하고 로날드가 행복한 척해요. "Gina and Ronald pretend that (they) are happy."
3 패트릭이 항상 돈이 없는 척해요. "Patrick always pretends that (he) has no money."
4 제임스가 제시카를 싫어하는 척해요. "James pretends that (he) dislikes Jessica."
5 앤서니가 공부에 관심이 없는 척해요. "Anthony pretends that (he) is uninterested in studying."

Exercise 19.7

1 교수님을 함께 만나는 거예요.
2 우리 모두 콘텍트 렌즈를 끼는 거예요.
3 이제부터 같이 사는 거예요.
4 물가가 높은 거예요.
5 조지가 솔직한 거예요.
6 제임스가 똑똑한 거예요.
7 새 차를 산 거예요.
8 지갑을 잃어버린 거예요.
9 지나도 파티에 초청한 거예요.
10 한국어를 전공한 거예요.

Exercise 19.8

1 늦게 일어나는 바람에 수업에 지각했어요. "(I) was late for the class because (I) got up late."
2 갑자기 비가 오는 바람에 옷이 젖었어요. "(My) dress got wet because (it) rained suddenly."
3 차가 고장이 나는 바람에 회사에 못 갔어요. "(I) could not go to the company because (my) car broke down."
4 감기에 걸리는 바람에 공부를 못 했어요. "(I) could not study because (I) caught a cold."
5 바람이 부는 바람에 모자를 잃어 버렸어요. "(I) lost (my) hat because the wind blew."
6 소금을 많이 넣는 바람에 음식이 너무 짰어요. "The food was too salty because (I) put too much salt (into it)."
7 코를 고는 바람에 잠을 못 잤어요. "(I) could not sleep because (he) snored."
8 길에서 미끄러지는 바람에 허리를 다쳤어요. "(I) hurt (my) waist because (I) slid on the road."
9 차 사고가 나는 바람에 전화를 못 했어요. "(I) could not make a phone call because there was a car accident."
10 새벽에 일하는 바람에 감기에 걸렸어요. "(I) caught a cold because (I) worked at dawn."

Exercise 19.9

1 월급을 받을 때 기분이 좋습니다. "When (I) receive (my) salary, (I) feel good."
2 영화가 시작할 때 팝콘을 먹읍시다. "When the movie begins, (let us) eat popcorn."
3 숙제를 할 때 음악을 듣습니까? "Do (you) listen to music when (you) do (your) homework?"
4 맥주를 마실 때 노래를 부르십시오. "Sing a song, when (you) drink beer."
5 스테이크를 먹을 때 와인을 마십니다. "When (I) eat steak, (I) drink wine."
6 스트레스가 많을 때 운동을 하십시오. "When there is a lot of stress, do exercise."
7 도움이 필요할 때 친구들한테 연락할 겁니다. "When (I) need help, (I) will contact (my) friends."
8 결혼식에 갈 때 양복을 입었습니다. "When (I) went to the wedding ceremony, (I) wore a suit."
9 비가 올 때 우산이 필요합니다. "When (it) rains, (you) need an umbrella."

10 시간이 있을 때 코미디 영화를 보십시오. "When (you) have (some) time, see a comedy movie."
11 날씨가 흐릴 때 기분이 나쁩니다. "When the weather is cloudy, (I) feel bad."
12 여자친구 생일일 때 무슨 생일 선물을 준비합니까? "When it is (your) girl friend's birthday, what kind of birthday gift do (you) prepare?"
13 심심할 때 서점에 갑니다. "When (I) feel bored, (I) go to a book-store."
14 어렸을 때 의사가 되고 싶었습니까? "When (you) were young, did (you) want to become a doctor?"
15 날씨가 더울 때 짧은 바지를 입읍시다. "When the weather is hot, (let us) wear short pants."

Exercise 19.10

1 친구하고 싸울 뻔했어요. "(I) almost quarrelled with (my) friend."
2 물에 빠질 뻔했어요. "(I) almost fell into the water."
3 약속을 잊을 뻔했어요. "(I) almost forgot about the appointment."
4 문을 잠글 뻔했어요. "(I) almost locked the door."
5 게임을 질 뻔했어요. "(I) almost lost the game."
6 우리 팀이 경기를 이길 뻔했어요. "Our team almost won the game."
7 길에서 미끄러질 뻔했어요. "(I) almost slid on the road."
8 아이들한테 화낼 뻔했어요. "(I) almost got angry at (my) children."
9 와인을 마실 뻔했어요. "(I) almost drank wine."
10 길을 건널 뻔했어요. "(I) almost crossed the road."

Unit 20

Exercise 20.1

1 혼자 가게를 열 수 있어요.
2 그들에게 희망을 줄 수 있어요.
3 무대 위에서 춤을 출 수 있어요.
4 집을 팔 수 없어요.
5 이 수학 문제를 풀 수 없어요.

Exercise 20.2

1 트럭을 운전할 수 있어요. "(I) can drive a truck."
2 더위를 느낄 수 있어요. "(I) can feel the heat."
3 와인을 마실 수 있어요. "(I) can drink wine."
4 한국 노래를 부를 수 있어요. "(I) can sing Korea songs."
5 미국 친구를 사귈 수 있어요. "(I) can make American friends."

Exercise 20.3

1 일본 노래를 부를 줄 알아요.
2 중국 음식을 만들 줄 알아요.
3 스칼릿이 열쇠를 가지고 있을 줄 알았어요.
4 일요일에도 가게를 열 줄 알았어요.
5 오늘 교회에 있을 줄 알았어요.

Exercise 20.4

1 김치를 만들 줄 알아요. "(I) know how to make kimchi."
2 골프를 칠 줄 알아요. "(I) know how to play golf."
3 자전거를 탈 줄 알아요. "(I) know how to ride a bicycle."
4 여기서 회사까지 갈 줄 알아요. "(I) know how to get to the company from here."
5 수영할 줄 알아요. "(I) know how to swim."

Exercise 20.5

1 제리가 유명할 줄 몰랐어요.
2 장 교수님이 한국 사람일 줄 몰랐어요.
3 케이트가 공부를 잘 할 줄 몰랐어요.
4 남자 친구가 있을 줄 몰랐어요.
5 조지가 경찰관일 줄 몰랐어요.

Exercise 20.6

1 형이 월요일에 일본으로 갈 줄 몰랐어요. "(I) did not think that (my) older brother would go to Japan on Monday."
2 매튜가 토요일에 가게를 일찍 닫을 줄 몰랐어요. "(I) did not think that Matthew would close the store early on Saturday."
3 수잔이 한국에 갈 줄 몰랐어요. "(I) did not think that Susan would go to Korea."
4 사이먼이 운동을 잘 할 줄 몰랐어요. "(I) did not think that Simon would be good at sports."
5 찰스가 오늘 런던으로 떠날 줄 몰랐어요. "(I) did not think that Charles would leave for London today."

Exercise 20.7

1 옷 사이즈가 맞을 리가 없어요.
2 날씨가 좋을 리가 없어요.
3 그 영화가 재미있을 리가 없어요.
4 앤드류가 게으를 리가 없어요.
5 윌리엄이 한국 역사를 전공할 리가 없어요.

Exercise 20.8

1 대학 생활이 재미있을 리가 없어요. "There is no possibility that college life is fun."
2 지하철이 편할 리가 없어요. "There is no possibility that a subway is convenient."
3 테니스가 쉬울 리가 없어요. "There is no possibility that (playing) tennis is easy."
4 택시 요금이 쌀 리가 없어요. "There is no possibility that taxi fee is cheap."
5 디자인이 예쁠 리가 없어요. "There is no possibility that the design is pretty."

Unit 21

Exercise 21.1

1 제리가 몇 살인지 아세요? "Do (you) know how old Jerry is?"
2 영화가 몇 시에 시작하는지 아세요? "Do (you) know what time the movie starts?"
3 어디에서 일하는지 아세요? "Do (you) know where (he) works?"
4 어디에서 버스를 타는지 아세요? "Do (you) know where (he) rides the bus?"
5 제임스의 방이 몇 층에 있는지 아세요? "Do (you) know on what floor James' room is?"
6 줄리가 왜 파리로 떠나는지 아세요? "Do (you) know why Julie leaves for Paris?"
7 집이 왜 시끄러운지 아세요? "Do (you) know why the house is noisy?"
8 방이 왜 더운지 아세요? "Do (you) know why the room is hot?"
9 이 국이 왜 짠지 아세요? "Do (you) know why this soup is salty?"
10 이 컴퓨터가 왜 싼지 아세요? "Do (you) know why this computer is inexpensive?"

Exercise 21.2

1 마이클이 무슨 일을 할지 아세요? "Do (you) know what kind of work Michael will do?"
2 어디서 저녁을 먹을지 아세요? "Do (you) know where (they) will have dinner?"
3 요즈음 로마의 날씨가 어떨지 아세요? "Do (you) know how Rome's weather will be like nowadays?"
4 비행기가 공항에 몇 시에 도착할지 아세요? "Do (you) know what time the airplane will arrive at the airport?"
5 내일 몇 시에 가게를 닫을지 아세요? "Do (you) know what time (they) will close the store tomorrow?"

Exercise 21.3

1 폴이 시험에 합격했는지 모르겠어요.
2 어디서 결혼식을 하는지 모르겠어요.
3 뭘 사야 할지 모르겠어요.
4 이름이 무엇인지 모르겠어요.
5 언제 결혼을 해야 할지 모르겠어요.
6 언제 소포가 도착할지 모르겠어요.
7 폴이 차가 있는지 모르겠어요.
8 시험이 쉬웠는지 모르겠어요.
9 가격이 비싼지 모르겠어요.
10 가방이 얼마나 무거울지 모르겠어요.

Exercise 21.4

1 "How noisy the house is, (I) cannot study."
2 "How congested the road was, (I) was late for the party as long as one hour."
3 "How difficulty the test was, (I) could not solve even one problem."
4 "How interestingly (they) see a movie, (they) do not even go to a toilet."
5 "How heavily (it) snows, (it) seems that (we) may not be able to go to school."

Exercise 21.5

1 몇 시까지 기다려야 할지 모르겠어요. "(I) do not know what time (we) should wait until."
2 어느 차를 사야 할지 모르겠어요. "(I) do not know which car (I) should buy."
3 얼마에 집을 팔아야 할지 모르겠어요. "(I) do not know at what price (I) should sell the house."
4 왜 여자 친구와 헤어져야 할지 모르겠어요. "(I) do not know why (I) should break up with (my) girlfriend."
5 무엇을 마셔야 할지 모르겠어요. "(I) do not know what (I) should drink."

Exercise 21.6

1 눈이 오기 시작한지 4 일이 됐어요.
2 캐나다로 이사온지 1 년이 됐어요.
3 한국어를 배운지 3 주가 됐어요.
4 담배를 끊은지 6 개월이 됐어요.
5 요리를 시작한지 10 분이 됐어요.
6 차를 산지 이틀이 됐어요.

7 제니퍼가 런던으로 떠난지 일 주일이 됐어요.
8 머리를 자른지 얼마나 됐어요?
9 집에 돌아온지 얼마나 됐어요?
10 그를 마지막으로 본지 얼마나 됐어요?

Exercise 21.7

1 점심을 먹은지 2 시간이 됐어요. "(It) has been two hours since (I) ate (my) lunch."
2 감기 걸린지 이틀이 됐어요. "(It) has been two days since (I) caught a cold."
3 편지를 받은지 1 주일이 됐어요. "(It) has been one week since (I) received the letter."
4 운동을 시작한지 4 일이 됐어요. "(It) has been four days since (I) started exercising."
5 취직한지 1 년이 됐어요. "(It) has been one year since (I) got employed."

Unit 22

Exercise 22.1

1 손님이 많더라구요.
2 서비스가 좋더라구요.
3 아파트세가 비싸더라구요.
4 다섯 시간 걸리더라구요.
5 집이 크더라구요.

Exercise 22.2

1 윌리엄이 부지런하더라구요. "William was diligent (you know)."
2 수잔의 오빠가 회사 사장이더라구요. "Susan's older brother was the company president (you know)."
3 톰이 택시를 기다리더라구요. "Tom waited for a taxi (you know)."
4 제인의 생일이 어제이더라구요. "Jane's birthday was yesterday (you know)."
5 캐서린이 반지를 사고 있더라구요. "Catherine was buying a ring (you know)."

Exercise 22.3

1 듣던 노래
2 타던 자전거
3 일하던 회사

4 좋아하던 음식
5 쓰던 칫솔
6 씩씩하던 남자
7 부드럽던 피부
8 어둡던 방
9 따뜻하던 날씨
10 손님으로 붐비던 가게

Exercise 22.4

1 대학교 때 읽던 소설책이에요. "(It) is the novel that (I) used read during (my) college days."
2 사귀던 여자 친구예요. "(she) is (my ex) girlfriend that (I) used to go out with."
3 한국에서 즐겨 보던 TV 드라마예요. "(It) is the TV drama that (I) used to enjoy watching in Korea."
4 10 년전에 살던 아파트예요. "(It) is the apartment where (I) used to live ten years ago."
5 중학교 때 입던 교복이에요. "(It) is the school uniform that (I) used to wear during (my) intermediate school days."
6 같이 일하던 동료예요. "(He) is (my) colleague whom (I) used to work with."

Exercise 22.5

1 아침에는 집이 조용하더니 오후에는 시끄러워요. "In the morning, the house was quiet, but in the afternoon, (it) is noisy."
2 지난 주까지 일본 드라마를 보더니 이번 주는 한국 드라마를 봐요. "(She) watched Japanese dramas until last week, but (she) watches Korean dramas this week."
3 한국어를 배우더니 한국 영화만 봐요. "(He) has learned Korean, and as a result (he) only sees Korean movies."
4 십 분 기다렸더니 음식이 나왔어요. "As (I) waited for ten minutes, the food was served."
5 어제 맥주를 많이 마셨더니 머리가 아파요. "Since (I) drank beer a lot yesterday, (my) head aches."

Exercise 22.6

1 시간이 있었더라면 만났을 거예요.
2 바쁘지 않았더라면 집에 들렀을 거예요.
3 행복했더라면 이혼하지 않았을 거예요.
4 비밀을 알았더라면 성공했을 거예요.
5 연습을 더 열심히 했더라면 경기를 이겼을 거예요.

Exercise 22.7

1 병원에 갔더라면 살았을 거예요. "If (it was the case that he) went to the hospital, (he) might have lived."
2 약을 먹었더라면 안 아팠을 거예요. "If (it was the case that she) took the medicine, (she) might not feel painful."
3 돈이 있었더라면 떠났을 거예요. "If (it was the case that I) had money, (I) might have left."
4 고기가 있었더라면 샀을 거예요. "If (it was the case that they) had meat, (she) might have bought (it)."
5 차가 있었더라면 만났을 거예요. "If (it was the case that he) had a car, (he) might have met (her)."

Exercise 22.8

1 궁금하더라도 묻지 마세요.
2 가렵더라도 긁지 마세요.
3 화나더라도 참으세요.
4 심심하더라도 집에 있으세요.
5 늦게 오더라도 잔소리 하지 마세요.

Exercise 22.9

1 피곤하더라도 졸지 마세요. "Even if (you) may be tired, do not doze off."
2 영화가 재미없더라도 꼭 보세요. "Even if the movie may be uninteresting, see (it) for sure."
3 기분이 나쁘더라도 웃으세요. "Even if (your) mood may be bad, smile."
4 무겁더라도 가져오세요. "Even if (it) may be heavy, bring (it)."
5 슬프더라도 울지 마세요. "Even if (you) may be sad, do not cry."

Unit 23

Exercise 23.1

1 아침을 먹기 전에 손을 씻으세요. "Wash (your) hands before eating breakfast."
2 시험을 보기 전에 잠을 충분히 자세요. "Sleep sufficiently before taking a test."
3 기차를 타기 전에 기차 표를 예약해야 돼요. "(You) must reserve a train ticket before riding the train."
4 레스토랑에 가기 전에 집에 들릅시다. "(Let us) stop by home before going to the restaurant."

5 출근하기 전에 신문을 보세요? "Do (you) read newspapers before leaving home for work?"

6 화장을 하기 전에 샤워를 해요. "(I) take a shower before doing makeup."

7 새 집으로 이사하기 전에 아파트에서 살았어요? "Did (you) live in an apartment before moving into the new house?"

8 전공을 정하기 전에 교수님하고 상담해야 합니다. "(You) must consult with (your) professor before deciding (your) major."

9 피터를 만나러 나가기 전에 전화합시다. "(Let us) make a phone call before going out to meet Peter."

10 차를 팔기 전에 아버지하고 의논하세요. "Consult with (your) father before selling (your) car."

Exercise 23.2

1 점심을 먹기는 커녕 아침도 안 먹었어요. "Far from eating lunch, (she) did not even eat breakfast."

2 등산을 하기는 커녕 집 밖에도 안 나갔어요. "Far from climbing the mountain, (they) did not even go outside of the house."

3 저녁을 먹기는 커녕 커피도 못 마셨어요. "Far from eating dinner, (I) could not even drink coffee."

4 새 차를 사기는 커녕 구경도 못 했어요. "Far from buying a new car, (I) could not even look around."

5 생일 파티를 하기는 커녕 선물도 못 받았어요. "Far from having a birth-day party, (I) could not even receive a present."

Exercise 23.3

1 두 사람이 자기에는 침대가 너무 작아요. "The bed is too small for two people to sleep."

2 영화를 다운로드 받기에는 제 컴퓨터가 너무 느려요. "My computer is too slow for downloading a movie (file)."

3 수영을 하기에는 날씨가 너무 추워요. "The weather is too cold for swimming."

4 영화를 보기에는 시간이 없어요. "(We) do not have time for seeing a movie."

5 전화를 하기에는 너무 늦었어요. "(It) is too late for making a phone call."

6 농구를 하기에는 키가 작았어요. "(My) height was small for playing basketball."

7 커피를 마시기에는 너무 어렸어요. "(I) was too young to drink coffee."

8 혼자 운전하기에는 너무 멀었어요. "(It) was too far (for me) to drive alone."

9 노트북을 사기에는 돈이 모자랐어요. "The money was short for buying a notebook."

10 선물로 주기에는 너무 비쌌어요. "(It) was too expensive (for me to) give (it) away as a gift."

Exercise 23.4

1 감기 걸렸기 때문에 학교에 못 가요. "(I) cannot go to school because (I) caught a cold."

2 아침을 늦게 먹었기 때문에 점심을 먹고 싶지 않아요. "(I) do not want to eat lunch because (I) ate breakfast late."

3 비가 오기 때문에 경기가 취소될 거예요. "(I guess that) the game will be cancelled because (it) rains."

4 버스가 불편하기 때문에 지하철을 이용해요. "(I) use a subway because a bus is inconvenient."

5 시험 기간이기 때문에 도서관에 사람이 많아요. "There are many people in the library because (it) is an examination period."

Exercise 23.5

1 살을 빼기 위해서 저녁을 조금 먹을 거예요. "(I) will eat dinner a little to lose weight."

2 의과 대학에 진학하기 위해서 준비하고 있어요. "(I) am preparing to enter medical school."

3 차를 고치기 위해서 정비소에 가고 있어요. "(I) am going to the repair shop to repair (my) car."

4 다음 경기를 이기기 위해서 매일 연습해요. "(I) practice everyday to win the next game."

5 한국에 있는 친구한테 전화하기 위해서 전화 카드를 샀어요. "(I) bought a telephone card to make a phone call to (my) friend in Korea."

Exercise 23.6

1 내년 봄에 결혼하기로 했어요. "(We) decided to get married next year's spring."

2 학교 기숙사에서 살기로 했어요. "(I) decided to live in school dormitory."

3 다음 학기에 한국어 수업을 듣기로 했어요. "(I) decided to take the Korean language class next semester."

4 내일부터 담배를 끊기로 했어요. "(I) decided to quit smoking from tomorrow."

5 다음 달부터 태권도를 배우기로 했어요. "(I) decided to learn Taekwondo from next month."

Exercise 23.7

1 토요일마다 테니스를 치기도 해요. "(We) also play tennis every Saturday."
2 가끔 까만 넥타이를 매기도 해요. "(I) also wear a black tie occasionally."
3 주말에 친구들하고 농구를 하기도 해요. "(I) also play basketball with (my) friends on the weekend."
4 심심하면 영화를 보기도 해요. "When feeling bored, (we) also see movies."
5 토요일 아침에 조깅을 하기도 해요. "(I) also jog on Saturday morning."

Exercise 23.8

1 매일 요가를 하기가 어려워요. "Doing yoga everyday is difficult."
2 프랑스 음식을 만들기가 어려워요. "Making French food is difficult."
3 시험에 떨어지기가 쉬워요. "(It) is easy to fail a test."
4 이사하기가 힘들어요. "Changing one's residence is laborious."
5 노래를 부르기가 좋아요. "(It) is nice to sing songs."
6 차를 타기가 편해요. "Riding a car is convenient."
7 일하기가 싫어요. "(It) is unpleasant to work."
8 요리하기가 재미있어요. "Cooking is interesting."
9 빨래를 하기가 귀찮아요. "Doing the laundry is bothersome."
10 매일 운동하기가 힘들어요. "Exercising everyday is laborious."

Exercise 23.9

1 좋기는요.
2 영화를 보기는요.
3 자주 만나기는요.
4 따뜻하기는요.
5 부지런하기는요.

Exercise 23.10

1 내일 오전 10 시에 돌아옴. "Will be back at 10 a.m. tomorrow."
2 오늘 저녁 스테이크임. "Tonight's dinner is steak."
3 차 고쳤음. "Repaired (your) car."
4 집에 안 갔음. "Did not go home."
5 옷 샀음. "Bought the dress."
6 어제 머리 잘랐음. "Had a hair cut yesterday."
7 우리가 지갑 보관하고 있음. "We are keeping (your) wallet."
8 잃어버린 개 찾았음. "Found the lost dog."
9 룸메이트 구함. "Seeking a roommate."
10 영화 재미없음. "The movie is uninteresting."

Unit 24

Exercise 24.1

1 누나가 "제발 일찍 일어나라" 라고 했어요. "(My) older sister said 'For heaven's sake, get up early.'"
2 앤드류가 "빨리 따라오세요" 라고 했어요. "Andrew said 'Follow (me) immediately.'"
3 이사벨이 "정말 우유를 잘 마시네요" 라고 했어요. "Isabel said '(You) really drink milk well.'"
4 리사가 "저녁에 저희 집에 들르세요" 라고 했어요. "Lisa said 'Stop by our house in the evening.'"
5 선생님이 "오늘 수업 끝" 이라고 했어요. "Teacher said 'The end of class for today.'"
6 폴이 "피자 먹자" 라고 했어요. "Paul said 'Let us eat pizza.'"
7 마리아가 "찌개가 맵다" 라고 했어요. "Maria said 'Pot stew is spicy.'"
8 브래드가 "우리 금요일에 만나자" 라고 했어요. "Brad said 'Let us meet on Friday.'"
9 니콜이 "이따 시간 있으면 전화해" 라고 했어요. "Nicole said 'Call (me) if (you) have time later.'"
10 지나가 "집에 안 가세요?" 라고 했어요. 'Gina said 'Don't you go home?'"

Exercise 24.2

1 모니카가 뉴욕에 4 계절이 있다고 했어요. "Monica said that there are four seasons in New York."
2 앤서니가 내일 소나기가 내리겠다고 했어요. "Anthony said that (it) would shower tomorrow."
3 사브리나가 집세가 올랐다고 했어요. "Sabrina said that house rent went up."
4 제이슨이 오늘 스파게티를 만든다고 했어요. "Jason said that (he) would make spaghetti today."
5 조디가 내일 다시 전화하겠다고 했어요. "Jodie said that (she) would call again tomorrow."
6 스티브가 언제 직장을 그만뒀냐고 물었어요. "Steve asked (me) when (I) quitted (my) job."
7 줄리아가 언제 집에 오냐고 물었어요. "Julia asked (them) when (he) would come home."
8 에스더가 이 차가 누구 거냐고 물었어요. "Esther asked (me) whose car this is."
9 제리가 잘 지내고 있냐고 물었어요. "Jerry asked (me) how (I) am getting along."
10 데이지가 몇 시냐고 물었어요. "Daisy asked (her) what time it is."

Exercise 24.3

1 에릭이 버스를 타자고 했어요. "Eric suggested that (we) take a bus."
2 나오미가 오후 2 시에 만나자고 했어요. "Naomi suggested that (we) meet at 2 p.m."
3 클라라가 같이 요가를 시작하자고 했어요. "Clara suggested that (we) start yoga together."
4 조지가 이번 주말에 같이 영화를 보자고 했어요. "George suggested that (we) see a movie together this weekend."
5 나탈리가 그 친구를 도와 주자고 했어요. "Natalie suggested that (we) help that friend."
6 아비가일이 빨래를 하라고 했어요. "Abigail told (me) to do laundry."
7 케빈이 열심히 공부하라고 했어요. "Kevin told (her) to study hard."
8 다이에나가 20 분안에 내려오라고 했어요. "Diana told (us) to come down within 20 minutes."
9 져스틴이 화내지 말라고 했어요. "Justin told (him) not to be angry."
10 일레인이 열쇠를 찾으라고 했어요. "Elaine told (them) to find keys."

Exercise 24.4

1 샘이 오늘 밤 떠난다고 했어요.
2 리사가 몇 시에 자냐고 물었어요.
3 폴이 한국 음식을 먹자고 했어요.
4 선생님이 조용히 하라고 했어요.
5 수잔이 오늘 밤 전화할 거라고 했어요.

Exercise 24.5

1 음식이 맛있다고 생각한다.
2 서비스가 좋다고 생각한다.
3 커피가 너무 진했다고 생각한다.
4 내일부터 운동을 시작해야겠다고 생각했다.
5 존한테 이메일을 써야겠다고 생각했다.

INDEX

Page numbers in **bold** refer to those pages in the book where the relevant grammar point is discussed in detail.